Additional Praise for

THE BOY IN THE MOON

"Honest and deeply moving."   —*Tucson Citizen*

"A stark, lovely memoir . . . fiercely plainspoken and lyrical."
                                        —*The Boston Globe*

"Unforgettable . . . Crisp, observant, and, occasionally, sub-
versively funny . . . In the end, as in the beginning, Brown
questions the value of a life like Walker's, 'lived in the twilight and often in pain.' He sometimes locates it in Walker
himself. Another answer is this book."
                              —*The Plain Dealer* (Cleveland)

"Brown presents a moving and deeply felt account of his life
with his son Walker, who is one of fewer than 300 people
in the world who were born with CFC, cardiofaciocutaneous syndrome. . . . [T]he book describes Brown's fascinating
worldwide investigations into the various living situations
offered to people with CFC as well as his visits with other
families whose children have CFC."   —*Publishers Weekly*

"[An] intimate glimpse into the life of a family that cares
around the clock for a mysterious, profoundly disabled child,
that gets so close to the love and despair, and the complex
questions the life of such a child raises . . .. It is a beautiful
book, heartfelt and profound, warm and wise."
                    —Jane Bernstein, author of *Loving Rachel*
                                        and *Rachel in the World*

"Eloquent as a love song, rich as the most generous, finely tempered philosophy, *The Boy in the Moon* asks some profound questions. What makes us human? What connects us to the most impaired members of our community? Who benefits more, the caretaker or the cared-for? The answer to all these questions lies in the wonderfully realized—poignant, dignified, funny—portrait of Walker, whom Ian Brown calls 'my teacher, my sweet, sweet, lost and broken boy.' It's hard to imagine a reader who won't also learn important things from Walker: This is a book that expands the mind and heart, and a joy to read."   —Katherine Ashenburg, author of
The Mourner's Dance and *The Dirt on Clean*

"If you read to get a sense of how other people experience being alive, *The Boy in the Moon* is the real thing: an intimate, profoundly eloquent, soul-wrenching memoir. In seeking to understand what goes on in his disabled son Walker's mind, Ian Brown allows us into his own. By turns lyrical, quirky, spare, unsparing, confessional, journalistic, irreverent, grim, angry, and sometimes hilarious, Brown writes out his thoughts, feelings, and experiences as father, son, husband, and ambivalent visitor to the international community of the 'disabled.' An extraordinary book, this is literature that opens up new emotional and psychological terrain."
—Helen Epstein, author of
Children of the Holocaust and *Where She Came From*

THE BOY IN THE MOON

A FATHER'S JOURNEY TO UNDERSTAND

HIS EXTRAORDINARY SON

To James & Courtney — Fellow travellers... Best, Ian Brown

Ian Brown

 ST. MARTIN'S GRIFFIN ⚲ NEW YORK

Some of the material in this book was first published, in different form, in *The Globe and Mail*. Permission to use that material is gratefully acknowledged. Grateful acknowledgement is made to the following for permission to reprint previously published material. "Anecdote of the Jar," from *The Collected Poems of Wallace Stevens* by Wallace Stevens, copyright © 1954 by Wallace Stevens and renewed 1982 by Holly Stevens. Used by permission of Alfred A. Knopf, a division of Random House, Inc. "Summer 1983" by Mary Jo Salter. Used by permission of the author. "Do Not Be Ashamed" by Wendell Berry, copyright © 1999 by Wendell Berry from *The Selected Poems of Wendell Berry*. Reprinted by permission of Counterpoint.

www.stmartins.com

The Library of Congress has cataloged the hardcover edition as follows:

Brown, Ian, 1954–
    The boy in the moon : a father's journey to understand his extraordinary son / Ian Brown.—1st U.S. ed.
    ISBN 978-0-312-67183-9
    1. Brown, Walker, 1996– 2. Brown, Ian, 1954– 3. Brown, Walker, 1996–
4. Brown, Ian, 1954– 5. Genetic disorders in children—Patients—Canada—Biography. 6. Genetic disorders in children—Patients—Family relationships—Canada. 7. Parents of children with disabilities—Canada—Biography. 8. Genetic disorders. 9. Fathers and sons. 10. Handicapped children—Canada—Biography. 11. Parents of handicapped children—Canada—Biography. 12. Father-son relationship. 13. Genetic disorders.
    RB155.5 .B76 2011
    618.92/0042092—dc22

                                                                    2011378371

ISBN 978-0-312-67541-7 (trade paperback)

Originally published in hardcover in Canada by Random House Canada, a division of Random House of Canada Limited

First St. Martin's Griffin Edition: July 2012

D 10 9 8 7 6 5 4 3 2

This book is dedicated to
Walker Henry Schneller Brown
and his many, many friends.

What madness came upon you, what daemon
Leaped on your life with heavier
Punishment than a mortal man can bear?
No: I cannot even
Look at you, poor ruined one.
And I would speak, question, ponder,
If I were able. No.
You make me shudder.

SOPHOCLES, *Oedipus Rex*

I like imbeciles. I like their candour. But, to be
modest, one is always the imbecile of someone.

RENÉ GOSCINNY

one

For the first eight years of Walker's life, every night is the same. The same routine of tiny details, connected in precise order, each mundane, each crucial.

The routine makes the eight years seem long, almost endless, until I try to think about them afterwards, and then eight years evaporate to nothing, because nothing has changed.

Tonight I wake up in the dark to a steady, motorized noise. Something wrong with the water heater. *Nnngah.* Pause. *Nnngah. Nnngah.*

But it's not the water heater. It's my boy, Walker, grunting as he punches himself in the head, again and again.

He has done this since before he was two. He was born with an impossibly rare genetic mutation, cardiofaciocutaneous syndrome, a technical name for a mash of symptoms. He is globally delayed and can't speak, so I never know what's

I

wrong. No one does. There are just over a hundred people with CFC around the world. The disorder turns up randomly, a misfire that has no certain cause or roots; doctors call it an orphan syndrome because it seems to come from nowhere.

I count the grunts as I pad my way into his room: one a second. To get him to stop hitting himself, I have to lure him back to sleep, which means taking him downstairs and making him a bottle and bringing him back into bed with me.

That sounds simple enough, doesn't it? But with Walker, everything is complicated. Because of his syndrome, he can't eat solid food by mouth, or swallow easily. Because he can't eat, he takes in formula through the night via a feeding system. The formula runs along a line from a feedbag and a pump on a metal IV stand, through a hole in Walker's sleeper and into a clever-looking permanent valve in his belly, some-times known as a G-tube, or mickey. To take him out of bed and down to the kitchen to prepare the bottle that will ease him back to sleep, I have to disconnect the line from the mickey. To do this, I first have to turn off the pump (in the dark, so he doesn't wake up completely) and close the feed line. If I don't clamp the line, the sticky formula pours out onto the bed or the floor (the carpet in Walker's room is pale blue: there are patches that feel like the Gobi Desert under my feet, from all the times I have forgotten). To crimp the tube, I thumb a tiny red plastic roller down a slide. (It's my favourite part of the routine—one thing, at least, is easy, under my control.) I unzip his one-piece sleeper (Walker's small, and grows so slowly he wears the same sleepers for a year and a half at a time), reach inside to unlock the line from the mickey, pull the line out through the hole in his sleeper and hang it on the IV rack that holds the pump and feedbag. Close the mickey, rezip the sleeper. Then I reach in and lift all 45 pounds of Walker from the depths of the crib. He still sleeps in a crib. It's the only way we can keep him in bed at night. He can do a lot of damage on his own.

This isn't a list of complaints. There's no point to complaining. As the mother of another CFC child once told me, "You do what you have to do." If anything, that's the easy part. The hard part is trying to answer the questions Walker raises in my mind every time I pick him up. What is the value of a life like his—a life lived in the twilight, and often in pain? What is the cost of his life to those around him? "We spend a million dollars to save them," a doctor said to me not long ago. "But then when they're discharged, we ignore them." We were sitting in her office, and she was crying. When I asked her why, she said "Because I see it all the time."

Sometimes watching Walker is like looking at the moon: you see the face of the man in the moon, yet you know there's actually no man there. But if Walker is so insubstantial, why does he feel so important? What is he trying to show me? All I really want to know is what goes on inside his off-shaped head, in his jumped-up heart. But every time I ask, he somehow persuades me to look into my own.

But there is another complication here. Before I can slip downstairs with Walker for a bottle, the bloom of his diaper pillows up around me. He's not toilet-trained. Without a new diaper, he won't fall back to sleep and stop smacking his head and ears. And so we detour from the routine of the feeding tube to the routine of the diaper.

I spin 180 degrees to the battered changing table, wondering, as I do every time, how this will work when he's twenty and I'm sixty. The trick is to pin his arms to keep him from whacking himself. But how do you change a 45-pound boy's brimming diaper while immobilizing both his hands so he doesn't bang his head or (even worse) reach down to scratch his tiny, plum-like but suddenly liberated backside, thereby smearing excrement everywhere? While at the same time immobilizing his feet, because ditto? You can't let your attention wander for a second. All this is done in the dark as well.

But I have my routine. I hold his left hand with my left hand, and tuck his right hand out of commission under my left armpit. I've done it so many times, it's like walking. I keep his heels out of the disaster zone by using my right elbow to stop his knees from bending, and do all the actual nasty business with my right hand. My wife, Johanna, can't manage this alone any longer and sometimes calls me to help her. I am never charming when she does.

And the change itself: a task to be approached with all the delicacy of a munitions expert in a Bond movie defusing an atomic device. The unfolding and positioning of a new nappy; the signature feel of the scratchy Velcro tabs on the soft paper of the nappy, the disbelief that it will ever hold; the immense, surging relief of finally refastening it—we made it! The world is safe again! The reinsertion of his legs into the sleeper.

Now we're ready to head downstairs to make the bottle.

Three flights, taking it in the knees, looking out the landing windows as we go. He's stirring, so I describe the night to him in a low voice. There's no moon tonight and it's damp for November.

In the kitchen, I perform the bottle ritual. The weightless plastic bottle (the third model we tried before we found one that worked, big enough for his not-so-fine motor skills yet light enough for him to hold), the economy-sized vat of Enfamil (whose bulk alone is discouraging, it implies so much), the tricky one-handed titrating of tiny tablespoonfuls of Pablum and oatmeal (he aspirates thin fluids; it took us months to find these exact manageable proportions that produced the exact manageable consistency. I have a head full of these numbers: dosages, warm-up times, the frequency of his bowel movements/scratchings/cries/naps). The nightly pang about the fine film of Pablum dust everywhere: Will we ever again have anything like an ordered life? The second pang, of shame, for having such thoughts in the first place. The rummage in the ever-full blue and white dish drainer (we're always washing something, a pipette or a syringe or a bottle or a medicine measuring cup) for a nipple (but the right nipple, one whose hole I have enlarged into an X, to let the thickened liquid out) and a plastic nipple cap. Pull the nipple into the cap, the satisfying *pop* as it slips into place. The gonad-shrinking microwave.

Back up three flights. He's still trying to smash his head. Why does he do it? Because he wants to talk, but can't? Because—this is my latest theory—he can't do what he can see other people doing? I'm sure he's aware of his own difference.

Cart him into the bed in his older sister Hayley's room on the third floor where I have been sleeping, so I can be near him. Hayley, meanwhile, is downstairs with her mother in our bedroom so they can get some sleep. We take turns like this, reduced by the boy to bedroom Bedouins. Neither Johanna nor I has slept two full nights in a row in eight years. We both work during the day. After the first six months, I stopped noticing how tired I was: my days and nights simply became more elastic and similar.

Lay him down on the bed. Oh, fuck me dead—forgot the pump! Build a wall of pillows around him so he doesn't escape or fall off the bed while I nip back into the other room. Remember 4 cc's (or is it 6?) of chloral hydrate, prescribed for sleep and to calm his self-mutilation. (I tried a dose once: the kick of a double martini. William S. Burroughs was thrown out of school as a kid for experimenting with it.) Reprogram the pump, restart the familiar mild repetitive whine, his night pulse.

At last I sink into bed beside him and pull the wriggling boy close. He begins to hit his head again, and because we know of no acceptable way to restrain him mechanically, I hold down his small right hand with my large right one. This brings his left hand up to his other ear—"he's a genius for finding ways to hurt himself," his teacher told me the other day. I grab his left in my left, which I have threaded behind his head. He begins to kick himself in the crotch with his right heel, so hard it makes me wince. I run my big leg over his little leg, and lay my right hand (holding his right hand) on his left thigh, to keep it still. He's stronger than he looks. Under his birdy limbs, he's granite. He'll mash his ears to a pulp if no one stops him.

There is a chance, of course, that none of this will work. Every once in a while, the chloral hydrate rebounds and transforms him into a giggling drunk. It's not unusual to have to perform the entire routine again an hour later. When he has a cold (eight, ten times a year), he coughs himself awake every twenty minutes. Sometimes he cries for hours for no reason. There are nights when nothing works, and nights when he is up and at it, laughing and playing and crawling all over me. I don't mind those nights, tired as I am: his sight is poor, but in the dark we're equal, and I know this makes him happy. In the night, there can be stretches when he is no different from any normal lively boy. It makes me almost cry to tell you that.

Tonight is a lucky night: I can feel him slip off after ten minutes. He stops grunting, strokes his bottle, turns his back and jams his bony little ass into my hip, a sure sign. He falls asleep.

I hurry after him. For all this nightly nightmare—the years of desperate worry and illness and chronic sleep deprivation, the havoc he has caused in our lives, threatening our marriage and our finances and our sanity—I long for the moment when he lets his crazy formless body fall asleep against me. For a short while, I feel like a regular little boy's father. Sometimes I think this is his gift to me—parcelled out, to show me how rare and valuable it is. Walker, my teacher, my sweet, sweet, lost and broken boy.

———

In the early years, after Walker was first diagnosed with CFC syndrome at the age of seven months, the estimated number of people who suffered from the syndrome changed every time we visited the doctor. The medical profession—at least the handful of doctors who studied cardiofaciocutaneous syndrome, or knew what it was—was

learning about the syndrome as we did. The name itself
was nothing more than an amalgam of the syndrome's
most prominent symptoms: *cardio*, for ever-present murmurs and malformations and enlargements of the heart;
facio, for the facial dysmorphia that was its signal characteristic, a prominent brow and down-sloping eyes;
cutaneous, for its many skin irregularities. The first time
a geneticist ever described the syndrome to me, he told me
there were eight other children in the world with CFC.
Eight: it wasn't possible. Surely we had been blasted out to
an unknown galaxy.

But within a year, after our doctors had begun to sweep
the medical literature for references to CFC, I was informed
there were 20 cases, because more had turned up in Italy.
Then there were 40. (The speed with which the number
changed made me sneer at the doctors: they were trained
medical professionals, surely they ought to know more than
we did.) More than 100 cases of CFC have been reported
since the syndrome was first described publicly in three
people in 1979; some estimates are as high as 300. Everything
about the syndrome was a mystery, an unknown. It was 1986
before it had a name. Symptoms ranged wildly in severity and
kind. (Some researchers believe there may be thousands of
people with CFC, but with symptoms so mild the condition
has never been noticed.) Some CFC children hit themselves,
though most didn't. Some could speak or sign. All but a few
were anywhere from mildly to severely retarded. Heart
defects ranged from serious to unimportant. (Walker had a
mild murmur.) Their skin was often sensitive to touch, to the
point of agony. Like many CFC children, Walker couldn't
chew or swallow easily; he couldn't speak; his vision and

hearing were compromised (he had narrowed optic nerves, one more than the other, and skinny ear canals subject to incessant infection); he was thin and wobbly, "hypotonic" in the medical jargon.

Like virtually all CFC children, he had no eyebrows, sparse curly hair, a prominent brow, wide-set eyes, low-set ears and an often charming cocktail-party personality. The CFC features grew more noticeable, more "abnormal," as he grew older. I assumed my little boy was an average example of the condition. It turned out I was wrong. It turned out the average didn't exist—not here.

Nor did those conditions change. Today, at thirteen, mentally, developmentally—I'm terrified even to write these words—he's somewhere between one and three years old. Physically, he's better off than many CFC children (he doesn't have frequent seizures, doesn't have ulcerated intestines); cognitively, less so. He could live to middle age. Would that be good luck, or bad?

Minus a few new genetic details, this was and still is the sum total of what the medical profession knows about CFC. It isn't widely studied, as autism is. Most parents of CFC children know more about the affliction than their pediatricians. The CFC population isn't large and politically powerful like that of Down syndrome, which more than 350,000 people live with in North America, and which occurs once in every 800 births. CFC shows up no more often than once in every 300,000 births, and possibly as rarely as once in a million. The Office of Rare Diseases at the National Institutes of Health characterized CFC as "extremely rare," way out at the far, thin end of the statistical branch, alongside bizarre genetic anomalies such as Chédiak–Higashi syndrome, a bleeding disorder caused by platelet dysfunction and white cell abnormalities. There were only two hundred known cases of Chédiak–Higashi, in part because so few born with it ever survived.

Raising Walker was like raising a question mark. I often wanted to tell someone the story, what the adventure felt and smelled and sounded like, what I noticed when I wasn't running through darkness. But who could relate to such a human anomaly, to the rare and exotic corner of existence where we suddenly found ourselves? Eleven years would pass before I met anyone like him.

two

Early on I learned my son could lift my mood, that I responded to his unusual emotional valence. Many days, even now, follow a pattern:

I arrive home from work tired (possibly from being up with him the night before), even defeated: some ship has not only failed to come in, but turns out not to have sailed at all. The daylight is fading. Walker is playing with Olga, his nanny since he was born. Her last name is de Vera, but she's always just Olga to us. If she hasn't already returned with him from a three-hour walk outside (he loves the outside) and given him a bath, I can. I used to do it every other day, back when he was with us all the time. Bathing him brings me back to myself.

I run the bath; fetch him from Olga downstairs (he follows her steadily from the kitchen to the laundry in the basement back up to the kitchen, intermittently conducting self-guided tours of the living room, dining room, piano, front hall, and stairs of our narrow city house; for a long time, until he was six, the stairs were his favourite lounging space); eagerly unburden him of his clothes (the buttons, the zips, the geometry problem of extracting his stiff arms from his sleeves, keeping him on his feet, preventing him from slumping to the ground while I am upside down undoing his shoes, wishing we had bought the Velcro model instead of the lace-ups); ditch his diaper and perform cleanup if called for. Done. Lift him into the bath, watch him like traffic so he doesn't submerge while I undress in an instant, jump in with him.

Then: we recline in the tub, the smooth of his naked back against my chest. He is as calm as a pond. His nipples are minute, literally the size of rivets. They make me nervous, I don't know why. (I can only imagine.) His shoulder blades and the bones of his back are oddly soft, plastic, bendable, as if covered by some miracle upholstery. The skin of his arms and thighs feels almost manufactured too, too much matte and not enough flow, the cells rampaging, overbuilding, one of the more direct results of the genetic miscues that made him this way.

His body changes so slowly I often forget how much it *has* changed. The older he gets, the more noticeable are his deformities—they warned us about that, back when he was a baby. He has a small pot-belly now, which he never did before. When he was younger he was nothing but rope, whereas now around his middle, there is a quarter-inch pinch of flesh, like a roll in a sock. His skin is actually softer than when he was a baby, as if time were running in reverse.

At first, when he was an infant, baths upset him. But if you got the temperature right and sat quietly with him for long enough, slowly replacing the cooling water with hot, he calmed down long enough to enjoy it, briefly, until you rinsed his hair or delivered a new shocking sensation to his exterior: CFCers hate new stimuli, their nerves seem to be permanently scalded. Over time, he grew to like the bathwater; it seemed to free his all-too-loosely-linked limbs, lighten the load gravity imposed on them. The irony was that water had been one of his original nemeses: too much amniotic fluid in the womb, some of it aspirated before birth; also too much fluid in the brain, filling his overlarge cerebellar cavities.

He laughs more when he's in the bath. Of course I like to think he laughs because he's with me, but that's absurd. He'll laugh with almost anyone.

Another day. This morning we're up before breakfast, while everyone else sleeps. We've started to let him get up when he wants to, to give him the illusion of choosing. Walker and I are in the kitchen, and I am making my daily inventory of his body: his ears (he has cauliflower ears from hitting himself, prone to constant infection), his nose (don't ask), his general well-being. He's playing with a Baggie filled with pop-can tabs. Olga saves them. I don't know why she saves them but there are hundreds of pop-can tabs, secured and wrapped and secreted around the house—awaiting some strange catastrophe for which Olga endlessly prepares.

Maybe the catastrophe of her eventual absence? Olga saved our lives. She had been looking after the dying mother of a prominent capitalist when we found her through the Filipino nanny mafia. Hayley was a year old. Olga had worked around the world as a caregiver and a maid, after being forced to leave nursing college in Manila to provide for her family. When Walker appeared two years later, trouble from day one, Olga enveloped him. He was a shorter version of her: compact, intent, difficult to distract. She washed his clothes and kept his room and managed his meds and fed and changed and walked him for hours on end and sang him to sleep; and if she didn't, she helped us do it. She did laundry the way pilgrims perform religious rituals, precisely and at least twice a day. Only at night and in the morning and on weekends, when she went home, did the house feel less secure: we were on our own again, Olgaless. Nothing fazed Olga—not screaming nor illness nor filth nor disaster. She wrote down everything Walker-related—number and nature of bowel movements, duration of walks, his mood, medicines and dosages four times a day, spells and fits, the odd proverb, our various whereabouts—in a coiled notebook she kept on the microwave:

> *Nov. 19 A.M.*
> *Walker Brown*
> *10:30-chloral*
> *11:00-Peptamol / Claritin / Risperidone*
> *Poo=Yes=M=Reg*
> *Bath=Yes*

If she wasn't looking after Walker, she rubbed Hayley's back and feet. Hayley called her "Olgs." She had no special qualifications to look after a boy as complex as Walker— beyond endless patience, an imagination, an eccentric sense of humour, cast-iron reliability, a love of the cellphone and a massive heart that did not distinguish between the needs of one person and the next. On the rare occasions Walker fell asleep, she devoured every newspaper in the house at the kitchen table. She was my age, exactly. Every couple of months she and forty Filipina girlfriends would stack themselves into a package-tour bus and drive to Orlando or Las Vegas or Chicago or New York or Atlantic City and back, in five days. After that, maybe even Walker was a vacation.

The Baggie full of pop-can tabs that Walker is mauling is metallic pulp: he pulls it and grasps it and flattens it, working it continuously between his flank-steak hands like a robot's rosary, a thing to calm the future. Like something out of *Blade Runner*. I don't know why he does it, what it means to him; I have to be content instead with the only certainty I have, which is that he likes to touch the bag, a lot. This is one unusual thing about having a boy like Walker: he has his own life, his own secret world, always has. It gives him a grave, adult air, even as a boy. He has things to do, objects to press.

Is it the sharp tabs under the softness of the plastic bag— two equal and opposite feelings at the same time? Maybe a plastic bag filled with pop-can tabs is Walker's version of negative capability, the objective correlative of Keats's ideal of equal and opposite notions held in the mind at the same time without having a nervous breakdown, without choosing one over the other. An idea reduced to something physical. Or maybe I'm reaching. He gives me no choice but to reach this way. He and I invent our world together every moment I am with him. *How are you, Walkie? What are you doing? Ah, you're banging the bag of pop-can tabs, trying to find some music somewhere. Is that it?*

There are worse ways to pass time.

Everything about him compels me, unless it terrifies me, and sometimes it does both. Today, up in his room, before we clump downstairs one step at a time, hand on the banister— he always leads with his left foot—we have a pillow fight. It lasts twenty minutes, longer than I've ever known his enthusiasm to endure. For the first time in ten years, I discover that he loves to be batted with a pillow. Astonishment—how did I miss this?—pleasure, a little boredom when it drags on too long, but (overall) happiness because he is happy. Before the chloral hydrate seeped into his system, while he was still standing beside his bed trying to defecate (his morning chore, right out of bed, whammo!), his defecation look on his impassive face (and the act does have its own look), he was cranky and upset, rasping his fingers at the site of his G-tube as if it were an open-pit mine. Not breaking the skin; just abrading it, minor stuff by Walker's self-punishing standards. The skin was white, chafed. I imagine it was painful, though he seems not to feel pain much, another sign of his syndrome. In any event, I love to come down the stairs with him. It feels like progress. I hate his room, that forgotten lair on the third floor. I hate the wall-to-wall sky blue carpet, and the Babar posters (which never change, like him), and the crick-crack wooden craft-show belt rack that's always falling apart (he's never owned a belt that has fit him, that was small enough for the tiny waist above the long-limbed legs). The multiple chests of drawers (unmatched, wicker versus IKEA) packed with clothes we can't bring ourselves to throw away; the $10,000 veil bed hulking against one wall like an altar, encased in a tent of mesh, to prevent him escaping; the $1,200 stainless-steel IV tree standing in the corner of the room like neglected Uncle Bertie (but which we can't throw away, in case an emergency arises, in case we need it again: Christ, what if we need it again?); the rocking chair my mother gave me as a boy, now broken, one of her few connections to my son. And of course Clarence the Clown, the nightmarish plastic clown's head that comes apart in slices, the eyes, the nose, the mouth, while Clarence talks to you, letting you rearrange his face, sad, happy, Cubist, terrorist. Is that telling—that a toy whose face he can rearrange and distort should be my dysmorphic boy's favourite? Or is the appeal that he can turn the electronic voice on and off, unlike his own? You tell me. I hate his room because it feels like an out-of-date museum, a place that, like my son, rarely progresses.

He has the body of an old boxer: square, really, like a shirt box on end. His arm cans—rigid fabric tubes that prevent him from bending his elbows, so he can't deliver smashing upper cuts to his skull all day long—prevent him from developing big biceps, but he has tough lumps of muscle on his forearms. His face is heavy in the lower jaw, full in the cheeks: he has no chin to speak of. Curly hair, but no eyebrows, where he's as bald as a spaceman. A wide nose, characteristic of this syndrome (and of many others, too). Thick lips, especially the lower one, "patulous," the doctors called it, back when he was still a novelty. Square teeth, yellowed from the formula, but undecayed. Hands like gloves, huge for his size. The helmet he wears more and more of the time now is royal blue, a polished slippery foam—the blows glance off it. It came with a rainbow-coloured strap, someone else's gesture at inclusiveness. (Is Walker as strange to the outside world as a transgendered person? I sometimes wonder.) He can hurt himself and others swinging his arms, butting with his head; he even hits Ginny, our border terrier, unintentionally. She doesn't hold it against him. I, too, always give Walker the benefit of the doubt.

There are now two and three-quarter rooms in the house dedicated to his belongings. He expanded his domain gradually, but his empire is still the same size today, three years after he moved out, at the age of eleven, to the group home. He spends a week and a half there and then three days at home, but we keep our version of Walker's world intact. Because of course we can never let him leave us, even if he wants to. There's an entire room on the third floor, next to his bedroom, dedicated to the storage of toys he's never played with and clothes he's never worn—the archaeological history of our futile belief that this or that plaything would pull him out of his closed-off world, into our own more public space. They rarely did.

There are drawers of clothes Walker was given by outsiders as presents—clothes that required too much threading or buttoning, clothes made of the wrong fabrics for his ultra-sensitive skin, decent intentions that had flummoxed dozens of people as they racked their brains wondering what on earth they could buy our strange and limited boy. The dinosaur castle that cost a hundred dollars and occupies him for five minutes a month, if he's up here within sight of it. Mr. Wonderful, the doll that when you press its stomach says all the right things: "Honey, why don't you take the remote. As long as I'm with you, I don't care what we watch." That held his focus for fifteen seconds. My wife, however, got a couple of laughs out of it.

On the other hand, a gable from an old gingerbread house stuck to a paper plate—petrified and long inedible—attracts him whenever he sees it. As does a plastic bag of Christmas ornaments, another Olga invention, good for a few hundred dozen hand-rolls a day. Panels and puzzles and balls and sparklers and buzzers and Plasticine, activity boards, pop-goes-the-weasel boxes, enough educational toys to change the future of Africa, dolls, stuffed animals, costumes—all languish like a reproach in a series of white laundry baskets.

Downstairs in the basement, in the old sauna we use for storage (who has had time for a sauna?), are even more unusual objects, the truly frightening stuff we were lent by the social services departments of various levels of government for the therapists to use when they came by the house. When Walker was an infant there was a good chance that whenever I stepped into our house I would find a woman in her thirties or forties in denim coveralls, sitting on the floor of my living room, patting him, stimulating his cheeks, manipulating his hands, patiently repeating the same sound or the same gesture over and over and over and over again. Every time I walked in and saw such a woman I felt both a pang of grief, as I remembered once more that I had a son who needed her help, and a surge of hope and gratitude—because perhaps this session would be the breakthrough that would send him on his way to a normal life. I still feel both lurches when I see him with a new, fresh, undefeated teacher.

To this day in the sauna, for instance, there is a set of plastic yellow half-buckets, each three inches high, each with a different gizmo in the bottom. One, for example, has a yin-yang wheel, a black and white swirl with a knob to twirl it. I understand the yin–yang wheel: infants respond well to contrast, to black and white patterns. Around the edge of the yin-yang wheel, in turn, are metal rivets, which ding whenever the yin-yang wheel is churned. *Ding ding ding ding ding!* Something vaguely Nepalese, Tibetan. Surely that would work for my little Buddhist? The gizmo, in any event, is inside, on the bottom of the yellow bucket. There are two holes in the bottom of the bucket, too, possibly finger grips, possibly drool-drains, possibly both. I have never been able to understand, quite, how to use this device, and I have never seen it hold Walker's attention for more than two seconds—literally, not even for two seconds. But we keep it anyway, because maybe (as noted) this will be the magic bucket, the contraption that changes everything. A paper label has been laminated onto the outside of the yellow demi-bucket:

FINE MOTOR DEVELOPMENT MATERIALS
TWIST, TURN AND LEARN
FULL CHIME MODULE #10

And beneath that, rubber-stamped in ink:

METRO SPECIAL
PROGRAM [VISION]

I don't know which is more depressing: the awkward clunky design, the incomprehensible finger/drool holes, the bureaucratic stamps (#10, one of many), the full chime designation (perhaps the quarter-chime module would have worked more effectively?), or the even more bureaucratic division (vision) within the larger division (metro special program), with its inference of large and all-seeing provincial and national programs above, each nesting down, like a know-it-all, to smaller and smaller sub-jurisdictions until finally, at last, we reach this tiny, ugly, brutal, awkward, clumsy, two-holed yellow plastic corner of the system that has been reserved for my unfixable boy. The touching hopefulness and yet utter hopelessness of that label, the grunting Neanderthal conception of human nature (stimulus/response, good/bad, on/off) it reflects. Or is it just that there are four more yellow plastic activity buckets downstairs, just like this one but different? A plane with a movable propeller. A clown with a spinning bow tie. A bunch of flowers on wobbly stems. The major clichés, because children respond well to clichés— at least normal children do, but not Walkie. Each yellow bucket as awkward to operate as the next one; each one a reminder of how dark and murky and flat-out basic our understanding of childhood development actually is, how little we know. But stackable: the buckets have that going for them, they're stackable. I know stackable, how crucial stackability is in a house full of junk and disappointment.

Every time I look at the yellow activity buckets (and I put them in the sauna so I wouldn't have to look at them) I see the history of Walker's life in their minute details. They are only a few of the carefully labelled contraptions the educational councils and special assistance boards and special access groups lent us—*lent* us! Expecting us to wash them and give them back when the problem was solved! As if the problem would one day be solved. As if when that day came we would be able to find them again in the avalanche of toys we lived under, figure out which of a dozen agencies they had come from, and where that agency was now, wash them up and then load them into the car—maybe Walker would come along—and drive them back! Lovely dream. I wish it worked that way, my God more than anyone I wish it worked that way.

Instead, the yellow buckets live in the unused sauna, make me feel guilty to this day, one more task I have not had time to accomplish. There was a clearly delineated system designed to teach skills to Walker. Acuity of vision! Gross motor skills! Hand–sound associations! The ability to stick his finger in a goddamn hole! Why could I not hew to the system? Surely other parents did—that's why the system was designed the way it was. So I was once convinced, in any event.

Never mind that the system never taught the boy anything.

The most mysterious of the loaned and purloined devices is the red and white triangular box. This contraption has a tape-laminated label too:

TOYS FOR SPECIAL CHILDREN
PLASTIC PRISM
#5 Catalogued

The three long sides of the triangular box are red; the end caps are white. Four of the five sides are designed to stimulate The Child in a different way.

One side has a mirror—a mirror so scratched it resembles a patch of pavement, but a mirror nonetheless.

Another side has two buttons on either side of a light. The light is in the middle of a depressed circle.

A third side has another depression, in which there is a smiley face pattern in tiny red lights; below the face there is a wooden roller that does not roll, but that clicks when pushed.

Finally, on the bottom of the contraption is a string that once upon a time lit up the face lights. In my experience the lights never worked, but that is the theory. The theory is that if The Child pulls the string, the face lights go on, whereupon The Child will be stimulated to move his or her hand toward the roller below the face, and the roller will make its little noise. The intention and theory of the device are represented by a formula:

string + lights = face recognition with voice/noise association

The purpose of the toy, then, was to teach Walker to associate faces with voices, to pattern into his mind the concept that a face and a voice might be related. At least that is my best guess. I tried to call the manufacturer, to learn just what the device was supposed to teach my boy, who sometimes smiles at me when I put my face next to his and call his name, but the manufacturer's name is not on the toy. Perhaps this would have been too distracting.

I still remember the day, back when Walker was an infant, when my wife came up with the idea of storing a toy basket on every floor of the house. I thought it was a stroke of genius; I thought we had the problem licked. But all these years later they're still there, stuck and full, as we often are.

three

What irritated Dr. Norman Saunders, Walker's pediatrician, was that the hospital hadn't called him soon enough after Johanna delivered an obviously troubled baby five weeks early. Certainly something seemed off that day. It was the twenty-third of June, 1996, a Sunday. I was at work, hosting a three-hour weekly public radio show. Johanna called me after the second hour: she was in labour. Her voice was only a notch off its usual calm. My brother drove her to the hospital, one that specialized in women's health. I finished work, and met them there. Her own doctor was on holiday; the delivery would be supervised by one of her doctor's partners, a tall mild man named Lake. Walker wasn't his fault, of course, but I never forgave him anyway.

Something else was off that day, besides my wife's regular doctor: the way the boy, the moment after he came out, slumped in the obstetrician's hand. He wore a strange defeated look, as if he knew something was wrong. His skin was jaundiced. His lungs hadn't opened well, and the interns whisked him off to a table, where for several minutes they pressed an oxygen mask to his tiny mouth and nose. For several years afterwards I wondered if forced oxygen had contributed to his delays—as it can. "Whew," I heard the tall intern whisper to his colleagues a few moments later, "I'm glad he started breathing when he did." That's when the steady low-grade panic began, the worry that has marked Walker's life since that day. The lurch of his life. The signs were there from the beginning. That strange flock of wild, curly hair, piled in a strip on top of his oblong head—an unexpected pattern. The other day I found myself riding my bicycle past the hospital where he was born and nearly spat at it. I hate the place, even the yellow bricks it's made of. But, we reasoned, he was premature; naturally he was lethargic. (No one spots CFC at this stage.) He refused his mother's breast on alternate feeds and one of his testicles hadn't descended and he could open only one eye. Still, by the time he saw Dr. Saunders for his first checkup two days later, the kid had gained 300 grams.

Even on that inaugural visit, however—I know this now from examining Walker's medical records—Dr. Saunders began to note odd details in my son's chart. *Palate unnaturally high. Flaccid muscle tone. Small palpebral fissures*, or eye openings; *lowered, rotated ears*; a fold in the skin on his nasal bridge. Hayley had been a star baby. Saunders wasn't so enthusiastic about her brother.

Two days later, Walker had lost most of the weight he'd gained. Johanna was beside herself, deep in a hormonal trance in which her only concern was to get the boy to eat.

He didn't seem to be able to suck, and he needed an hour to ingest half an ounce of milk. When he did get it down, he threw it up. His body didn't want to survive. "We do want this child to live, don't we?" Saunders snapped one morning on yet another of our visits to his office. I decided it was a rhetorical question.

Saunders' question implied another, unstated: "This child cannot live without going to extraordinary lengths; do you want to go to those lengths and live with the consequences?" Even if he had asked it outright, I can't imagine my answer would have been anything but yes. All the ethical theorizing in the world can't change the pressures of the moment: the squalling baby on the examining table, his distended stomach, the doctor's obvious concern, his father standing gormlessly by. The call of the physical child and his need.

It was only later, alone, at night, having battled for hours to get him to sleep, only to find myself sleepless, that I sometimes considered the cost of his life, and the alternatives. Had the doctor been asking me if I wanted to let Walker's life end, as nature would have ended it on its own? I sat on the back steps of our little house in the heart of the city at 4 a.m., smoking and thinking the unthinkable. Criminal thoughts, or at least outlandish ones: what if we don't take extraordinary measures? What if he gets sick and we don't work so hard to get him better? Not murder, just nature. But even as I considered these grave plans, I knew I could never enact them. I'm not bragging; my hesitation wasn't ethical or moral. It was a more medieval urge, instinctual and physical; fear of a particular mode of failure, fear of retribution if I ignored the dull call of his flesh and his body and his need.

In any event I felt like an ox slipping into its yoke. I could feel the heavy tragic years coming on ahead of me, as certain as bad weather; there were nights when I even welcomed them. At last a fate I didn't have to choose, a destiny I couldn't avoid. There was a tiny prick of light in that thought, the relief of submitting to the unavoidable. Otherwise, they were the worst nights of my life. I can't explain why I wouldn't change them.

Before Walker was born, after the birth of our first child, Hayley, my wife and I had the usual modern conversations about whether we could handle another. I loved Hayley, she was the best thing that ever happened to me, but I wasn't sure we could afford a second child. I wanted Hayley to have allies in her future fights with us, even liked the idea of a larger family, but Johanna and I were both writers, and never had much money. I wanted some reassurance I would not have to give up my ambitions. A friend said, "Tell your wife you don't want to be a stay-at-home dad," which I did, to which Johanna said, "I know." It was my porosity that worried me more, my susceptibility: I was a sucker for a point of view. And of course there was the immensity of the decision itself, to bring a child into the world—a major step in life that could end in failure or, worse, heartbreak. As a young single man, I had often seen married couples arguing in the street, or eating dinner together in restaurants, silent for half an hour at a time. Why do that? I thought to myself. Later, after I married, I saw couples harried by children, and wondered: why do that? And to see a couple with a handicapped child filled me with horror. Not the sight of the child, but the thought of the burden. I couldn't imagine anything worse.

The argument about a second child ended the way that argument often does: we let nature take its course and quickly produced a brother for Hayley. She was three when Walker was born. Some part of me wasn't at all surprised that Walker was handicapped: he was my comeuppance, my education. From the first night I took him in my arms in bed to feed him, I could feel that chain between us, that chain that said we were linked, that I owed him.

After Walker was born, I thought the conversation about more children might abate, but instead it intensified: now Johanna was driven by a new need, for a third child. She wanted to bracket Walker with normality. She wanted to insulate Hayley from the loneliness of being raised with a severely disabled brother, who would never be the company for her that a normal sister or brother might. But it was unthinkable and I was the one who said no. The guilt that came afterwards was as inevitable as the weather.

———

Walker saw the doctor three more times that first month. He was puking like a pro; he never slept. His mother was a ghost. Dr. Saunders was now noting anatomical details every visit: oval, spade-like thumbs, mild blepharophimosis (smallish, down-slanted eyes), orbital hypertelorism (eyes widespread too). He always used the scientific terms on the boy's chart— it made for more accurate communication with other doctors. They were serious words, embodying a professional standard of exactitude. But Walker Brown was a hard boy to be exact about. Both his testicles, on the other hand, were now palpable, a small victory.

"It's still too early to get worried," Saunders told Johanna.

He had a talent for reassuring mothers, one of the reasons he was considered one of the best pediatricians in the city. He was just turning fifty, trim, well dressed (he insisted on wearing a tie), and he knew how to make easy conversation. Most of the mothers I knew had crushes on him. They tarted themselves up for the trip to his office when their kids needed a booster shot.

What his patients didn't know was that their beloved Dr. Saunders had a long-standing interest in rare afflictions and their human consequences. His wife, Lynn, had been a special-education teacher. Pediatrics didn't pay as well as most other specialties, but it was hopeful medicine: most kids he could fix with swift and certain action. The times when he couldn't reached a long way into Saunders: he saw something heroic in those children and in their lives. (Shortly before he died of colon cancer in the spring of 2007 at the age of sixty, he inspired the creation of the Norman Saunders Initiative in Complex Care at Toronto's Hospital for Sick Children.) Privately, Saunders was obsessed with eighteenth-century British naval history and heroes. With the most broken kids, Saunders, too, became a navigator in unknown waters, an explorer.

But his watchfulness with Walker drove Johanna crazy. She'd arrive home from an appointment and struggle through the door with a baby bag and a stroller and some new device to try to feed the boy, hand him to Olga and say, "I'm so upset with Norm. Normally he knows what he's doing. But with Walker he just looks at him."

What Saunders was doing was trying to figure out whether the just-offness of the boy's appearance—to say nothing of his limpness and failure to thrive—were signs of a syndrome. And if so, which one? There were thousands of medical syndromes and at least six thousand rare diseases. On its own, blepharophimosis (the extra fraction of space between Walker's eyes) suggested any number of them: Van den Ende–Gupta syndrome, say, or Ohdo syndrome, or Carnevale syndrome. At the time the Internet was still a new device, into which geneticists poured lists of symptoms daily, which in turn made diagnosing a syndrome both easier and more complicated than it was before. It was like trying to find a particular plant in a vast garden of exotic flowers, each one more bizarre than the next.

Slowly but steadily, Walker passed sixteen weeks of age. As the first autumn of his life greyed into winter, Saunders began to refine a diagnosis—not yet that something was wrong, but that something wasn't right. The child was becoming more alert; his eyes, at least, were now tracking objects, even if his head was a bit laggy. He had started smiling. Good signs, the doctor thought.

But at night at home, Saunders was leafing through medical literature on rare afflictions. He didn't like what he found: specifically, a research paper with pictures of children who looked almost exactly like Walker Brown. The anomaly was newly described and shockingly rare, a random genetic misfire that produced a wide-ranging group of related symptoms collectively known as cardiofaciocutaneous syndrome. The global effort to sequence the complete human genome was still years in the future; clinical genetics, its predecessor, was still mostly a detective game of observation and hunches. Symptoms overlapped with other syndromes, and misdiagnoses were common. Shprintzen syndrome looked like CFC—Saunders almost fell for that one—but it wasn't the same: those kids had eyebrows. Noonan syndrome was far more common than CFC, and shared many features, but usually produced much milder developmental delays. Ditto Costello syndrome, with the difference that Costello children had "softer" features (whatever that meant) and were more prone to certain cancers than CFCers. Many geneticists believed CFC and Costello syndromes were only variants of Noonan; others insisted they were separate anomalies. My wife and I kept hoping someone would be specific, and specifically helpful, but the only thing geneticists seemed sure about was how little they knew.

———

By the late fall of 1996, from what Norman Saunders could see, Walker had nearly all the signs of CFC. The potential consequences were sobering: learning difficulties, hearing loss, intellectual impairment, language impairment. "Socialization skills may surpass intellectual skills," one researcher noted, rather gracefully. Ten percent developed psychiatric disorders in the teen years.

That November, Saunders referred Walker's case to the genetics department at the Hospital for Sick Children. At home, what had begun as a normal concern for a preemie baby had mutated into a twenty-four-hour state of turgid alarm. There was something wrong with our boy.

Any parent of a child with a syndrome remembers the day he or she is told to see the genetics department. It is the second circle of diagnostic hell. What has been, to that point, a matter of health, something you could fix, is suddenly a matter of science, carved in genetic stone. I still remember the way that day closed in, the way time gelled, went still. There had been an accident miles earlier on the divided-cell highway; we had to go back. The shock was similar to that of losing one's wedding ring in the sea: you knew it was gone, it was unrecoverable. This *wasn't* something we could fix, it felt ancient, primordial. One day Walker was part of life, the next he was a misstep of evolution. I hated the idea, but I now understood fate, what the Greeks talked about. Suddenly, nothing seemed to move much, and I felt a decade older.

The building that housed the genetics clinic at the Hospital for Sick Children resembled a futuristic spaceship: stainless steel, clean, no nicks or flaws. Normally, the clinics and emergency departments and institutes and programs we visited with Walker were tiny madhouses—chaos, children crying in several registers at once. Mothers tearing their hair out. Social workers with clipboards. Doctors, the male ones, anyway, trying ever so delicately to avoid the fray. Machines beeping: I once counted ten different tones of *ping*.

The genetics clinic, on the other hand, was like the sperm factory in Woody Allen's *Everything You Always Wanted to Know About Sex* (*But Were Afraid to Ask*): clean, pristine, well ordered, neat. Nothing out of place. And quiet! No wonder: there were never any people around. It felt like a department where certainty reigned, where you might get a few answers. (Little did I know. To this day, despite repeated genetic testing, we have no confirmed genetic diagnosis of Walker's CFC, even though his doctors are convinced that is what he has.)

Saunders referred us to Genetics in November; the request wound its way through the medical system, and by February we had an appointment. The geneticist's name was Dr. Ron Davidson; his son was a geneticist too. He was a tall man with a confident voice, and he confirmed Saunders' inkling: Walker had cardiofaciocutaneous syndrome. He was eight months old. That qualifies as an early CFC diagnosis even today.

"Now that we know what's wrong, we'll know what to put right," Johanna said, touchingly, as we sat in Dr. Davidson's office. She believed in medicine. She had wanted to be a doctor, had been a pre-med student for a year, before physics and organic chemistry finished those aspirations off.

The doctor was upbeat. "His developmental milestones are being achieved at a rate that is well within the normal range," he wrote in a confirming letter after meeting Walker. (There were always confirming letters, following doctor's visits. We have rafts of them.) True, "the feature of the CFC syndrome that raises most concern is the chance of learning problems," but even here there was hope, in the doctor's view. As the number of cases reported has increased, several affected individuals have been reported as having completely normal learning histories and normal intelligence."

The syndrome was not hereditary: the chances of having a second CFC child were microscopic, although Walker had a fifty–fifty chance of having a CFCer of his own. "However, by then we will know a great deal more about the condition and the mutation that causes it, and there will undoubtedly be a variety of options available to him and his wife." Walker's wife! I have to say, I never believed it.

four

His infant head was overlarge and shaped like an olive, but the rest of him was as light as a loaf of bread: I could carry him in one hand. I called him Boogle, or Beagle, or Mr. B, or Lagalaga (because he made that noise), or simply Bah! (He liked *B* sounds.) As he grew older, we developed a private language of tongue clicks that only he and I speak. All we ever seem to say is, "Hello, it's me, I'm clicking to you, and only to you, because only you and I speak Click"; to which he (or I) reply, I think, "Yes, hi, I see you there, and I am clicking back, I like it that we speak our private language, in fact I find it hilarious." This is very enjoyable for both of us.

I could clap my hands and he would clap back; he especially liked it when I clapped his hands faster than he ever could on his own. It was impossible to take a decent photograph of him, except by chance, and then he looked like

Frank Sinatra Jr. on a tear. He smelled warm, baked: his head to this day has the tasty whiff of a Zagnut bar. He never crawled, but began to walk at two-and-a-half.

The house was a well-organized nightmare. You couldn't survive as the parent of a handicapped child if you weren't organized, and my wife was. There were the famous laundry baskets of toys on every floor; plastic activity boards hanging off the backs of chairs in the kitchen and the living room; tubs of syringes and feeding lines upstairs and down; caches of diapers in a chest by the front door; troops of medicine bottles and ointment tubes marching through cupboards and across dressers and countertops.

He loved to touch things. The bottom three slats of every window blind in the house were mangled. His most developed consciousness seemed to live in his hands, in what he could manipulate—the genius light switch, the fascinating toilet-paper tube, anything that beeped or flickered. What he could touch, he knew.

The best part was the way he exploded with laughter and rocked into a ball of glee at some mysterious thing, which passersby loved. (For a while, I suspected he was rubbing his penis between his thighs, a traditional source of merriment for all boys.) As he grew older, he became slyer. He loved to clear tables and flat surfaces, especially closely guarded ones. He went for glasses of wine, which seemed to catch his eye, so we called him the temperance man. He would distract you, then wipe the deck and throw his head back with pleasure, momentarily cleverer than anyone else. Was that his secret project, to show us he was sometimes smart enough to fool us? That would not surprise me. His desires were invisible, unspoken, but that did not mean he had none.

He became a great wanderer, a lucky one. Here is one evening:

He is five. (At his stockiest, he looks three.) I leave him in an enclosed hallway at the foot of some stairs in a friend's elegant house while we eat dinner. I know he can't climb stairs and I know he can't open a door.

Ten minutes later, I hear a tinkling sound. A beautiful sound, the noise of the air breaking, but unusual enough to go and see what it is. It's Walker. He has done the unimagined and climbed the stairs and opened the door and is now gleefully and deliberately smashing the last of seven wine-glasses on a Noguchi coffee table. Not a scratch on him. We come to call that evening Kristallnacht.

It was not a particularly funny joke, but if you spend a lot of time with a disabled child, with a child who was not supposed to live and whose survival nevertheless radically changed your life—especially if said child is your child—you feel you can break the rules. The boy recalibrates the world. The crisis of so-and-so's unhappiness about her job or his inability to meet a woman who will pay him what he considers to be a sufficient degree of attention pales next to the crisis of how to stop Walker from beating his own brains out. The opinion of other people matters less and less the more you walk down the street with a boy whose lumpy looks attract attention, stares and smiles alike. One's life is suddenly marked by other exigencies.

I use the word *retarded*, for instance, though never to describe a disabled person: it's insufficiently descriptive applied to a human being. But it's evocative if you're describing an inanimate design, or an especially recalcitrant aspect of bureaucratic behaviour. Sometimes I'll use it at a party, and I can sense the person I am speaking to rearing back, however imperceptibly, at the sudden presence of what is supposed to be an unusable word; I can see him note the usage, and I can see him decide not to react, because he knows I have a disabled son: he must think, well, if anyone can use it, he can use it. It needs to be repurposed.

He loved women, the prettier the better. Even as an infant he would raise his arms to be picked up—he couldn't sit up on his own until he was nearly a year old—or, later, climb into a woman's lap and immediately peer down her neckline. Then he would feel her up. I thought it was accidental, but Johanna's friends remarked how intentional it seemed. He loved anything shiny, fingering it close to his wonky eyes. Our friends called him "the jeweller."

Our close friends, that is. To others, at least for the first few years, I never mentioned Walker's difficulties. I wasn't ashamed of him. But I didn't want sympathy and I didn't want him to feel he needed it either.

He stayed in my mind. Not only darkly, or as worry, but as a mental talisman. So did my daughter, of course. But I was always catching up to Hayley, whereas Walker moved slowly and could be tracked from standing. His aura, the fact of his existence, turned up everywhere, unexpectedly: in the lyrics of a Neil Young song at the gym ("*Some are bound to happiness / Some are bound to glory / Some are bound to loneliness / Who can tell your story?*"), between the lines of a Norman Mailer essay read during one of my bouts of insomnia. He turned up in other people's conversations. Once, at a cocktail party—this would have been the summer Walker turned three—I overheard a man I had known well for a long time trying to explain to another friend how people communicated with my son. "It's hard to describe," he said. He had a drink in his hand. "His father has his own babbling language. It seems to work as well as anything else." I couldn't tell if he approved or not, but it was the first time I heard what Walker and I did with each other described as language.

I often wondered if we were imagining Walker's progress, inventing the connections we thought he was making. Did he really say "Heh-Heh" when Hayley was nearby? Or was he just breathing? When I said goodbye to him, and leaned over and kissed him, did he really say "Bye"? *Or was he just breathing*? Johanna heard it too: "He just said goodbye!" she would say, followed by "I'm going to cry," experiencing yet again the instantaneous hyperplasia that marked our days. He made people feel things. But did *he* feel anything? Did the outline of a boy I saw beneath his stolid surface, beneath the dead-calm pond of his mind, actually exist? Or was it wishful thinking? I was often convinced our effort to perceive a whole being in his stunted parts was an act of almost reckless faith, no different from that of any other zealot—from, say, the mother of the Houston TV evangelist I once met, who told me in no uncertain terms that heaven existed, that she was going there, and that God had already decorated her part of it, as he did for each of his faithful, according to her personal tastes. "My heaven will be full of water," she said matter-of-factly, as if she were describing her favourite resort. "Because I love water." Coarse speculation, but how was she any different from Johanna and me? Who doesn't *want* to believe there's a heaven? But that doesn't mean it exists.

And yet this constant questioning, filtered through Walker—does he mean what he's doing, or not?—was also a model, a frame on which to hang the human world, a way of living.

The summer Walker turned twelve, we took our first long holiday without him. It was the same summer he learned to respond most of the time to a request for a high-five. While Walker was in Toronto at a respite camp, Johanna, Hayley and I took a week away at my brother Tim's house in the town of Rockport, on Cape Ann, north of Boston. Tim and I had spent our summers in the town as boys, with our parents and sisters; we learned to swim there and sail, to eat a lobster properly, to take pleasure in the feel of the sea. We became independent there, and friends.

The house was on the ocean, a square, immaculate dwelling that looked out over the Atlantic onto Thacher Island, a shoal so dangerous it sported not one but two lighthouses. It's one of my favourite places on earth, and it always makes me think of Walker: he had been with us the first summer we stayed there, before Tim owned it, the first summer he and I rented the house together. Walker was born in June, five weeks premature, but we drove to Boston in August anyway, Walker barely six weeks old, back before we knew something was wrong, when he just seemed like a difficult kid to feed. We thought we could manage anything then. For two weeks my wife sat in a chair in the kitchen of the rented house by the sea, trying to express fluids into our weird little son while gazing out at the twin beacons.

The chair had green cushions and bamboo arms. I looked at it so often that first summer of his life I made a water-colour of it, a painting my wife later framed and hung on the wall of our bedroom, near my side of the bed. For a long time it was the first thing I saw when I woke up in the morning. She meant it as a compliment, but I couldn't help but wonder if it wasn't an admonishment: don't forget about the boy.

Now he was twelve; we were back by the sea, our first time without him. The chair was gone too. The first morning I woke up before anyone else and climbed down over the granite rocks to the ocean for a swim, naked. The ocean was rough and it was hard to get into the water, and hard to get out again. Afterwards I made my way back to the outdoor shower and rinsed away the salt and got dressed and made coffee and read the paper and looked at the sea. I was by myself. It felt like paradise. I didn't even think of the hours I had spent in that room with the boy, twelve years earlier. I am glad there is still a place, a sanctuary of sorts, where my concern for him cannot reach me, where I can forget him at least momentarily. But I always miss him when this happens, and he always gets there, as he has now in my memory of that kitchen by the sea. Such a luxury, the luxury of no concerns! Of not having Walker on or in or under my mind! Without him, for a short stretch I could do everything as I once did it, in deliberate steps, the way you can when you don't have a handicapped child.

But even there Walker found me. That morning,* having returned from my swim in the sea, wandering through the house, I began leafing through a *catalogue raisonné* from an

---

* That same morning *The New York Times* featured a front-page story, "For Families of the Ailing, the Chance to Relax." The story was about couples

exhibition of Edward Hopper's paintings. Hopper had lived down the road in Gloucester, had created some of his most famous pictures from the grave and uncompromising local light. In 1947, Mrs. Frank B. Davidson asked Hopper what he thought of abstract art. The great representationalist wasn't impressed. "There is a school of painting called abstractionist or nonobjective," he told Mrs. Davidson, "which is derived largely from the work of Paul Cézanne, that attempts to create 'pure painting'—that is, an art which will use form, color and design for their own sakes, and independent of man's experience of life and his association with nature. I do not believe such an aim can be achieved by a human being. Whether we wish it or not we are all bound to the earth with our experience of life and the reactions of the mind, heart, and eye, and our sensations, by no means, consist entirely of form, color and design. We would be leaving out a good deal that I consider worthwhile expressing in painting, and it cannot be expressed in literature."

The first time I read the passage that morning—it was still before breakfast—I thought, this is exactly my error with Walker. I'm trying to see in him things that aren't there, events

---

seeking temporary respite from caring for their sick and aging parents. Nearly 10 million North Americans take care of someone with Alzheimer's or another form of dementia. The consequences of caring for someone who is handicapped, the story claimed, were serious: depression, hypertension, diabetes, sleep disorders, heart disease and "death." For anywhere from $120 to $200 a day, grown children (most were in their fifties) could leave their ailing parents in the care of a respite facility. The offspring quoted in the story spoke of these breaks as if they were miracles, though they all admitted to feeling guilty for needing the service. "What kind of daughter am I, leaving her for four days?" one of the women interviewed remarked. "I felt I was being selfish. Why do I need this time away from her?" Oh, I knew that feeling.

"independent of life and my association with nature." We were the abstractionists where Walker was concerned, insisting there was a painting, a coherent idea, albeit in radical form, that no one else could see. I kept rereading the passage, and the more I read it, the more I began to think that there was very little difference between what Hopper tried to do on canvas or paper and what we tried to do on the blankness of Walker: we described what we saw, and then tried to determine what it meant, how it made us feel, and whether it was realistic.

An hour can pass that way, triggered by the mere thought of him.

At home on his neighbourhood tours with Olga, Walker had a vast circle of acquaintances. Strangers approach me even now and say, "You're Walker's dad." It makes me feel his brilliance. He was well dressed too. Olga bought him the latest gear at Gap for his birthdays and I occasionally snuck out on my own to pick up something. I can't describe the pleasure it gave me to buy his first big-boy shirt: he looked so sharp and cool. I bought him an orange skateboarder sweater, I bought him his first jeans, his first khakis, his first sneakers, his first baseball cap, a flight jacket with a fur collar, a T-shirt from wherever I travelled. I bought him an undershirt that was smaller than my hand, a pair of sunglasses he despised. Hat and gloves (all hurled aside with vigour), socks, beaded Indian belts. All the emblems of a normal boyhood. My longing, not his. One day I'm going to take him with my father and brother to buy his first tie. I know it's futile: the bib he wears to catch his drool will cover it. But that might be the only male ritual we pass down to him.

From a notebook I kept:

27 December 1997. Have to pay more attention to Walker's diet. He had a doctor's appointment before we left for Christmas here in Pennsylvania, and our pediatrician was surprised that he still can't or doesn't walk, crawl, strive to pick up objects and stuff them in his mouth, feed himself, swallow anything with chunks in it, or stack blocks. He was even more appalled that Walker still weighs only 20 pounds—half or at best two-thirds of what he ought to at this age, a year-and-a-half. The new fear is that his inability to put on weight will affect his intellectual development, even such as it is. So I spent a fair bit of time trying to figure out how to make egg custard, which a nurse thought would put some meat on his bones. But he has a bad cold, and bad swallow control, which means that he throws up half the time after a meal. I can see a GI tube looming in his and my future. Mostly, though, I fear for his loneliness. Lately I've begun to think that he is aware of it too—suddenly aware that he is not like everyone else, albeit unconsciously.

I seem to be on the verge of crying, so I will go.

By the time Walker was three, his medical chart was ten pages long.

A pattern of afflictions had emerged early: bad chest, pneumonia, constipation, endless earaches, scaling skin. He didn't sleep. We thought of him as affable, but he cried half the time.

At least at the doctor's office you could ask questions. Returning home again was like entering a long hallway where the lights wouldn't go on. My wife said she felt "as if a soundproof curtain has dropped over us." Certainly any crisis with any child brings that curtain down: your focus shortens, you aim straight ahead. The difference with Walker was that the curtain was permanent. Before Walker, the future had looked like a series of discrete challenges, each to be overcome, resulting in (possibly callow) glory. After Walker was born, the future appeared unchanging, sad, full of obligation until we died—which only raised the gloomy prospect of what would happen to him then.

Early on—this too is common in the families of CFC children—we agreed Hayley shouldn't be held responsible for Walker as an adult. But she took him in her stride. One day, I asked her why she thought Walker couldn't walk and talk at the age of two. "I could walk when I was one because I was born with two eyes open," she said. "But Walker was born with only one eye open." She was four.

The CFC diagnosis was something to go on, but having a label still didn't improve Walker's health. Dr. Saunders' notes became repetitive: *congested* and *coughing* and *otitis* and *failure to thrive* appeared in every entry. At eighteen months Walker neither spoke nor understood any words, couldn't walk, had no gestures except raising his arms for "up" and the occasional smile. DEVELOPMENTAL DELAY, Saunders wrote, in capital letters on his chart. There wasn't time in the day to wait for Walker to take in the trickle of food he could swallow, and Saunders ordered the installation of a G-tube. Until he grew stronger, he wouldn't be able to eat; because he couldn't eat, he couldn't grow stronger. The G-tube made it easier to administer the growing list of medicines Walker needed for his reflux and his ear infections and his sleeplessness and his jitters and his rashes: Gentian violet, hydrocortisone, amoxicillin, azithromycin, clarithromycin, erythromycin (ever wider on the spectrum of antibiotic strength), cisipride, Keflex,

Betnovate, Flamazine, lactulose, Colace, chloral hydrate. They sounded like the names of ambassadors to an intergalactic conference of aliens. His chronic constipation (his muscles were too weak to move things along normally), made worse by the equally necessary chloral hydrate, often required not one but three drugs—lactulose as a sugary starter, Colace as the dynamite, and suppositories, the blasting cap itself. You had five minutes to take cover.

Nothing was ordinary. Like most kids, he had diaper rash—but because this was Walker, my compromised son, it was the Chernobyl of diaper blights, requiring a day in hospital. There was so much wax in his ears that we could have started a museum. For a period of ten months, he developed agonizing blisters on his feet that thwarted his already thwarted walking. They were three inches across, yellow, and showed up whether he was wearing socks or no socks, shoes or no shoes. They disappeared as quickly as they came. The doctors never did figure out why.

The diagnosis of CFC meant more appointments: the ear specialist, the eye doctor, the dermatologist, the gastro-reflux expert, the neurologist, a foot doctor, occupational and behavioural and oral therapists, the geneticist, the cardiologist, the feeding and sleep clinics, even the drooling clinic. Their conclusion (and I'm quite serious): "Mrs. Brown, your son drools." The dentist needed to place Walker under full anaesthesia to clean his teeth. Oral therapy was important if he was going to learn to speak, but two years yielded nothing; we switched to sign language, but he wouldn't make the eye contact essential to learn sign, and his fine motor skills were too coarse to do it anyway. By then he was beginning to bang his head as well, which didn't encourage his therapists.

The eye doctor couldn't get an accurate reading on what his eyes needed, and Walker couldn't say. Ditto his hearing. Added to the eleven times he was at Dr. Saunders' office in 1998 alone, along with trips to Emergency, Walker logged a medical visit a week. And that was if he was more or less healthy.

Better to concentrate on his gross motor abilities, the experts told us: if he learned to walk, at least, he could vary his environment and stimulate himself that way, and would be that much less dependent on others for the rest of his life. That was the phrase: *for the rest of his life.* To teach him, we undertook a costly and radical Venezuelan therapy three times a week for two years. The MEDEK method entailed hanging him upside down and pulling his legs into unnatural positions. The only MEDEK specialist in the city, Esther Fink, lived forty-five minutes away by car, in a north Toronto neighbourhood heavily populated by Hasidim with a substantial number of disabled children of their own. It was another world, and I was suddenly part of it.

Walker hated the sessions, started screaming the moment we pulled into Esther Fink's driveway, but he learned to walk. At least he had that. He could be what his name said he was. Maybe that was why we insisted.

The strange thing was that all this darkness could be relieved by a few pinpoints of light. A reaction alone was notable; a smile or one of his glee sprees charmed my afternoon.

I remember how proud I was the first day he went to school. By the age of three he was enrolled in Play 'n Learn, a daycare program that integrated normal and disabled children. I could spot the parents of the delayed kids in the school parking lot when I dropped Walker off: they were the ones who looked as if a bomb had just gone off in the back seat of the car. They were starved for contact and longing to tell the truth. One afternoon, I ran into a woman whose severely disabled fourteen-year-old daughter had died two years earlier. "Do you know the first thing I did—on the way back from the funeral?" she said. "I said to my husband, 'Pull over. Let's have sex.'" She later divorced him.

From Walker's first Play 'n Learn report card:

Walker enjoys exploring objects by manipulating them. He turns objects through his fingers as he looks at them, and has also begun to bang objects together.

Play 'n Learn's theory was that integrating normal children and their disabled counterparts would sensitize the normals and inspire the delayed. The school boasted a full-time sensory integration therapist (CFC children are often overwhelmed by their senses and have to be conditioned to them, even to someone else touching their skin) and an occupational therapist, to teach basic concepts of sociability such as sitting down with others at lunch. To my surprise, Walker slowly became bolder, more outgoing. The staff (all women) were dedicated teachers of the disabled, optimists who saw hope in everything.

Typically, he produces open vowels and consonant–vowel combinations—which may include any of the sounds [b, n, d, 1, y] with an "ah." Although he will not initiate an interaction, he enjoys having his peers around. When a peer is holding his hand, he seems to be content.

It was the last line that crushed me. He needed someone to moor him.

The provincial government in Ontario, keen to show it was serious about education, insisted that all children be graded. Grades meant standards. The first time Walker arrived home from Play 'n Learn with a report card in his backpack, we learned he was improving at math. Math! And improving! We laughed like hell, and then we kissed him and said, "Well done, Walker! Two plus two is four!" We did that for a long time, held on to it like a rare, delicious treat. Not that we believed Walker could do math as we defined it. But it was a story he had brought us that anyone could appreciate, a detail of his life that made it out from behind the soundproof curtain.

What I couldn't tell was what the routines meant to him. Did he know he was "painting" when the teacher was guiding his hands? He had a friend, Jeremy, but did he know what a friend was? He sat at the table with the other kids for Snack— a stretch of time named Snack, I loved that—but did he feel the communal buzz? What went on inside that thickened skin, behind that swollen heart? I didn't care if he never threw a ball or tormented his sister or skied beside me or told a joke or dated a girl (though I would love it if he did). What I cared about was whether he had a sense of himself, an inner life. Sometimes it seemed like the most urgent question of all.

———

From the day he came home from the hospital as a baby, at two days old, nights were hard. If it was Johanna's turn to put him to bed and sleep with him, I drove Olga home. The next night we'd switch. Our nights off from Walker duty were big events: I planned my week around them, however

unreliable that plan was. (If one of us had to travel for work—
something both of us did at least a few days every month—
the other took Walker alone, night after night. That was
exhausting, but it made us appreciate the nights that he slept:
they felt like beautiful and unexpected gifts. A clear four hours
for us was like a night's sleep for anyone else.) After dropping
Olga back at her apartment, I was free. I could go for a drink,
a walk. Most of the time I snuck back into the house quietly,
turning the heavy front door lock by hand, leaving my shoes
by the door, hoping to get to bed without waking him,
without hearing him crying or pounding his head. He had a
knack for worming his way into my brain just as I opened
a book or began to write a letter, and once I heard him, I was
hijacked. I couldn't bear the sound of his steady agony. But if
he was asleep and I could stay awake, I could read, and did,
voraciously. I have never appreciated words and books and
time and the life of my mind more than I did on those stolen
late nights. Dante, *The History of Mental Retardation*, books
about deafness and about stuttering, novels about cowboys
and reprobates, diaries of diplomats, Casanova's memoirs.
(Casanova claimed he didn't speak until he was five, and then,
when he did, he was lying on the *vaporetto*, moving down the
Grand Canal in Venice. "The trees are moving!" he said, if
my memory serves me. His parents, rather than being
amazed that their lagging boy finally had spoken, immediately berated him for being an idiot. "The boat is moving!"
they cried. Whereupon Casanova uttered his second sentence: "Well then it is possible the earth moves around the
sun!" I admit there were days when I hoped for a similar out-
burst from Walker. Certainly I collected stories.) I read
Chesterfield's letters to his son, and Chesterton's dull

detective novels, and anything that took me away: Elmore Leonard and Chandler and Roth and Updike, books about fathers and collecting and obsession, essays about any variety of inner life, lives of artists and millionaires, and of course every scientific paper about CFC. And newspapers. One of my favourite photographs of Walker from those days shows him sitting in my lap in a reclining lawn chair on the deck of a friend's cottage north of Toronto, beside a still lake. I am reading the newspaper, holding its pages open, frowning. Walker is leaning back against my chest, laughing like mad. We were both happy then.

We fantasized about holidays, Johanna and I, but getting away was complicated. He was three years old before we left him and Hayley with Olga overnight. But we didn't like to do that: Olga worked hard enough as it was; it was too much to ask for more. Instead, we took him with us: me, Johanna, Hayley, Walker, and often Olga—our little caravan of care.

One early CFC study speculated that the protective myelin coating on the nerves of children with CFC was insufficient, which resulted in too much information coursing through their brains: their lack of output was the result of too much input, an insufficiently controlled and organized neural network. It made sense to me. In a car or in a plane, looking out the window, stimulated, Walker never stopped moving. It was all he could do to be contained by gravity. On a plane he looked out the window and laughed, looked at his hands, looked out the window again, laughed again, picked up his knees, balled into the seat, rolled on his side, hauled himself up again, looked out the window again, whacked himself in the head, fell flat on his side, laughing uproariously, and then stretched himself out on the smooth, slippery chair (he loved the frictionless slidey-ness of the upholstery). Then he did all of it all over again, and then he started crying. That was two minutes' worth of action. He didn't seem to be able to control whatever came over him, and a lot did.

He loved an airplane takeoff and our car pulling out of a parking spot. He liked to lower the electric windows in the back seat and throw things out of the car when he thought no one was looking. (Which was frequently.) Sometimes when I worked at home on the dining room table, plowing my way through incomprehensible papers on genetics or neurology, he walked into the room, sat on my lap, accepted a jiggle or two, and then, ten seconds later, got up and walked away. I could hear Olga in the kitchen, and I thought, *how long will this last?*, even as I was grateful for the interruption. Ten minutes later he was back, to do it all again. Strange rhythm of the mystery boy.

Those were the good days. On the bad ones he stayed with me, hanging on to my arm or lying near me, moaning or wailing or crying. When it snowed too much for him to go outside in his stroller he pitched fits, lying on the floor and slamming his head against it. I know the precise shape of that noise from memory.

On the good days my wife and I snatched the time we could get to ourselves. Our friends Cathrin and John had an old lakeside cottage north of Toronto, in a region known as Muskoka, an hour and a half by car. They invited us north again and again, often with another couple, Tecca and Al. It became a second world for us, a sanctuary of weekends. You could see for miles across the water from their island into the endless feathery green of the trees.

We took Hayley and Walker and Olga, and Olga watched our boy, sat with him in the screened-in porch of a little sub-cabin by the shores of the lake: the tune and words to "Do Your Ears Hang Low?" floated from that veranda across the water again and again and again like puffs of love. There was often a breeze to thrill him. Late in the afternoons he might paddle in the water, never too enthusiastically, but he loved the company at waterside. He loved to glide out in my lap in a kayak, dragging his hands over the side like an insect feeling the watery surface of its world. I rambled at him, talking in his ear. "See the trees, the way the greens are different? Or see the waterslide? You'd really like that," He loved being spoken to. He loved a lot of things, or seemed to. I nattered on in his ear, endlessly, but I didn't mind that he never answered. He made me stretch for him; for inexplicable reasons I am grateful to him for that, always will be. Where would I have gone, without him? He was such a little boy, featherweight, dependent: whoever was with him was his world, and I loved being his world, if he let me. His curly hair against the underside of my chin as we floated together in the boat.

In the evenings, after dinner, sitting out on the screened-in porch, Walker joined us again. I remember the first time he did it, how deliberately he visited everyone: climbing up into Cathrin's lap, laying his head against her shoulder, then climbing down and moving on to fondle Tecca's silver bracelet (it was she who dubbed him "the jeweller"), moving on from there to Al, to John, to me, to his mum, his sister, her friends, his world. He made his rounds. Then he glided back to Olga, or wandered past the lights and sounds of the stereo, or opened the screen door to the evening outside. I imagine—that's the only word I can use—he wanted us to know that he loved us. His grown-up friends look back on those days now as a unique, impossible trip we all took together. "Those summers were an extraordinary time," one said to me the other day, "though I'm not sure I knew just how extraordinary at the time."

The rest of the time I read and talked and swam and cooked. And drank: I often drank gin heartily when it wasn't my night with him, for the instant lift-off. (I had no time to lose.) Every free minute felt like a sapphire, and yet also stung me with a rebuke: not because I was being irresponsible, but because his need never went away. We frantically tried to relax as much as we could in the time we had. It was only thirty years ago that a child like Walker might not have survived, and his affliction was still a mystery, to the medical profession as much as to us: how could I not wonder what I was supposed to be doing with him? Johanna and I traded nights at the cottage too, one of us sleeping with Walker in a tiny bedroom on the ground floor of the main residence, while the other enjoyed a night alone in the luxury of a sleeping cabin by the water—free to stay up late, have another drink, live briefly what felt like the exotic life. Trains hooted by in the night on the far shore.

In the morning after a bad night with Walker—I had a raging theory that he never slept well with me because he slept like a log every other night with his mother—after he had finally fallen asleep, or at ten in the morning after Olga had come up from her cabin to take over, I stumbled down the path to the lake. I can still see my long-legged wife in those days: already stretched out by the water, greedily tanning and reading. I was happy for her, and angry at her, and exhausted, but the same pang shot through me anyway: where was the boy? (We called him "the boy.") Why wasn't she with him? Why wasn't I? The admonishments were on a circuit, and they ran incessantly beneath our surfaces.

five

It was nearly impossible to take a good photograph of Walker. The trick was to wait for a crucial intersection when at least three things happened at once: a moment when he was calm and his body felt organized and relaxed; a moment when his internal battles abated and he wasn't hitting himself; and a moment when he was alert and energized. Such moments didn't occur often. When one did, and you happened to have a camera on hand, and you managed to get a picture before the moment evaporated, then, maybe, you got a picture you wanted to look at, that you didn't have to look away from. They were our real treasures, proof of the Walker we were convinced was there, under his fuss and pain.

The first time it happened he was nearly three and he was sitting in the bath. By that point in his life, his calm in the bathwater was almost biblical. Eight gallons and three quarts was the ancient Hebrew measure of a bath: that was about right for Walker, until the warmth hit his chest, whereupon he got nervous again. The trick was to stay within his narrow zone of comfort.

That first good photograph was a fluke, taken as he looked up from endlessly turning a toy in his hands. I had bought sinking submarines and squirting whales and swimming frogs, but he liked the measuring cups and sieves that let the water trickle out. He liked the noise they made.

The first shots Johanna liked, unequivocally, were taken when he was seven. Seven years of trying to catch Walker in a pose she wanted to look at.

It was a hot day in the summer, and Walker, per usual on hot days, was wearing little more than a shirt and a diaper. He was lounging on his back on the couch in the TV room, in an orange T-shirt, wearing a pair of my sunglasses, which Hayley had slipped onto his head. This in itself was daring: Walker was hell on glasses and sunglasses alike, and took

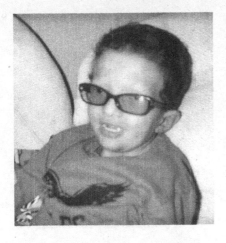

no time at all to break their arms and shatter their lenses. Johanna had recently interviewed Robert Evans, the late film producer. By then Evans was in his seventies, but he still personified the sixties Hollywood mogul—tinted shades, cravats, starlets on his arm, a voice that seemed to have been strained through smoke and money. Nothing fazed Evans, nothing embarrassed him. As soon as she saw the shots of Walker, Johanna started calling him Walker Evans, and pinned them to the kitchen cupboard, a reminder of his charm. It was his Nothing Fazes the Boogle look. I imagined he was reminiscing about Natalie Wood. When I look at it now I remember the chant he had in those days (he doesn't do it any more), a *rah-rah-rah-rah-rah-rah* routine that was clearly his way of telling a story, when he knew he had the floor. He could have been on the telephone, luring someone into an obvious deal. There was to be no interrupting him on this one. He had no words, but he had tone down.

It was a miraculous shoot, in any event, that steamy day in the TV room: the very next shot in the series conjured up not Evans, but the comedian Drew Carey, who has since assumed Bob Barker's role as the host of *The Price Is Right*. Evans and Carey—two men who, apparently, were more than willing to play a role, even degrade them- selves, to be in showbiz.

In the Carey shot he looks more wary, confident but watch- ful, taking in some inanity across the sound set. A normal photograph made it possible to imagine he was normal too.

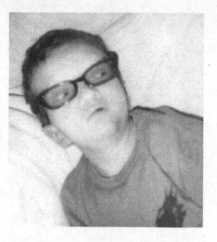

My favourite photographs were of his more private moments. When he was barely a year old, we rented a cottage on an island in Georgian Bay, a few hours north of Toronto. It was an isolated place forty minutes by boat from the nearest marina, surrounded only by other cot- tagers on other islands, accessible only by water. It was so quiet when the wind was low I was afraid the other cot- tagers could hear Walker's crying, or even my shouting. But the quiet changed him; up there he transformed, became surer of himself, less distracted. Sometimes he looked out toward the orange sunsets at the end of a fine day, with the breeze blowing, as if he could see something a thousand miles away across the water of the bay—the long view. He knew the place, knew its feel, anyway, even if he didn't know where he was precisely, or couldn't show it. We have a photograph of him there, in Olga's arms, the only time she ever came up in seven summers (it was the one place she wouldn't go: she hated snakes, and the island had rattlers), his weird tuft of hair golden in

the sunset light: the God child, Johanna called the picture,
and he looked it. It was the first place I ever imagined him
to have an inner life, a life private from the rest of us. And
it was there, one afternoon, as everyone napped after a day
swimming—the Canadian version of paradise—that
Johanna snapped a shot of him on the soft blue couch in
the living room, the afternoon sun glowing through the
wraparound windows:

He looks utterly normal, the spitting image of his father
as a kid, and of his grandfather before him. Perhaps that's
why I liked it: it was proof of our bond. I see his slim thighs,
his tan—a tan! He has laid his head on his hands, and his
knees are up; he's wearing a pair of checked shorts
(Hayley's castoffs), and a blue sweatshirt. It's as close as we
got to a picture of what might have been. It even feels
slightly dishonest.

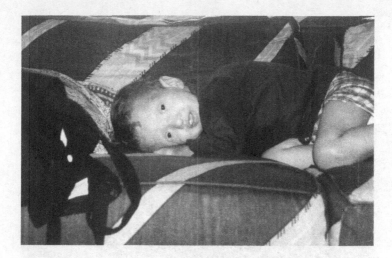

In my favourite photograph of them all, he is six. He'd started at a new school by then, and had blossomed. Beverley Junior Public School was ten minutes by car from where we lived, and right next to a tiny office I had in those days: I could stand outside and look over the fence at him, swinging in the playground. It was a gorgeous school, huge and open, designed with skylights and low windows for the children who spent most of their day on their backs. There was space.

The snapshot was taken just after he started. Walker is standing in the sunroom of our house, gazing intently at my old manual typewriter. He has his hands and fingers splayed across the keys. It was the feel of the keys on his itchy palms that drew him, of course, the give of the keys, the sensation of manipulation. But he looks as if he's making progress, an illusion not uncommon to people who make their living as writers. He's dressed in the red plaid shirt I gave him, and he's ready to type, with plenty to say

and the glint of someone eager to say it. Maybe he had seen
his parents hunched that way so often. It's a charming
scene; who knows, maybe what it depicts is genuine curiosity, a moment of clarity in that fogged-in head. Or so I
think—until the charm falls away, and the space around my
eyes begins to ache, and I can't look at the picture any
longer. Every instant of joy with him is like this, lined at
some eventual depth with the lead of sadness, a reminder
of—well, never mind that. No need to go too big too fast.
But I have to put the pictures of him aside now; that's as
long as I can stand it. It took me ages to let these fantasies
go; I daren't let them back.

———

During bad stretches, my wife and I made two or three trips
to the hospital a week. Infections of the ears, gasping colds,
epic constipations, rashes, bleeding, dehydration *and* constipation (on at least one memorable occasion), toothaches,

and—most of all—unstoppable crying. One evening I was at the Hospital for Sick Children at 11:30 a.m., stayed until midnight, and was back again the next morning from 9 to 12.

Reality goes 3-D in the inferno of the emergency ward at a children's hospital. The default noise level, for starters, is usually half a dozen children crying at once, each in a different key and scale. Rossini would have made an opera from it. The staff bounce from one crisis to another, human balls in pastel blue and green fatigues, utterly dedicated to the welfare of the children: overeager residents, overworked nurses as calm as reeds, the doctors hovering above it all, trying not to fall too deeply into the actual screaming pissing puking aching fray. And of course the equally raucous sound, one you can't always hear but can always feel as a roaring in your ears—the anxieties of the parents. Some of them are so graceless as to talk back to the doctors and nurses and worry and push their kids ahead of yours because their need is greater or they have been waiting longer. There are two categories of mothers in Emergency, the ones who hate being there and the others who secretly love it, because here they are finally among other people who recognize the pre-eminence of their child. Emerg was the full sociological pageant: otherwise healthy-looking kids with strange bruised welts on their unsuspecting legs (blood disease); single mothers with four pallid, ill-nourished children from homes I could see in my mind, with too many extension cords in the bedroom (the youngest has been running a temperature of 102 for four days straight); huddled, well-dressed families unfamiliar with the drama of post-operative consultation (camping accident, knife in the head, narrowly missing the optical nerve, no damage to the sight or mind but some permanent impairment of movement in the left arm).

Who were the lucky ones this time? Who would stay, and who would breathe a sigh of relief and go?

My own worry ponged back and forth. Is it a cold? No, it's cancer. No, it's a cold. The doctors were always flummoxed by Walker's condition, always asked the same questions, wanted the same details over and over again.

Yes, he eats entirely by stomach tube.

Yes, we've tried feeding him by mouth.

Chloral hydrate. Yes, by prescription.

It's not his ears. I know it's not his ears because I was here yesterday about his ears, and it's not his ears, he doesn't cry like this if it's just his ears.

Yes, Doctor, I waited. I waited for five days, with him screaming all the time, before I even thought of bringing him here.

All those stuffed animals in the hospital store in the lobby of the brilliant children's hospital in the middle of the downtown of the brilliant genius city! And yet the place was filled with doctors who couldn't help my boy. I developed a degree of skepticism toward the medical profession that tended to show itself after the fourth doctor in a row told me something I already knew. Sometimes they saw my skepticism and agreed with it, quietly admitting their own helplessness, which made me like them again. Sometimes they spotted my frustration, and stayed away.

I learned an almost geological patience. I knew the hospital like I knew my own basement, all the tricks of the place: the most convenient end of the parking garage (the second level, before the first was even full, near the north elevator), where to validate parking, the best time to line up for the best coffee (before 7:45 in the morning, or after 11), how to work the prescription counter in the pharmacy to minimize the wait. I knew how to find Physio and MRI and Dentistry from memory. I knew what I would see roaming the floors of the place—the children themselves, with their strange afflictions, heads the size of watermelons with bright red newly stitched surgical gashes running from ear to ear, braces and casts, greyish-yellow skin, the resigned eyes, a resignation deeper and more profound than any adult's could ever be.

I knew what to do in response. I knew to smile. Smile for every one of them. Nothing too obvious; I knew what it was like to have someone pander to Walker, I didn't want that special treatment. But an openness, a lack of hostility and fear nonetheless, that was the trick. It was a form of meditation. But always I was looking, and silently asking: what happened there?

In some ways, for all the tension, Emergency was easy—because there was an ease to the department as well, a straightforward, fact-based calm devoid of worry. Here in Emerg, worry is beside the point: you're in the maw of it now, it's as bad as it gets, you have to get through it. I knew doctors who admitted privately to the secret appeal of emergency medicine: they were too busy to contemplate the sadness of it all. Their work profoundly unreflective, liberating in its mindlessness.

You can sit and wait in that calm for a long time as a parent, without minding. You look around. The technology, everywhere, on carts, an entire science on wheels, but also replicated at the bedhead in room after room, the same clean new tubes and bottles and valves over and over again, because of course our individual weaknesses are the same. Countless heavy-gauge yellow plastic waste-collection bags, for toxic bloods and spent dispensers, an entire industry (safe disposal!), money to be made from the garbage of the trauma of the body. The smells: antiseptic, coffee, puke, muffins, fresh linen, shit, worry, fear, grief. The last the worst: a dry smell, like stale ground, like hot pavement. And hand-washing, again and again, the splurt of the sanitizer, the Saran-Wrappy sound of a pair of hands spreading goo over themselves, the holy ritual of precaution. Choirs of crying. Clacking gurneys. Ambulance drivers making light banter with victims. Curtains hiding unknowable despair. The questions: Is it curable? Can they see my fear? And the inevitable comparison: Is my child better off than that child?

Through it all, you hold your child's body, hold its flesh and heat close to you, like a skin of fire, because you need to hang on to what life there is. The need to eat drives us, sex makes us shameless, but touch is our truest hunger. Just hang on. Just hang on. Just hang on. Just hang on.

And gradually, without you noticing it, something changes, and you don't have to hang on quite so tightly any more, or else there is nothing left to hang on to. The crisis passes or resolves. All of it incommunicable and yet, much later, impossible not to talk about ad nauseam.

If you're lucky they let you both go. The most liberating sensation of all, when you finally leave the hospital again in the early morning, before the sun is entirely up, the sidewalk still damp from the dew, your child safe again, for now. The way the world seems to start over. By the time you find your car—level two, near the north elevator—you're making plans again.

Throughout these years, on half-sleep, my wife and I fought a lot. Like most CFC parents, we argued more about sleep than about anything else: who had been able to sleep when and who hadn't, who deserved to sleep in and who didn't. It's mostly the same argument. It goes like this: in the middle of the night, though it's Johanna's turn with Walker—and it could easily be the other way around—I can't sleep and head downstairs to the living room to read. Five minutes in, I hear Johanna: "No, Walker, no!" A minute later, she appears at the foot of the stairs—naked, her skin still lightly tan (even in January), exhausted. Walker has been up for three hours and has just head-butted her and erupted with laughter. "Can you take him?"

I sigh (a mistake) and say (another mistake), "I had him last night for three hours straight in the middle of the night."

"Forget it." She stalks off. "Never mind! Sorry I asked!"

I follow her upstairs, recanting.

I pass her and get to Walker's room first and lie down with him. By now my poor wife is so tired she refuses to let go. She shouts, I shout, I close the door. She comes in again, so I nudge her out, close the door again and bar it with my foot. I'm not exactly rational. When I open the door again, I can hear Hayley, in our bedroom (the endless game of musical beds, to accommodate the boy), asking what's happening. I begin to apologize profusely to her mother. It's not entirely sincere, but sometimes in these volatile battles it does the trick.

But there are other times too—moments of unstoppable pleasure. The four of us in bed together on a Saturday morning, Walker on his knees, towering for once over us all. This is something, you see: every time he is happy, he is as happy as he has ever been. Hayley, a delicate and skilled ballet dancer, twisting with Walker to music on the stereo, Walker on the moon with joy. Minutes from his life. Everyday occurrences for a normal child. But I know their true value.

Shortly before Walker turned two, we heard about a CFC study being conducted at the famous Children's Hospital of Philadelphia. We drove ten hours to get there. At the end of a day of examinations we finally met a doctor who told us something we didn't know. His name was Dr. Paul Wang, and he was a developmental pediatrician.

Wang conducted a series of tests. He was a slim man with a high forehead and a quiet voice. He showed Walker some line drawings, a light, a puzzle; Walker threw them on the floor. After an hour, the doctor was done. Walker wandered over and climbed into my lap.

"As you know," Wang said, "there are three general levels of cognitive delay, or retardation—mild, moderate, and severe, sometimes called profound."

"Which one is Walker?" Johanna asked.

"If Walker continues at his present rate of development, then he might be diagnosed with moderate mental retardation as an adult."

"Moderate?" Johanna said, and put her hand to her mouth. She was already crying. (I hope I held her other hand.) "I was hoping for mild. Will he ever be able to read? Or . . . drive a car?"

"I doubt it." This was bad news. Moderate retardation is still catastrophic, and there was nothing to say it wouldn't get worse as he got older. He would need lifelong supervision, support in his living arrangements. "At this point, little definitive information is known about children with the CFC syndrome." The doctor judged Walker's overall development to be at the ten-month level. Ten months. Less than half his age. "As he gets older, of course, the differences will become more noticeable."

Wang turned to me. "Do you have any questions?"

"Just one. We rented a cottage this summer for the first time, north of Toronto. It's a very remote place, very quiet. An island, no one around but us. Walker seems to love it. It changes him, calms him. It means a lot to me, that place, and how it changes him. Will I ever be able to explain all that to him?"

Wang shook his head. "Not rationally, probably not. But"—he stopped, thought—"it sounds like he already understands it." Another pause. "The Buddhists say the way to enlightenment, to pure being, is by getting your mind out of the way. I'm not trying to be trite, but Walker already knows how to do that. He is pure being. He may be developmentally delayed, or moderately retarded, but in that way, he's already miles ahead of most of us."

That was the first time someone suggested Walker had a gift the rest of us didn't.

Gradually, as the endless routine of caring for him and watching him and stopping him and stimulating him became familiar, my fear subsided, and my grief was transformed into an unusual loneliness. Life with him and life without him: both were unthinkable.

As much as I tried to consider alternatives, I couldn't imagine not caring for him every day: couldn't imagine a day without the morning wake-up, the cleanup, the dressing, the school, the return home, the tired wailing, the sudden change and the bursts of sunny happiness, the feeding, the pointless teaching, the hilarity, the hospitals and doctors, the steady worry, the night rambles, all repeated every day until it ended, however that happened. There was nowhere we could afford to put him, and there was nowhere to put him anyway.

Our friends offered to take him, to give us a weekend away. We did that twice in twelve years. Each time it was a different couple, our closest friends, a single night each time. They volunteered many times before we agreed: caring for Walker was a complicated thing to ask someone to do, after all, what with all the tubes and feedings and drugs, and the incessant hitting and crying. They wore one look on their faces when I dropped him off—attentive, but eager—and another thirty-six hours later when I picked him up, the look of someone who has just had 150 house-guests for the weekend, during which the entire plumbing system has exploded. I saw the same stunned gaze a few weeks ago on the passengers of a plane that crash-landed safely and miraculously on the Hudson River. Those were the looks our friends had after a weekend with Walker. I understand completely. But I will always be loyal to them because they tried—they tried to reach down into our darkness and hold us. I cannot tell you how deep that well felt, how far down they had to reach. I never asked them again. It was, as I always said to Johanna, too much to ask.

"I wish people we know offered to take him more," she said one night.

We were talking in bed, one of the rare nights Walker fell straight to sleep. Lying next to each other in the darkness was so rare by then, it felt exciting again. I could feel her warm skin against mine, thrilled by the relative novelty of a grown-up at my side. The room was so dark we couldn't even see one another, but we spoke into the black night anyway. A small act of faith, and someone to listen.

"I mean, no one in my family or your family has ever offered to take him for a single night. My mom, once. That's it." I was shocked, not just by the truth of what she said, but by the very audacity of what she was suggesting. Asking someone to take Walker! Who the hell did she think she was! My parents were in their eighties, and they were afraid of Walker, afraid they wouldn't know what to do. My sisters lived in distant cities. My brother, who lived in Boston, and his partner, Frank, offered, but I couldn't bring myself to impose on them: they had no children, their house was too perfect to wreck. My wife's sister was single and lived in Los Angeles; we had no family living nearby, and no extensive community in the city. It wasn't just too much to ask, it was too much to imagine.

"Our closest friends have taken Walker into their lives as if he were one of their own kids," I said. "All those weeks at cottages, dinners at their homes. They didn't have to do that."

"But one night? I would have done more than that for them."

"But you know what it's like to do it. You have a kid like Walker. They don't. Most people are terrified."

Speaking the words into the black night, our bodies touching, remembering luck and good fortune.

It was too much to ask.

At dinner parties, we ate in shifts, one of us eating, the other wandering hand in hand with Walker, to keep him calm. If he got carried away and stroppy, if he began to whack his head uncontrollably, I sat him on my shoulders or strapped him into his stroller and took him outside: we'd leave and come back twenty minutes later. If I caught a whiff of a diaper, I whisked him away. We insisted on maintaining ordinary routines and customs. "He's fine," friends said to me when they invited us over for dinner or drinks, but I knew his buzz-saw scream and I didn't want to be responsible for other people hearing it; I didn't want them not to invite us any more, because they were all we had. In those days I still thought Walker was a reflection of me, I didn't think of him as a separate being. When he was calm Walker made his way from guest to guest, crawling into their laps, playing with their watches and their bangles, drooling onto their pants and shirts. He was a steady reminder not just of his presence, but of the existence of all children like him, the children we so often try to forget. For this reason we tended to select our dinner guests carefully. If he attached himself to someone, I intervened: "Here, I'll take him." Many objected and told me to go away; many did not. You could see the reserve in the eyes of the latter, in their posture: they kept talking, but they didn't resist giving him up. Who could blame them?

Johanna was better that way: she let other people look after him, wander with him, sit with him. She seemed to feel it was his, her, our due, whereas I literally leapt to take him off their hands. I didn't want anyone to reject him, so I tried to take rejection out of the picture from the start. He felt like my boy that way. I was not going to let anyone hurt him, he had been hurt enough, and so I would wrap his guilelessness in my constant presence to protect him against everything, even rejection. We were in it together, he and I, it didn't matter about the others. You could hammer away at me, but you'd never get through to him. Like taking a beating: bury yourself, hunker down, survive until the blows stop raining. It was the least I could do as his father, and at least I did that.

That was why we took him with us, on planes and in the car. In the car was easier: Hayley and Olga and Walker in the back seat, Johanna and I in the front, and everything we needed divided into two loads, the stuff we could pack away in the wayback (that was what we called it) and the detritus we had to have close at hand, for Walker. The at-hand pile comprised the stroller, at least one jumbo pack of thirty-six diapers, a box or two of formula, a small Coleman cooler of medicines, two changes of clothes and bibs and neckerchiefs in a carryall (because he drooled and puked) for the trip itself, a bag of toys and distractions—and that was, as I say, not counting suitcases and his folding playpen/bed. If we were in the car we could take more, of course, adding a second hamper of toys and his plastic "jumper," a purple and green and yellow plastic rolling contraption with a fabric seat suspended in the middle, in which he could sit and propel himself across the room. He loved that goddamn thing. "Do you like to jump-jump-jump?" Johanna would ask, and he would grin and jump, jump, jump.

We flew with him, too, but to do so was truly hairy, a form of extreme travel we undertook only to see Joanne and Jake, Johanna's mother and stepfather, in Pennsylvania for Christmas (we set the playpen up between the twin beds in the overheated guest room, the windows open wide even in winter, and tended to him together at nights, trying to shush him so the others wouldn't wake); to Florida to visit Walt Disney World. (Jake, a devout Catholic, bought indulgences in Walker's name and prayed to Padre Pio, a local candidate for sainthood.) We never knew if Walker's ears would react and make him cry the whole way, or if being confined in the plane would drive him (and us) crazy, or if he would instead just sleep or lie in his seat and gaze out the window at the clouds, a smile pasted across his face. We never knew.

In a pinch we tried babysitters. When Olga was away or unavailable, on New Year's Eve and the big holidays, we hired a sitter from respite agencies that specialized in looking after disabled children. They were first-rate caregivers, mostly unflappable, but until you met them or knew who you were getting, it felt a bit like dropping your kid off with a hired invertebrate. I mean, who is available to babysit on New Year's Eve? Several were on the eccentric side. A patho-logically shy, limping giantess stranger would arrive at the door, and I would pretend that it was the most normal thing in the world to hand over my disabled son (and often my daughter) to a stranger for six hours. "Ah, hello, One-Eye. How are you, nice to see you, come on in, I'm Ian."

A terrified *eep* from One-Eye would be the only acknowledgement.

"And this . . . is Walker! Can you say hi, Walker?" Of course I knew he couldn't say hi, but what was I supposed to say? *Here, you two seem well matched.* Instead I said the only thing I could say: "Let me show you his room."

There would then follow our standard explanation of the Walker routine. Here is his food, his clothes, his diapers, his changing room, his room, his playroom, his bed. Then the routine itself: he gets this syringe at this time, and 4 cc's of this at that time, and then two cans of formula every four hours, which you administer like this, attaching this bit here to that bit there and this gizmo into that nozzle—et cetera.

"Hayley knows what to do," we said, pointing to our lovely four-year-old daughter. It was a little like trying to explain the plumbing of a large complicated house in five minutes before you flew out the door. Because of course we also *wanted* to fly out the door.

But that was when One-Eye would unpack her . . . bag. Bag? The One-Eyes always carried a carpet bag of contraptions. Puffers and inhalers (their own); bottle of hand cream; snacks (including in one instance an entire loaf of bread; "What's she going to do?" Joahnna said, after we left. "Have a picnic?"). One woman—she came back several times—found the stairs too much to handle, and we returned after midnight to find her camped out in the living room, Walker alive and well and, always, wide awake. Hayley developed favourites—the woman from the Maritimes who told funny stories about growing up in the country—and others, such as the woman who insisted that Hayley give her all the red sour worms in a bag of candy, and that they be transported to her fingers, one by one. We lived in a world of our own, an underworld of Walker's making.

six

But let me ask you this: is what we've been through so different from what any parent goes through? Even if your child is as normal as a bright day, was our life so far from your own experience? More intensive, perhaps; more extreme more often, yes. But was it really different in kind?

We weren't disability masochists. I met those people too, the parents of disabled children who seemed to relish their hardship and the opportunity to make everyone else feel guilty and privileged. I disliked them, hated their sense of angry entitlement, their relentless self-pity masquerading as bravery and compassion, their inability to move on, to ask for help. They wanted the world to conform to their circumstances, whereas—as much as I could have put words to it—I simply wanted the rest of the world to admit (a minor request!) that our lives, Walker's and Hayley's and my wife's and mine, weren't any different from anyone else's, except in degree of concentration. I realize I was delusional. People often said, "How do you do it? How are you still capable of laughing, when you have a son like that?" And the answer was simple: it was harder than anyone imagined, but more satisfying and rewarding as well. What they didn't say was: why do you keep him at home with you? Wasn't there someplace where a child like Walker could be taken care of? Where two parents wouldn't carry the whole load, and could have a moment or two to work and live and remember who they were and who they could be?

I asked myself those questions too. I knew Walker would have to live in an assisted living environment eventually, but that was surely years away. I approached the subject casually, even at home. "We should put him on the waiting list for a long-term place," I'd say, off-handedly over breakfast. I tended to think about the problem in bed at night.

"Oh," Johanna invariably replied, "I'm not ready for that."

"No, no, not now," I would say. "Later."

Just as Walker turned two, he began to grab his ears and bite himself. He didn't stop for a year and a half. We thought he had a toothache, an earache. He did not. *Self-mutilating* appears for the first time in his medical chart in March 1999, shortly before his third birthday. He quickly graduated to punching himself in the head. He put his body behind the punches, the way a good boxer does. Hayley called it "bonking," so we did too.

The irony was that he had been making progress, of sorts: finer pincer movements with his fingers, a little eating. (He loved ice cream. If you could get him to swallow it, ice cream made him smile and scowl—from the cold—at the same time.) He could track objects and wave goodbye, and often babbled like a madman.

Then he flipped into blackness.

Was it self-hatred? I wondered about that. We enrolled him in a famous rehabilitation clinic, the Bloorview MacMillan Children's Centre (now Bloorview Kids Rehab) in north Toronto, where he was seen by a behavioural therapist. Everywhere else when people saw his bruises they wondered what we were doing to our child. *Cannot communicate*, Dr. Saunders noted.

Sometimes Walker was in agony as he smacked himself and screamed with pain. At other times he seemed to do it more expressively, as a way to clear his head, or to let us know he would be saying something if he could talk. Sometimes—and this was unbearably sad—he laughed immediately afterwards. He couldn't tell us anything, and we had to imagine everything. More specialists crowded into our lives. Walker was diagnosed as functionally autistic— not clinically autistic, but he behaves as if he is—as well as having CFC. Dr. Saunders tried Prozac, Celexa, risperidone (an antipsychotic designed for schizophrenia, it has been known to allay obsessive-compulsive behaviour in children). Nothing worked. Once, in Pennsylvania, he bit his hand to the bone and, after an hour of surgery to repair the damage, spent a night in hospital. (The bill was $14,000.)

Dr. Saunders' notes began to track longer and longer stretches of horror. *"Bonking" ears x 2–3 days*. I remember that morning, especially the grief-stricken look on Walker's face as he bashed himself. He looked straight at me. He knew it was bad and wrong, he knew he was hurting himself, he wanted to stop it and couldn't—why couldn't I? His normally thin gruel of a wail became frightening and loud. From June 2001 to the spring of 2003, every entry in his medical records mentions his unhappiness, his irritability.

Did he know his window for learning was closing? Was his vision dimming? *72 hours aggressive behaviour. Unhappy crying x 5 days.* Even Dr. Saunders' handwriting became loose and scrawled, distracted by the chaos of those shrieking visits. *Screaming all day, needs to be held.*

I dreaded the doctor's waiting room, with its well-dressed mothers and well-behaved children. They were never anything but kind, but walking in with Walker yowling and banging his head, I felt like I'd barged into a church as a naked one-man band with a Roman candle up my ass and singing "Yes! We Have No Bananas."

Mother tearful, Dr. Saunders noted on December 29 of that awful year. *Urgent admission for respite.*

I remember that day too. We drove Walker home from the doctor, fed Walker, bathed Walker, soothed Walker, put Walker to bed. I heard his cries subside in stages. Normally Johanna was relieved when he dropped off to sleep, but that night she came downstairs from his bedroom sobbing, her arms wrapped around herself.

"He's gone away," she said. "My little boy has gone. Where has he gone?" She was inconsolable.

So perhaps you can understand why, the very next morning, I began to look in earnest for a way out. I didn't tell Johanna, but I had to find a place for Walker to live, somewhere outside our home. I didn't realize it would take seven years, that it would be the most painful thing I have ever done and that the pain would never go away.

On my desk at work is a picture of Hayley reading to Walker. This was up north, on the quiet island. They are lying side by side on a bed, and Walker is looking up at the book in Hayley's hands, as if riveted by every word. I don't know if he understands a syllable. But he can hear her voice, is thrilled to be with her and clearly grasps his smart big sister's affection. He has become the moment and it has become him, because he has nothing else to be. Walker is an experiment in human life lived in the rare atmosphere of the continuous present. Very few can survive there.

The photograph reminds me of a poem I once read in a magazine, by Mary Jo Salter:

None of us remembers these, the days
When passing strangers adored us at first sight
Just for living, or for rolling down the street.

Praised all our given names, begged us to smile.
You, too, in a little while, my darling,
Will have lost all this,
asked for a kiss will give one,
And learn how love dooms one to earn love
Once we can speak of it.

My boy Walker has no worries there. He never asks, yet is loved by many. But I doubt it feels effortless to him.

"I hear parents of other handicapped kids saying all the time, 'I wouldn't change my child,'" Johanna said one night as we were lying in bed, talking as we fell asleep. "They say, 'I wouldn't trade him for anything.' But I would. I would trade Walker, if I could push a button, for the most ordinary kid who got Cs in school. I would trade him in an instant. I wouldn't trade him for my sake, for our sake. But I would trade for his sake. I think Walker has a very, very hard life."

seven

For seven years we talked about Walker moving away to a home for the disabled. Or, to be more accurate: for seven years I tentatively raised the subject of Walker moving into a home, and neither of us could face the possibility. We had to do it, but we couldn't do it.

The dilemma reminded me of an experiment I once read about. Rats were placed in a Skinner box. The floor of the box was then electrified, and the only way the rat could escape the shock was by jumping onto an elevated platform. Unfortunately, any rat that used the platform was punished with a sharp blast of super-cooled air directly into its anus— an experience of which rats are not fond, apparently. Rats subjected to this inescapable dilemma quickly began to display classic schizophrenic behaviour. I knew how the rats felt.

By the time Walker was nine, he was pushing sixty-five pounds, and getting bigger, as we were getting older. I was fifty; Johanna was forty-one; Hayley was suddenly a teenager. Carrying Walker upstairs was like hauling a canvas bag of iron pellets, all the weight in the bottom of the sack. Three hours of sleep a night for four nights running was beginning to have an effect: visual migraines became a new feature of my life. How long could we keep it up? Despair seemed to come in cycles, especially when Walker's health was compromised.

I kept my ears open for news of stable group homes and reliable assisted living centres for the intellectually disabled—but every time I pursued a lead, it disappeared behind an excuse: no room, no funding, wrong for little boys. One famous community for the intellectually disabled to the north of the city had a waiting list of twenty years and didn't accept children. I joined the local association for community living, hoping somehow to ingratiate myself with the organizers and find early leads; instead, the organizers informed me that the average applicant for a spot in the city's network of communal homes was a forty-year-old with Down syndrome and aging parents who were themselves increasingly in need of communal living arrangements. I came away from that conversation thinking that the future was a long way off. No wonder we wanted to keep Walker with us: the scene beyond the walls of our own home, in the world of public housing for the profoundly disabled, sounded like a novel by Zola.

We had lived with this dispiriting state of affairs in the background for years. Back when Walker was two, in the dark days when he began hitting himself, a friend with a disabled daughter of his own introduced me to a man I was told would solve my problems. He worked as an advocate for the handicapped. I'd heard of such people: they were almost legendary creatures, spoken of but rarely seen. An advocate was a kind of personal manager and agent—someone who took on specific cases (but by no means any case) and ran interference for that soul in the vast, complicated special-needs bureaucracy. The advocate helped families figure out what they needed, organized an appropriate plan of attack on the bureaucracy, then lobbied for care and support and money. Advocates tended to work on salary for social service agencies, usually non-profit organizations financed by charities and government grants.

Before I met the advocate, I had imagined there was one public government system through which every case of disability passed. I couldn't have been more wrong. "It's every man for himself," the advocate told me. He was in his thirties, and was wearing a suit and tie. "What you get, someone else doesn't get." He told me of children who had been negotiated into group homes, and others who had their own apartments and $1 million a year to pay for support staff: it depended on how one asked, who one asked, how one haggled. "But Walker has a lot of needs, so that's good," he said.

The trick was to hold out until you got the deal you wanted, because if you took too little from the government, it was hard to go back and get more. On the other hand, if your child was offered a placement in a decent home and you turned it down, you went back to the bottom of the waiting list. The net result of this negotiating was an uneven, secretive, unpredictable game that rendered the parents of a disabled child at once anxious and grasping, as well as pathetically grateful for anything they were eventually awarded. New and ever more exotic strains of guilt began to assail me. If Walker lived full-time in a good group setting, the cost would run at least $200,000 a year. If he lived to the age of fifty, the total would be $8 million. I didn't have $8 million dollars, but there were eight million people in Ontario, the Canadian province where I lived. Was Walker worth a dollar a person? Such calculations filled my head at night.

The advocate knew every play in the social services book. By the end of the hour and a half we spent together, I was convinced he was a genius, and said so. "I'd like you to represent Walker, if you can and would and have room for one more client," I said, practically tugging my forelock.

"I'd love to," he said. "He needs an advocate. There's just one thing: I'm getting out of the advocacy business, and going to work for the ministry." It felt as if the walls of the room had suddenly fallen down. A new Conservative government had taken power, and the province's social service agencies figured they needed one of their own deep in the funding apparatus. Nearly ten years passed before I met someone else like him.

From an entry in my notebook:

November 25, 2003
A call from Walker's school. "We're at some kind of crisis point,"
Alanna Grossman, the principal, says. He's gone from biting
himself to punching his head, in addition to his regular circus of
tics and antics.

We meet at the school at 9 a.m. Present are Grossman; Walker's
two young teachers, Thomas and Dean; a psychologist from the
school board, a strict, punctilious woman in a tartan bib dress; two
educational assistants; me; and Johanna, still fresh from the
morning battle of waking and cleaning and dressing and soothing

and feeding Walker, and thus having had no time to change out of her pyjamas, which she's wearing under her overcoat. An army, to care for a boy. "He needs stimulation," the psychologist says, by way of explaining why he hits himself. How she knows this I have no idea. "We want his hitting to be more of a choice."

These people all meet about Walker once a week. He's endangering himself eight days out of ten. "He can follow routine, but gets upset if it's imposed on him," Dean says. "Sometimes being firm works."

"But at the same time we want him to choose," the psychologist interjects.

I want her to choose another profession.

"I refuse to believe this is his personality," Johanna says. "And that's why I'm so frustrated at not being able to create a communication system for him."

Tartan-Bib: "Is he too dependent on holding?"

This is what I think is going on: Walker wants to be reassured that he's a human being. He hates how strange and different he is. Now the psychologist wants to deny me the only way I can tell him he's not.

Without an advocate, waiting for something to happen that will help us out of the nightmare of caring for a boy whose needs are growing as our capabilities shrink, we're thrown back on the ad hoc services the government provides as a stop-gap to a more permanent solution. There are respite care services—caregivers who will come and stay with Walker for half a day twice a week—but they too need to be sought out, applied for and approved. Everything we need requires a form: which form? Where do we get it?

Who has time to get it? Where do we send it? Once it is sent, we wait.

A number of brilliant university students pass through Walker's life in this way—women my stuffed brain remembers only as Gwen and Elizabeth and Del. Gwen is a medievalist from Texas, a brilliant and creative woman with a sexy-librarian look and a hulking, pleasant boyfriend. Elizabeth is the first *Buffy the Vampire Slayer* fanatic I ever met: she could talk wittily and endlessly about her heroine, and taught me to take such pop culture obsessions seriously. Del is the sweetest: a quiet, dark-haired, dedicated university student of childhood education, sister to a disabled boy herself. Hayley adores them all like big sisters, and Walker no more fazes them than a busy street does. They are so young and hopeful and energetic, and I am so grateful for them. Gratitude springs out of me like crabgrass out of a lawn, riots of it.

But they all have their own lives, and they never stay long. There are some tax deductions available, but both Johanna and I work, so our income is generally too high for us to be eligible, we discover after we fill out the schedules. There are programs to cover the costs of assistive devices, but they require mountains of paperwork, not to mention background checks: the government seems to think I might have reason to scam a netted bed and an IV stand. Just what I always wanted! In any event one of us ought to fill out these forms—but both of us are working and looking after Walker full-time. When we both begin to freelance, to give ourselves more flexible hours, the forms do get filled out—Johanna spends four hours a week on paperwork—but we make less money, whereupon we can apply for those tax deductions. The entire system resembles a Rube Goldberg contraption.

And that's only the bureaucracy dedicated to the disabled. The non-disabled bureaucracy is another galaxy altogether. At the age of five, Walker begins to attend Beverley Junior Public School—a famous local institution dedicated entirely to intellectually disabled children, where the ratio of students to teachers is a mere three-to-one. The school is a bright, airy space designed for children who can't see out of normal windows or walk easily through a standard door. Its effect on Walker's confidence is instantaneous: within a month he progresses from needing to be carried from room to room at school to walking on his own. But within a year, the provincial government announces its intention to close the school. The school is only for the disabled—a "segregated" facility, in the parlance of disability education—and doesn't conform to the province's policy of supporting (much cheaper) "inclusive" schools, where, theoretically, the disabled learn alongside the abled, and each gets used to the other. Inclusive schools are often excellent, and much preferred by a certain generation and political ilk of educators. But even those educators will admit integration isn't for everyone, that dedicated facilities can be more helpful for children as delayed as Walker.

But the provincial government is against Beverley School for bigger reasons, as well: the school doesn't conform to the Ministry of Education's arcane square-footage rules. To justify cutbacks to the province's education budget, the minister of education has ruled that schools have to support a certain number of students per square foot of floor space. This allows the Conservative government to build newer, more "efficient" schools in the suburbs, where their political support is, and shut down schools in the downtown cores of larger cities, where the irritating liberals tend to live. Beverley doesn't conform to the square-footage rule because its handicapped students need more space, for their wheelchairs and foam mats and ventilators and light rooms and IV stands and wagons, and so the institution is slated for closure. Public outrage eventually forces the government to keep the school open, but the government's priorities are clear: the disabled don't vote, and so don't deserve much individual attention. They don't fit the formula—any formula.

We cobble together what Walker needs regardless. Among Olga, ourselves, respite care, the university students, ad hoc programs, the odd agency, school and luck, we manage to survive ten years. The routines become more familiar, but the stress seldom abates. We can't save any money, we can't make any real plans, we can't travel farther than a car or a stroller can take us (now that Walker is bigger, planes are dangerously harder to manage), or anywhere there isn't a good hospital nearby. We try to live as if everything is normal. But the routine is as crippling as the position I have to sleep in with Walker. And the future looks dreary and spare. The money we spend on Olga, the $12,000 a year we spend on formula alone, the money we spend on diapers—all of it could be paying for Hayley's university education. She gamely says she'll try to win a scholarship instead, but she is already an anxious child, the fallout of living in a house where something is always about to burst. I dream incessantly about money, about having misplaced my belongings, about being chased and gunned down.

And then, suddenly, there is a glimpse of sky in the overcast future. In the fall of 2003, we're invited, once again, for Thanksgiving weekend to the cottage of our good friends John and Cathrin. Our steady companions, Allan Kling and Tecca Crosby, as well as another couple, Lorrie Huggins and Colin MacKenzie, old pals, are guests as well. We don't get to talk to them much, however, because Walker is in a terrible state. He never stops crying, never stops hitting himself, never stops requiring the attention of not one but two (and sometimes four of five) people, for three solid Canadian autumn days.

Two weeks later, after intense lobbying from Tecca and Cathrin, Lorrie calls me—me, not Johanna. Lorrie knows where she'll find the colder, more receptive heart. "I have someone I want you to meet. A woman who's an advocate out of Surrey Place," she says, referring to a local institute that specializes in the study and treatment of autism. "I think she may be able to help. Because you need it." To Lorrie's fresh eyes, our lives—Walker's and ours—are a nightmare.

An advocate, again. The woman will come to the house, suss Walker out, see what we're like, investigate our lives. If our "needs"—the word wears permanent quotation marks in my mind—are great enough, she will try to help us find the corner of the special-needs world where Walker will be able to stand and live and be. But I don't hold out much hope.

———

April 4, 2004
We now have an advocate for Walker's cause. Her name's Margie Niedzwiecki. "We'll begin to make initial applications for long-term care," she said the first time we met, just before Christmas of

last year. I must have looked shocked. "You don't have to make that decision now," she quickly added. "Think about it."

Any such application will take years, in any event. To my surprise, the mere fact that Walker is both mobile and dependent makes him a complex case. There are homes for medically fragile kids, but Walker might zoom around turning off their respirators, just for the fun of pushing the buttons. Then there are places for intellectually compromised kids, but they can't handle Walker's fragility, his small-boyness.

The shortage of places of either kind is epidemic. Every month in Toronto alone, 2,400 disabled people are looking for a place to live among seventy-six group homes. Some wait eight years. Those number seldom change.

Our best bet, Margie says, is to get help from a new branch of an established social service provider that specializes in "children who are unusual and hard to serve."

I'm sickened by the idea of Walker living anywhere else, but my guilt is by now a luxury. We must act. He can't be alone for even a minute, twenty-four hours a day. Eventually he'll have to move. Margie says it's a good idea to begin the transition early. At eighteen, it will be too hard.

The first visit takes place in our living room. Margie's older than us, maybe early sixties, and tall, with shoulder-length grey hair. She is extremely calm, and listens about ten times more than she talks. She doesn't use social services jargon, which immediately puts her in my good books. Even Johanna agrees to sit and talk to her about long-term care—a surprise.

"Walker responds to love," Johanna tells Margie. "We want him to go somewhere where they love all of him, not just some of him."

But she doesn't mean it. Like me, she doesn't want him to go anywhere at all.

My father and Walker have something, some indefinable thing, between them. The old man's in his nineties. He still goes to work, still performs fifteen minutes of calisthenics every morning, but he feels his weakness, and he hates it. He gave up his car at the age of ninety-three, after hurting his neck, and still thinks he's going to drive again. It won't happen, but the car is his great equalizer: he can no longer walk as fast as some people, but in a car he's the man he was. His name is Peter; his second name, Henry, I gave to Walker.

I drive out on weekends to help my parents. They live alone in a small house by a river, the last remnant of country land on the fringe of an omnivorous suburb. He needs me and my car for errands. The barber, the liquor store, various recycling drop-offs, the grocery store, the hospital for weekly visits to have my father's varicose veins wrapped, keeping my mother happy—these are his pleasures now. He's desperate to stay mobile, hence the three-act exits from the car: door open, legs swung to the side—*"Can you manage?"* *"Yes, yes."*—the arms spread to the sides of the door frame, as if he were about to parachute to the distant ground from the bay of a Cessna. The rock back, the catapult up and . . . out! Steady! Counterweight to prevent the pitch forward! Has he . . . yes! Hurrah. The human slingshot, enacted merely to fetch milk or pay the bills at the bank—one of two banks he and my ninety-four-year-old mother use, so as not to risk keeping all their money in one place.

My father's skin is as vulnerable as onion paper in a bible. I used to clap my arm around his shoulders when we met; he flinches if I forget and try it now. I could dislocate something. Dislocation is to be avoided at all costs, in all its forms. Routines cannot vary—the bank, the empties, then the grocery store, in that order—and neither can the route. "Why are you going this way?" he asks in the car, as if I had questioned the existence of carbon molecules themselves. He arrives forty-five minutes early for scheduled appointments. He carries a handkerchief to wipe spittle from the left side of his mouth when he thinks I'm not looking. Old age isn't just something he dislikes: he's personally offended by it. His mood is altered, slightly peevish. As his strength has failed, so has his famous reserve: he's crabbier now, except with Walker. They seem to understand each other's frailty; they have patience for each other.

Each time they meet, the same thing happens. The boy stands in front of the old man, and my father holds his hands and looks into his eyes. "Hello," he says. They are both smiling. My father knows what to do without ever having been told. "Hello there, Snodgrass." As he used to say to me, and to my brother. Then Walker climbs into his lap and doesn't move for twenty minutes. Walker recognizes him, I don't know how because he doesn't see his grandfather often. It isn't that my parents don't like him; they simply can't take the worry. They send him cards on his birthday and ask us to buy appropriate presents at Christmas, and they ask after him every time I visit, but the chaos of Walker coming to their house and aiming straight for a vase of calceolaria on my mother's antique game table—no, that is not relaxing. His nose alone can drive my germ-warrior mother to distraction.

She loves him, there is no doubt of that. She—her name is Cissy—loves him like a thing in nature, like her clematis plant or her roses or the river at the foot of her garden, as if he ran in her veins as a thick, normal residue. It's the farm girl in her, the labourer who takes nature as it comes. But the farm girl—stout, strong, brave, even fierce—is also intimidated by his scientific needs, by his tubes and doses. She is afraid she will hurt him more. The day I told her just how disabled Walker would be—this was after our trip to the children's hospital in Philadelphia, after we learned his reading and many other abilities would never progress much beyond those of a two- or three-year-old—she was sitting on the small love seat in the television room of her impeccable house. She looked at me, her hands in her lap, expressionless, then she shifted to the edge of the seat.

"Well, we'll just have to love him as he is, then."

Not a gift she extended my way, when I was growing up: perhaps Walker has made her more tolerant. (If so, he's a miracle worker.) It's not much of an answer: *We'll just have to love him as he is*. But it is the only answer that is always there, waiting. My mother has a talent for striking the flinty bottom of the truth.

My father, on the other hand, is his grandson's friend. They sit hand in hand. If Walker whimpers, he will hear a brisk and nautical "Come on, now!"—my father's years as a lieutenant-commander in the Royal Navy called back to service. It often works. The grandfather and the grandson are content to wait with each other. Maybe they are waiting for the same thing— but what is it? That is the sort of thought you have when you see them. This man who became me who became Walker. That stumbling, that hesitation, that indecision—the old man's, the boy's, and mine.

My father is not an emotional man: he was sent to boarding school in 1918 at the age of four. His favourite brother, Harold, died on a ship in battle; another brother left home, was never heard from again; neither is ever discussed. But

Walker softens him. The older my father gets the truer this is. He sees the broken boy, and begins to understand that power isn't all he thought it was cracked up to be.

And now I am preparing to put his grandson in a home.

———

Mid-April 2004
Another meeting at Surrey Place, a Toronto institution that specializes in autism, where a behaviour therapist has been working with Walker.

These meetings are always the same: playroom, indoor–outdoor carpet, pastel walls, half a dozen smart women with clipboards, all between thirty and fifty, all dressed in denim shifts or loose-fit stone-washed jeans with elasticized waists—good for working on the floor with children who drool.

Today's meeting is about Walker's head-bashing. There's always new lingo to be harvested.

"So it's intrinsic?"

"He is intrinsically motivated. He's obviously getting something out of it."

"His motor skills aren't fine enough for sign language."

"Pointing may be better for low performers."

For Walker to communicate by pointing, he needs ten sessions of "pointing instruction." It's a new "implementation," requiring new "intake" and therefore new forms.

One of the therapists tells me she spends half her time negotiating the bureaucracy of the rehabilitation world. But without these women to light the tunnels, I'd have succumbed years ago.

The behaviour therapist isn't encouraging. "The way to stop a kid like this from hitting himself," she says, "is with food and toys. But Walker just doesn't care about that stuff."

Back at home, Johanna is shaken. "That's when I thought, boy, they don't know anything. I see now: No one's been helping us, because no one can."

April 28, 2004

Six months in. Our advocate, Margie, introduces us to Lisa Benrubi and Minda Latowsky, the guts of Walker's new special-needs team. Margie has been working on Walker's case for six months. Lisa's the boss.

The three of them came by the house and sat in our living room, and listened to the story of Walker, so far. We know how to tell it. Unlike doctors, Lisa and Minda and Margie actually make eye contact. They seem to hear us, too. "How have you done this for ten years?" Minda asks—quite genuinely, it seems. Johanna cries, pretty much start to finish. I choke up myself, have to blow my nose. Afterwards, I apologise to Margie. "No," she says, "it's good you cried."

Minda will be our caseworker. Until this program came along in Ontario, a developmentally delayed child had to become a ward of the state—legally relinquished by parents to the Children's Aid Society—to qualify for a group home. Under the new program, we will still be Walker's parents—a relief and a requirement for us. That it might ever have been otherwise shakes me, makes me see the dark magnitude of what we're doing. We'll make all the decisions, but his care will be spread around. Minda, my new god, refuses to refer to any potential group home as "Walker's house." She says, "It'll be your house too."

The real problem is structural. Until recently, no one—certainly no part of the government-funding apparatus—was willing to admit that a child could be loved and still be too difficult to be cared for by his or her parents. Because until twenty years ago, children *this medically complex didn't exist. They didn't survive. High-tech medicine has created a new strain of human beings who require superhuman care. Society has yet to acknowledge this reality, especially at a practical level.*

And Walker is an especially needy example of the new human strain. There are high-quality residential homes but they typically have only 10 to 12 beds. At $250 a day—24-hour care, shelter, food, transportation—funding is limited and based on need. The contraptions alone are bank-breakers: Tumble Forms Feeder Seat, $729; BreezeLite helmet, $129; veil bed (for safety), $10,000. It took us nearly three years to find the money for the one we have at home for Walker, and we only managed it in the end with Margie's help. Meanwhile, I can qualify for a $500,000 mortgage in twenty minutes. "What I'd really like," Johanna said after they left, "is for them to give us the money, so we could have all the 24-hour care he needs, but at home."

I don't agree. I'm not sure a miniature hospital in our house would be an improvement.

But Johanna claims she has had a Walker revelation. "Sometimes it's not a choice between right and wrong," she says. "Sometimes it's a choice between bad and slightly less bad. That was a revelation to me—that some things are unfixable."

She may be coming around.

What was happening to our marriage? Many days it felt like a man with a lingering sickness he didn't know he had, getting weaker and thinner, but turning up for work every day nonetheless.

"We ask so much of each other, taking care of Walker," Johanna said one morning, explaining our mutual bad mood to me, "that when it comes to looking after each other, there just isn't anything left."

Estimates of the number of marriages that fail due to caring for a disabled child range from 60 to 80 percent. The ones that do make it through, according to other studies, are that much stronger for the challenge. I have no idea whether any of the research means anything. In our case the grit of resentment lay like a fine dust over everything. But the prospect of leaving each other was unthinkable: there was no way we could care for Walker if we didn't do it together.

With our nights divided, we were roommates as much as husband and wife. I saw Johanna in the house in the morning, carrying diapers and feedbags and heading out the door to appointments, her arms full of the sleepy boy, and at night again as she jogged him on her knee or held him away from Hayley's homework or spritzed formula into his G-tube, or (in the delicious moments when he was asleep) stretched across the pine table in the kitchen, her cup of tea at her side, stealing time with the newspaper (which of course I resented because I had not had time with the paper; just as she resented it when our roles were reversed). Her tea: I thought about that a lot when we were too trampled to talk, the way she reheated the cup over the course of a day, kept it by her side always, like a salve or tonic that kept her going. I became a student of her dressing gowns: the long kimono I bought her at a craft fair, the turquoise Japanese sweeper, the tiny silky one in the summer, the black all-purpose cotton she wore when winter chilled the house. My *wife*, that ancient word; the mother of my children, the mother of Walker. (There was the sourness again. *She wanted a second child.* I realize I was there at that moment of conception, but that didn't stop me from blaming the body that produced his body.) Johanna saw me from the same distracted, victimized distance: she worked at home, whereas I did not. I had a chance to slip away every day. She never escaped the burden. "She does everything," I once heard a friend say at a cocktail party, after someone asked how we managed. I resented the idea, because I knew it wasn't true: Johanna was almost always there, but because she felt everything deeply, a severe patch of pain or illness or unhappiness in Walker crushed her with sadness, and her sadness could then paralyze her. At times like that we relied on my more earthbound mantle, my bullheaded core.

Sometimes I was too tired to say hello to her in the morning, and I was often bad-tempered—she was like someone from the office that you see on the street, a nod, hello, a smile, and then you are apart again. ("Good morning," she would say, as I stumbled into the kitchen. I would grunt in response. "Good morning," she would say again.) I admired her, but it was hard to pony up the value-added considerations, slip in that occasional unanticipated favour or kindness that holds together any marriage that lasts. I saw her, us, more and more at a remove, from a distance: there are worse arrangements, but this one never seemed to change.

The negotiations over Walker were, and still are, endless. "Can you take Walker to his genetics/dental/nurtrition/physio/you-name-it appointment on Wednesday?" my wife will ask. She is organized, and direct. I prefer a more "neutral" approach: "Walker has a genetics/dental/nutrition/physio/you-name-it appointment tomorrow," I say, leaving my request unstated.

We argue about who will take him, who took him last time, who has more or less work, who has a deadline, who is contributing the most. Money talk is radioactive. It seems impossible that Johanna could contribute any more than she does, but I am not sure where to find the extra in myself to help more. We have our private moments, our intimacies, but they are so rare and so urgent they're like hallucinations. Nobody can say we aren't efficient.

In theory, having a handicapped child could bring a family closer together—a mutual project, a joint challenge, a bond. In practice, Walker deprives us of any privacy we ever had—and we are private people, introverts, readers and ponderers. Instead of bringing us together, Walker scatters us, making us both less private and intensely more so at once, desperate for a refuge where there are no interruptions, no surprises. I often worry I will never read an entire book again; my concentration seems permanently shattered. I long ago abandoned any plans I had of owning a cottage or a vacation house. It's all we can do to make it to the medical appointments.

Weeks go by without any real contact between us—and then we fight, perhaps to force some connection. The evidence of Walker's demanding presence never changes, the household stigmata of a disabled kid: the mangled window blinds, in whose jalousies he plays his fingers for minutes on end; the endless piles of laundry that self-propagate like jungle plants; his toothbrush in the kitchen drawer; the avalanche of potions and lotions and syringes and bottles held back by a cupboard door; all of it. With this chaos besetting us at every turn, would it be too much for him (for her) to put the fucking milk away?

Maybe it was us, not him: I often thought so. There were other families—I knew they existed because I read about them on websites—who seemed to cope well. We had been brilliant once, before the boy. I missed those days.

But: I still love my wife. I still admire her body, her brown skin; I still want to protect her. She still makes me laugh, tells a story brilliantly, remembers the lyrics to any song she has ever heard, can relate movies scene by scene, is capable of deep and lasting kindness. She is still a talented mother to Hayley. I can still make her laugh the way no one else can, can still reach the eccentric, private corners only a wife and a husband know. We lie in bed when we can, punning madly: I can hear her mind whirring to one-up me. I begrudge her time with the newspaper, but not her love of others; I forgive the dark fear she has felt on so many occasions, her struggle to love her broken boy. I was always willing to step in to help her through that black self-hatred. In that way the boy sometimes made us generous, too. You have no idea how much pleasure a person can offer to another with the words *That's okay, I'll take him to the doctor.*

An example: one night we attend a party. It's Christmas time and it's an office party in some dark bar in some darker corner of the city. Walker is still small, no more than three years old. I am sitting against the wall on one side of the room, half listening to a couple I know talk about religious fundamentalism, of all things. But what I am really doing is watching my wife—the secret hobby of so many husbands. I remember this moment because I am watching my wife briefly emerge from the cocoon of her endless obligations, from her endless life at home with a disabled child. She's famous among our friends for the good spirit she displays in the face of this hardship, but I know what it costs her. She is huddled at the bar beside a man I know, an old friend of ours, and she is laughing out loud, the last instance of which I can't remember, at least in my company. They look intimate: their shoulders are touching, their drink is the same, vodka with tonic. I know he is very fond of her, so much so that I once asked him—I admit I had had a drink—if he was in love with my wife.

"Yes," he said, "I am."

"In a way that's a problem?" I said.

"No," he said. "It's not a problem."

"All right, then," I said. "Crush away."

And this is the thing: I really don't mind. There is space in her privacy for my own tattered privacy, for starters. And how can I begrudge her that moment of friendship and freedom and even flirting, that tender intimacy, after all she has been through; how can I begrudge her some elemental attention, the frankly adoring gaze of someone fresh and new, someone with whom she doesn't have to negotiate every moment of respite? She never stops smiling in his tall company, and I am surprised to find myself pleased to see it. I am sure she has her secrets, and I am willing to let them stay secret, to let them remain hers and hers alone. I once came across a blog on the Internet written by the father of a disabled child, and he discussed such matters. "A disabled child teaches you to make your own rules," he wrote. I nurse a drink, and wonder what she does when I am not around. I know she wonders the same about me.

Mostly we forgive each other. Walker taught us how to do that.

January 25, 2005
My first visit to Stewart Homes, an independent, for-profit assisted-living organization that may—may, with the intervention of the special-needs group—have a space for Walker to live.

It was founded 30 years ago by Alan Stewart, who was himself a foster parent.

I was terrified at the door. I know what it's like to enter a room of handicapped kids: I was always astonished by the symphony of whoops and yowls that rolled over me when I visited Walker at school. But this is different: This is their territory, and the one who has to measure up is me. I stumbled into five children in a single room, but so isolated from one another, so deeply private, they might as well have been in separate galaxies. Gaspingly sad.

There are about eight children in each house—bungalow-style; spacious enough for the pumps and wheelchairs, lifters and toys; the floors seamless, carpet-free, for wheelchairs. The children are foreshortened or twisted, but self-possessed: This is their place, a haven where they are no longer oddities. The school is 20 minutes away by bus; the local doctor does house calls; there's a good hospital, a nurse on staff, a psychiatrist on call. One of the things Johanna doesn't like is the place's smell, a vague musk with top notes of humanity and the bathroom.

There's no room, of course. "Sometimes openings do come up in unpredictable ways," Diane Doucette, the director, tells us.

I think she means that children die. I am happy to wait.

April 8, 2005
Office of the special-needs project. Seven years after I first broached the idea of getting outsiders to help us raise Walker, Minda Latowsky has found him a place. It's on the edge of Toronto, in Pickering, 40 minutes by car.

There are two mobile children there already: Kenny, 13, a tall, skinny kid who suffered brain damage in a near-drowning, but who can understand and make himself understood by fluttering his arms *and vocalizing; and Chantal, tiny for eight years old, who speaks and understands. Kenny will be Walker's roommate—a big-boy concept, terribly exciting. The typical beginning is two to four trial visits, with Olga staying overnight at the new house to show the other workers the ropes with Walker, while Johanna and I are at work. "Then the move-in," Minda says. Then two weeks of no visits, to settle.*

"It'll be months before you realize you can put your coffee down, safe from flinging by Walker," Minda assures me. "But by then he'll be back at your place often." Johanna seems resigned, or at least numbed to our long-coming decision. But I'm a wreck.

I feel as if the shape that he gave my life, this deep fate he handed me, is melting away. For what? For the sake of my own comfort? Because there is no such thing as a perfect solution? When I think of this house without him, my body becomes a cave.

As the day of Walker's move to his other house approached— June 25, 2005, at the end of the school year—I sank into what I realize now was a sea of grief. I went to the doctor complaining of stomach cramps: his tests found nothing. Grief— "the curtain of silence," C. S. Lewis called it—was a shroud that separated me from other living people. It seemed impossible to me that anyone could understand our plight: if they didn't think we were monsters, they had to think us fools. Sometimes on the nights when it wasn't my turn to put Walker to sleep I went out to bars in the neighbourhood, but all I did there was drink, sitting in one place and keeping to myself and listening to conversations, trying to overhear a scrap of the normal. I hoped someone would talk to me— thankfully no one ever did—but I wanted a shred of my old callow life back.

Sometimes I even went to strip clubs. I did this at night, on the way home from driving our nanny Olga back to her apartment. I suppose I needed to feel something, anything other than the loss of Walker, however predictable and reptilian— and my lust, at its most basic, was that thing. In a strip bar you can sit beside your own desires for a while, the reliable ones and the surprises, and remind yourself of the old habits of this stranger you have become.

I missed his strangeness most of all. Before Walker, I imagined that the parents of a handicapped, disfigured child ventured out in public with trepidation: that the prospect of being looked at and ogled and even laughed at was agony. But the truth is, Walker loved to ride in his stroller, and I liked being in the street with him too—taking the air on the boulevard, chatting to him about the sights we passed. He responded to the sound of my voice. "Look here, bub, here's a big dog. And a girl, his owner. Look at her big fur hat"—that sort of thing. It made him laugh, and often he appeared curious—my favourite of his expressions. People watched us back, often couldn't help themselves from peering at Walker's lumpy face, his just-off features, his squirming tight body. They had a number of *ways* of looking. There was the glance-and-look-away: that was most common. Then there was the look-and-smile, to assure us we were accepted, that no stigma existed. Some people were openly horrified. Children stared bluntly, and some parents didn't even tell them not to. I have to admit I thought of them as animals, curs in the street.

Sometimes pregnant women, or youngish women who I imagined had begun to experience the lust to have a child of their own, came upon us clattering down the street, Quasimodo and his muttering minder, and clouds of alarm passed over their pretty faces. Then they sought out my face, to see if there was some hint in me that I might be the father of a kid like Walker: I could see them thinking they would be able to spot such a father. But I am quite normal to look at, and the clouds of alarm returned, and lingered. Deviance holds power over us because it strikes randomly.

The staring used to bother me. The worst offenders were teenage girls, who can't stop both hoping and fearing the entire world is gazing upon them in rapture—girls who want to stand out and fit in at the same time, a duplicitous transaction Walker doesn't allow the two of us. One spring, at the opening of the baseball season, I took him to see a Toronto Blue Jays game. His entire school at the time—the one designed exclusively for disabled children—came along: thirty bent and broken bodies, beeping and whooping and squawking in wheelchairs and carts, travelling in single file along the sidewalk for twenty blocks through the centre of the city. Now that was a procession that everyone watched. We broke up when we arrived at the stadium, and I wheeled my boy through the crowd.

It was School Day, or Bat Day, or some unimaginable combination of the two, and the stadium was overrun with teenagers. Again and again an identical ritual repeated itself: some tall thirteen-year-old girl in a pink or blue pop top and a white miniskirt and flip-flops, the leader of a tiny gang of three always shorter girls dressed exactly the same way, would spot Walker and me coming at them. The leader would lean over and whisper to her gaggle. Then they would all stare. Sometimes one would laugh. More often they would veil their mouths with their hands and pretend to hide their shock. I preferred open laughter to their smirking politesse.

The point is, I have known what it is like to be stared at, to be an object of fear and pity and even hatred. I hope Walker can't see it; he seems to ignore it, and gradually he taught me to ignore it as well. These days we stroll the boulevards as if they were ours. Walker has made me see how many of the rules we live by are simply made up.

I recall the actual day of his departure only through a baffle, as if my head is stuffed with pillows. The drive up—Johanna had carted his clothes and toys on several earlier trips—was quiet, a sunny Monday afternoon. We all piled into the house and half a dozen of the women who worked there welcomed him. Chantal, the eight-year-old, took him in hand right away. A tour of the bedroom and the rest of the house; the garden; details of his meds, feeding, instructions on the operation of the pump, all simply to reassure us. We stayed about an hour. Then we hugged and kissed him and hugged him again, me and Olga and Johanna and Hayley, and then we did it again, and then we forced ourselves to leave, saying goodbye loudly to all, trying to keep moving, trying not to stand still in case what we were doing caught up wth us. The ride back downtown without him, not sad or angry but extremely alert, as if we were driving through intense rain.

It was a good house, yes, of course, excellent. We reassured each other about that. We didn't go out that night, but instead stayed in and watched TV, marvelling at the quiet, at the velvety luxury of all the time we suddenly had. Huge folds of time that felt like curtains in the air. We could watch TV! Anything we wanted! And boy, we were looking forward to going to sleep. I kept thinking he was down in the basement playroom with Olga, where they often hung out—and then remembered the basement was empty, there was nothing below any more, just the white walls and the grey floor, no strange boy adventurer exploring its corners and shelves and cupboards over and over again, as if he knew they contained treasure, however hard it was to find. The pirate boy, in the bowels of our small home. He wasn't there any more. To this day I can't think of that night without a strange still pause coming over me, without wanting to mentally stick my fingers in my ears, so I can't hear his laughing, peeping, quacking voice.

———

We settled into the new routine. Walker was living in his new home: he came back to us every ten days for a three-day visit, plus long weekends and holidays. Minda called frequently to see how we were holding up. I was on the lookout for a hint of disapproval. Minda, after all, was a mother herself, and I couldn't believe she didn't somehow disdain, in her private mind, parents who couldn't look after their own children. Because that streak lived in me. But I was wrong: one afternoon nearly two years after Walker moved out, Minda explained what she had seen in our house that day she first came to meet us. We were having coffee in the suburbs, on our way back from one of the care-planning meetings we have about Walker.

"Physically," she said, "you and Johanna were shadows of yourselves. Here were two people who loved their child, who were trying to function as well as they could, who were working as well, who had another child as well. You think about it in future terms: should Hayley suffer as well? The emotion was palpable. And the struggle I could see in you and the pain you carried around—the roof was coming in."

She stopped talking. I refilled my coffee.

"You weren't people with an imaginary complaint," Minda continued. "Every family has something. It's just a question of levels, and how much a family can cope with. And how each family responds. And you have to be able to ask for help. Because wanting it and asking for it is a big difference. Because it means you can't do it on your own any more. Who wants to admit you've had a child and can't raise him?"

February 26, 2006

Picked Walker up today. He seems to have not one but two girl-friends: Chantal, who is now wearing a body brace for her scoliosis, and Krista Lee, a lovely fourteen-year-old girl in a wheelchair whom Walker adores. Chantal is bossier and pushes herself into Walker's ambit. Krista Lee waits, and so he goes to her.

Katie, one of the phalanx of men and women who work in the house, has even devised a way to stop Walker from hitting himself, without resorting to the foam helmet he hates—empty Pringles cans, reinforced with tongue depressors and electrician's tape and uphol-stered in bright fabric. The inside ends are stuffed with a ruffle of foam rubber. The cans slip over his arms, to his shoulders: these prevent him from bending his arms and levering his punches up to his skull. After years of misery, relief in a few cents' worth of cardboard.

I am still ashamed when people ask why they don't see Walker as much any more; I can't admit he lives mostly here. Johanna's more phlegmatic: she resisted his departure, but now that she has agreed to this arrangement, she backs it. "I feel as if he belongs to others now, as well as us," she said the other day, as we sat at the kitchen table, luxuriating in the newspaper. (Having the time to do so still feels as exotic as visiting Las Vegas.) He's certainly settling in. Not long ago Olga and Johanna drove Walker back "up there," as I call it, after a weekend here at home. Walker made a dervish entry, knocked over the trash can and buried his head in the breasts of Trish, his night worker. Then he took Johanna and Olga each by a hand, and gently but firmly escorted them to the front door. He wanted them to leave. Strange bout of liberation!

He's on a new dose of risperidone and a new drug for reflux, and his moods are more even. But it's his emotional confidence that's leaping forward. Living only in our world, I'm sure, he saw his limitations everywhere. In his new vacation home, as I think of it, surrounded by peers, he's as solid as anyone. I hope that is the gift we gave him by giving him up.

At our lowest point, we would try anything to feel better. I remember coming home one day to find my wife drinking wine and telling an elaborate story to Tecca and Cathrin, the friends who had been with Walker every stumbling step.

"I was at my chiropractor, Anita's," Johanna was saying, "and at the end of the session, she said, 'I have an idea about Walker. This is pretty woo-woo'—that was Anita's phrase, *woo-woo*—'but I wonder if you would take him to a shaman. A native shaman.' And I was so strung out on Walker that I said, 'Sure.' So two weeks later we set out to see the shaman."

"What, all three of you?" Cathrin said.

"Yes. We went to a native healing centre in an incredibly nondescript building. It looked like a rec room—industrial carpet, fake pine panelling. I was worried Walker might wreck the shaman's karma by freaking out. But as the shaman walked in, he became completely calm. So that was weird. He seemed to find some peace.

"There was a blanket in the middle of this basement floor. A woman, the shaman, was sitting on the blanket. There was an interpreter, a guy who explained what the shaman meant. You had to give her some money and some tobacco as an offering. So I gave her fifty bucks and put a pack of cigarettes on the blanket."

"What was Walker doing?"

"Walker scooted about between the shaman, me, Anita and the interpreter. I was nervous, but they didn't care, so I began not to care.

"The shaman lit a pipe. She lit some sage grass. She began a long introductory incantation. She spoke Walker's whole name: *Walker Henry Schneller Brown*. She called to the east wind, and then all the other winds, and then for Walker. By now there was a lot of smoke in the room, and I had a crashing headache. Then the shaman said: 'The gate appears.' And the guy, the interpreter said, 'Okay, it's starting.'

"The shaman said, 'I see a tree.' It was old and new. Parts of it were dead, and parts were alive. There was a light on the tree. It was full of singing birds. On the other side of the gate was a well, or pit. The shaman was singing all this, and the interpreter was interpreting. I'm condensing it. 'I see a well so deep you can barely see the water,' she said. And she said, 'I see a lot of elders.'"

I was still in the hall, jacket on, listening.

"The elders had come to see Walker, the shaman said. There were more than the usual number. Maybe they knew him? Maybe Walker was one of them. Maybe Walker was an elder. She couldn't tell. But they seemed to know him, anyway."

"The shaman said Walker was an elder?" This was Tecca.

"She wasn't sure. After the ceremony, the interpreter said the tree was Walker's life and the singing birds in it were all of us. The well was Walker's quest. And Walker's quest, the purpose of his life, was to see if he could see his reflection in the water at the bottom of the well."

"Get out." This was me.

"'That's what she said. 'This is the path that he has chosen for himself, to see if he can see his reflection. He may or he may not, but this is his quest.' Then the interpreter asked if I had any specific questions for the shaman. I said yes. What about this new group home, is this good for him? Should I let him go there?"

"And the shaman said, 'It will change his path. But his path is his path. He has to go down his own path.' Then I asked why he was injurious to himself, why he hit himself. And the shaman said he was trying to find the shape of his reflection in the well."

I wanted to lie down on the hallway floor.

"It was a huge relief to me," Johanna said. "Because for the first time, the only time, someone wasn't trying to fix him. They were just describing him. There was no judgment or fear. It was just very accepting. And I do think it was a turning point for me. Instead of trying to fix Walker or make him better or diagnose him or see what was causing his state, it was just what and who he is. This is what he's doing. It wasn't a triumph or a tragedy. It just was."

Silence. "Well," said Cathrin, "if I'd known he was an elder, I might not have let him look down my blouse all the times he climbed up into my lap. Turns out he's a dirty old man."

Tecca paused for a beat. "Dirty old *shaman*."

eight

The summer Walker turned eleven, living in his group home, I decided to get in my car and start driving. I felt compelled—though lured would be more accurate, strange as it might sound—to find some of the other people in the world like him. There were only a hundred of them, and they were scattered all over the world: Australia, Denmark, Britain, Japan, the United States. The nearest Canadian case I knew about was a thousand miles away in Saskatchewan. Thinking back on it now, it was another way to hold on to my boy, even as we were letting him go.

My first stop was California. That took a couple of weeks. Johanna didn't mind my absences: she never stood in the way when I tried to work my way closer to Walker. That had always been the case, since the early days when he was new and she was afraid, and I carried him through the dark places for her, until she was ready to love him. That earned me space. Or maybe, as she said one evening, "I think of Walker as Walker. And if I see other kids like him, then I'll start thinking of him as a kid with a syndrome." She preferred him as the only one of his kind. I wanted him to be like the world—or, though I didn't know it then, vice versa.

Emily Santa Cruz is hard to forget. She was the first person with CFC, other than Walker, I ever saw.

She was nine years old and in her mother Molly's arms, on the porch of their blue-and-white house in Arroyo Grande, halfway down the coast of California. Arroyo Grande is where the industrial farms of the dry-roasted Salinas Valley slip down to the cooler coast and the Pacific Ocean. Arriving there was like dropping into a new, more sympathetic atmosphere.

Emily had curly, black, standard-issue CFC hair, like Walker; slanty CFC eyes, like Walker; knobby CFC fingers; thick, brown CFC skin. I couldn't stop staring. Like Walker, she was spindly, and couldn't speak, but she could focus more than he could, and she wasn't as shy. It was a relief to find someone like my son, but a shock to see how stark the syndrome really is: I had no emotional attachment to Emily as yet, no need to find an "inner girl" or see her as anything more than she was, and so I saw only what was there: a small, bent, unusual, curious, twitching kid, afflicted but also clarified by her affliction. An elemental form of human being. Black-brown eyes; a grin as wide as a fender.

Even their house looked like ours, every surface cleared eighteen inches in, as far as Emily could reach; like Walker, she loved to throw things on the floor. Toys were scattered across the living room, the artifacts of her morning.

After Molly Santa Cruz had invited me in and asked to see some pictures of my son, we talked non-stop for eight hours. Emily was luckier than Walker in some ways—she could eat by herself—and not so lucky in others. A list on the fridge chronicled her seizures. It was pages long, single-spaced, and daily.

Sometimes Emily got out of her chair and crouched down on all fours next to us to peer at a toy. Sometimes she scrabbled a patch of wall with her fingers. The same squawks of excitement as Walker, the same chirps of desire.

Everything Molly told me was familiar. Emily liked to sleep without a blanket. For the first three years, she woke up every night, three times a night. "I think neurologically impaired kids like to get up at three or four in the morning," Molly said. Their lives were ruled by medical appointments: occupational and speech therapy twice a week, orthopedics every three to six months, a cardiologist annually, ophthalmologist twice a year, neurologist four times a year.

Molly was forty-five. She had a matter-of-fact way about her, the result of nine years of caring for Emily all day followed by evenings of work at her family's restaurant in nearby Nipomo. Her husband, Ernie, was fifty-six. He was a logistics specialist for a company that made Slime, a tire sealant. Leanne, Emily's older sister, was eighteen.

After we had been talking for an hour, Emily began to warm to me. She put her face two inches from mine and examined my notebook; I drew a picture of her and she looked at the picture and coughed, then laughed at her coughing. I rubbed her back: it was skinny and bony, her spine a thin dorsal ridge, like my son's. Should human beings ever discover benign and co-operative life on other planets, I wouldn't be surprised if they feel the same way I did that breezy California afternoon after meeting Emily, Walker's genetic cousin. I suppose it's simple enough: his universe felt slightly less lonely than it had before. My boy wasn't alone. Emily clapped her hands and climbed up into her chair again and began making a *brrrt*-ing sound through her lips, which she found even more hilarious than I did. She was nimbler than Walker, but periodically slipped off into the same private, unreachable places. Molly spoke to her as she would to anyone else.

"Do you think she understands you?" I asked.

"I don't think she understands a lot," Molly said. "But she's starting to understand. Especially at school, with the routine of every single day."

School was due to start in a week. When Molly mentioned it, a hungry look crept onto her face. Emily at school meant a chance to sleep in.

The strange thing is that when the incessant watchfulness of having a CFC kid does let up, it's hard to let go. Ernie Santa Cruz, Molly's husband, noticed it the first time he and Molly took a weekend away from Emily, when the child was five years old. They left her with Molly's sister, Kate, who lives fifteen minutes away in the Salinas Valley, not far from their parents, who descend from some of the first missionaries who settled California. Ernie had reserved a room in a great motel next to the Avila Hot Springs, and the setting was perfect. Their first weekend away in five years.

And yet what's the only thing Ernie can think about? Emily. Every few minutes, he has the same thought: what's Emily doing now? Is she sweeping the books off the bookshelf in the living room? Or is she alone in her room?

Ernie grew up in Whittier, California, Richard Nixon's hometown, attended state college in Chico for a degree in physical education, served in the navy in Japan and Vietnam. He coached girls' volleyball at the Arroyo Grande high school every afternoon. Leanne, his older daughter, was on the team. They'd won the regional championship twice, the league championship sixteen times. He'd been offered college coaching jobs, but he didn't want to travel far from Emily. He was a very steady guy.

Out in the backyard of their house in Arroyo Grande was an old shed. Next to it was an old chair. Next to the chair was Ernie's shrine. That was one word for it, anyway. ("He says this is his identity," Molly had said, as she gave me a tour of their place. She seemed both mystified and reassured. "He says this is his favourite place to be.") A plastic car, some rubber frogs, Dinky Toys, a meat grinder filled with cacti, a Corona beer bucket, some Mayan masks, Emily's old sneakers with hearts drawn on the toes. Emily, meanwhile, was walking around the yard and crouching down to the lavender plants and sniffing them and saying, "Buh! Wuh! Wuh!" Ernie liked to sit in the chair when Emily played in the backyard. He could sit there in his shrine and watch Emily be herself.

This was definitely—maybe—his last year coaching volleyball. "I see him getting a little more tired," Molly said. Ernie and Molly had always dismissed the idea of putting Emily into a group home. But that was changing. "We've always said we're gonna keep her with us as long as we can," Molly said.

By the time she got around to talking about such things, we were in her car, heading out to dinner at the restaurant her parents have owned for years. The long automatic irrigators had started up on the big farms next to the highway, as they do every evening, the water spritzing above the fields in the distance like wild thoughts.

"But we've started to think about it. We always said, it'll be easier next year with Emily. But it never is."

The thing about the CFC community, it turned out, was that everyone was isolated, and yet everyone knew everyone else. I met Molly and Ernie and Emily Santa Cruz, for instance, through Brenda Conger. Everyone knew Brenda.

In 1992, at the age of thirty-four, Brenda Conger had a husband, Cliff, a healthy two-year-old daughter named Paige and a job as a special-education teacher in Binghamton, in upstate New York. Then she got pregnant again.

This time, it didn't go well. Cliffie, her son, was born eight weeks early. According to the lumpy technology of the time, he showed no chromosomal abnormalities, but he had bigger problems. For instance, he couldn't breathe. He spent his first sixty-three days of life on a respirator in the intensive-care unit. Brenda says, "It was my worst fear as a special-education teacher, to have a special-needs child." The doctors predicted that the boy wouldn't live, and that even if he did, he would never walk or talk. For Brenda, it was agony. She started to pray, and not for the usual kind of salvation. "Take this child home," she would whisper to herself "And do it quickly."

Days and nights passed in a single blur. At last, after more than two months of watching their child breathe via respirator, the Congers and their doctors decided to take Cliffie off life support. "And apparently a guardian angel was at work,"

Brenda later told the local newspaper, "because on that day he started to breathe on his own. I was so mad at God on that day. That was not part of the plan. But that day I learned that Cliffie was leading the plan. And he had been since day one."

The Congers crashed into the hour-by-hour life of a family with a disabled child. Suddenly they had no time and less money. "We're middle-class. I'm a teacher. And if it doesn't snow, my husband—he owns a ski shop—doesn't have an income." The boy was three before doctors diagnosed him. Not that a diagnosis explained much: Cliffie was only the twenty-second case of CFC Brenda could find in the medical literature.

The syndrome, or at least a wide group of symptoms that seemed to be associated with a specific physical appearance like Cliff's, had first been publicly described at a March of Dimes conference in Vancouver in 1979, in a presentation titled "A New Mental Retardation Syndrome with Characteristic Facies, Icthyosis and Abnormal Hair." That the presentation had even been made seemed like a small miracle: the identifying team of clinical geneticists were spread across the United States, and had come together largely by chance. One of the members of the team was John Opitz, a legendary geneticist who had already identified and named half a dozen new syndromes. Opitz claimed to have seen his first case of CFC in the mid-1960s. Even so, it was 1986 before the affliction had a name. Conger found only a dozen scientific papers that mentioned the syndrome: most were just short reports of newly discovered cases. CFC was a mystery, and an arcane one at that.

That didn't stop Conger. A slim woman with reddish-blonde hair and worried eyes, she gives the impression of having two or three lists in her mind at all times—all things she has to get done by sundown. The year Cliffie was diagnosed, her brother, Carl, committed suicide. Her boy's troubles took her mind off the tragedy. "CFC has just been a lucky thing to be involved in," Brenda explained the afternoon I met her, eleven years later. "CFC is my therapy."

Within twenty-four hours of the diagnosis, she noticed an ad in *Exceptional Parent* magazine for something called the CFC Family Network. By 1999, Brenda, being Brenda, was running it. There were still only fifty known cases of CFC, but Brenda sent a newsletter to anyone who wrote in or answered the ads in *Exceptional Parent*.

In 2000, she organized the first-ever gathering of CFC families, held in Salt Lake City to be near John Opitz. Molly Santa Cruz showed up too, Emily in tow. "And it was like, 'Oh my gosh! These kids look like mine!'" Molly remembers. "Yeah, it was cool. There's nothing like meeting somebody who's been in the same boat you have."

Molly later became one of Brenda's board members. When they came across a paper by a San Francisco geneticist, Kate Rauen, who was investigating CFC, Molly called her up. With Dr. Rauen's encouragement, Brenda and Molly hired teams of phlebotomists to draw blood at the family conferences, which by then were happening every two years. In 2005, using the DNA they gathered from twenty-three individuals, Rauen eventually would identify the first genes known to be associated with CFC. She named Brenda and Molly co-authors of the discovery, only the third time non-scientists have been named as co-discoverers of a gene. (As a result, CFC International will have a stake in any future patents developed from their identification of this gene.)

These days Brenda Conger steers the world of CFC from the teeming offices of CFC International—the second-floor landing of her house, tucked in behind the stairs. She also oversees the Internet site on which CFC parents around the world discuss everything from seizure treatments to life expectancy, which even with luck won't reach past middle age.

"And that's comforting to me," Molly told me. "Because I don't want Emily to be getting old and I'm not here."

And Cliffie Conger, who doctors said would die before his first birthday? He's now seventeen. He goes to school, reads, talks and can drive a tractor.

———

Even the briefest meeting with another CFC child felt like the discovery of a new element. Kolosia Taliauli and her daughter, Vaasi, lived in a tiny apartment in a crime-ridden neighbourhood of Stockton, California. Vaasi was two and a half; she had spent 80 percent of her life in hospital. When Vaasi was born, Kolosia was a single mother with an eight-year-old son. She had to give up her job. California (a progressive state, where disabilities are concerned) now paid her $8.25 an hour to look after her own child. Medicaid covered everything else. Formula was delivered right to her door. "Sometimes, with a child with a lot of medical needs," her state-supplied nurse, Laurie Kent, told me, "it's better to be broke."

———

The first thing Daniel Hess did when he met me was shout and fling his glasses into the living room. It was an understandable reaction; I had interrupted breakfast with his grandparents, who were visiting from New York City. This was in Glen Ellyn, a prosperous suburb to the west of Chicago, where Daniel lives with his mother, Amy, his father, Steve, and his two younger sisters, Sarah and Laura.

Daniel was a six-year-old CFC miracle. He could talk. He was in school and could read at grade level, better than most of his classmates. He could even dress himself—he was wearing a very nice pair of green frog boots when I met him, to favour a sore ankle. Metabolically, Daniel is not so lucky: he suffers from ulcers in his intestines, serious allergies and immune problems, pervasive reflux and seizures.

Amy, who was about to turn forty, was a ball of purpose with blonde hair, and possibly (her mother claimed) the most organized woman in Chicago. She had grown up in Lake Forest, Illinois, and in Houston. Her father was an insurance executive. She had a degree in economics and anthropology from St. Lawrence University. She graduated in 1990, married in 1999, and had plans to work in the advertising business. Her husband, Steve, was the landlord of several buildings he had inherited.

Then in 2001, Daniel was born, four weeks early. He couldn't take Amy's breast, but he was her first child—what did she know? He slept three hours a night, aspirating and refluxing all the time. He was diagnosed with Costello syndrome, a genetic mutation that shares many symptoms and features with CFC—so many, in fact, that the syndromes are still often mistaken for each other, though the effects can be quite different. (Costello syndrome tends to produce softer facial features and less intellectual delay, but it is also associated with certain forms of cancer, which CFC is not. Kate Rauen and other scientists have identified genes associated with Costello syndrome as well.) She remembered the day he was diagnosed very clearly, partly because the diagnosis of Costello surprised her: to her mind, there were elements of Daniel's presentation that didn't fit the Costello template. Still, a diagnosis was a diagnosis, and she was already planning on researching outcomes that afternoon.

But on the way home from the doctor, as she led Daniel through the street by the hand, Amy ran into a woman she knew, from volunteer work they'd done together. The woman looked at Daniel and went white. "I have a friend who has a son who looks just like yours," she said. Amy faxed Daniel's picture to her friend's friend the moment she got home. The woman telephoned immediately: "Your son has CFC." Instead of researching Costello syndrome, Amy was on the phone to Brenda Conger that afternoon. This is not an unusual story in the world of CFC.

Amy Hess's acquaintance was right: Daniel had CFC, and the misshapen genes to prove it. The correct diagnosis didn't lift Amy's burden, but the knowledge that her son was the product of a spontaneous genetic mutation, virtually at the moment of conception, helped her in other ways. "It cleaned up the guilt of creating a child who suffers. You know, 'What did I do wrong? Was it because I had a manicure while I was pregnant, and the fumes did it? Was it because I was a skydiver and took a few jumps before I knew I was pregnant, and he suffered from a lack of oxygen?' So the diagnosis was peace."

Or at least as close to peace as the parent of a handicapped child can get—because even a firm diagnosis cannot clear away the ancient sense of culpability that has been attributed to these random genetic events for literally thousands of years—the lingering swamp notion that there is always a reason such a disability occurs, that it is a punishment, and thus deserved. European doctors in the 1500s attributed them to poverty (as have conservative politicians in North America in the past decade). Herodotus insisted deformity was caused by marrying insufficiently attractive partners. Martin Luther, who often behaved like an imbecile, believed the retarded and the deformed were siblings of the devil, beings born in the wrong realm, and that they ought to be drowned. Amy Hess was an educated and enlightened product of an age of science and progress, but the old shame worked its curse anyway.

"I've had a very, very blessed life," Amy told me one bright morning in Chicago. "I've had great parents. Great friends. Great jobs. Great schools. And I did think, it was my turn.'"

Amy is a worrier. Fortunately for Daniel, she coped by researching. She quit her job and transformed herself into a full-time medical detective. She enrolled him in an endless schedule of therapies—up to ten a week, from the time he was one month old until he was three, mostly paid for by the state's early-action program for children more than 30 percent delayed. "He needs every break he can get. I didn't want him not to learn at a crucial stage." There were stretches when Daniel was in some form of physiotherapy twenty-four hours a day, whether asleep or in his feeding chair.

A child who is at risk of not being able to speak will often be introduced first to sign language. To learn sign, the child has to be willing to make eye contact so he or she can see the signs being made. Daniel's speech and language therapists signed at him for four months before Daniel looked at them—but they signed away anyway. Amy kept detailed, typed records of every medical appointment her son attended, every medicine he tried. CFC is full of surprises, but Amy's systematic attention is a model of how it and similar syndromes should be approached. As far as providing services is concerned, there is no harm in being over-attentive.

The results are obvious. Daniel can watch TV and laugh; he can be reliably distracted. He has the same knobby knees as my boy, but Daniel can climb into the car with his dad and—armed with the uncanny spatial sense that lets him do jigsaw puzzles upside down—say, "We go your way, or Mummy's way?" Steve has lived in Glen Ellyn all his life and always takes the back roads, whereas Amy, a relative newcomer, sticks to the main highways. Daniel noticed. And of course there were Daniel's words. He never talked directly to me—I was an interloper, and he was watching TV—but he chattered away to everyone else. Of all the gifts I wish for my dear son, for him to speak a few words is the first I would want granted. I love Walker's Frankenstein walk, and his pulpy hands, which seem dearer for being the flawed things they are. But to hear him speak his own name? To hear him call *Hayley!* loud and clear, as opposed to the *Hehhh* he gets out now and then? To hear him say, *Ma, I love you?* My heart is banging at the thought. *Fuck you, Dada!* would be the Gettysburg Address.

And not because of what the words mean. The language of CFC children who can speak often has a faintly plastic or artificial quality, a less than genuine feel: they mean what they say, but one is sometimes left with the impression that they are using someone else's words to say it, that their language is more borrowed than self-generated. But at least it is language, proof of an inner life, evidence that they can sense context, that they have desires. I don't need Walker to say *I love you* to know he does. But if he spoke a word, it would be proof that he had something to say and that he wanted to say it, that there was a point to his saying it. Desire is intention. Intention is hope.

The autumn that Walker turned eighteen months old, my wife and I sat next to each other at the kitchen table and filled out the MacArthur Communicative Development Inventory. It was eight pages long. According to the inventory, Walker understood 115 words: *Are you hungry* and *Open your mouth*; *kiss* and *wet*; *yucky* and *you* and *breakfast* and *moon*. *Good*, but not *happy*. *Dark*, but not *broken*. Even *sky*. It helps to remember, of course, that it was Johanna and I who filled out the form: we saw his brilliance everywhere. But in fact he said nothing. Johanna and Hayley have dreams to this day in which Walker can talk like a trial lawyer. They wake up exalted, filled with excitement. In my mind, we chat nonstop. But in actual life, my son can't speak.

So there were times in the beautifully appointed and deliciously organized Hess house when I couldn't speak either, for envy and sadness. I wanted to get in my car and on a plane and fly straight to Walker. But for better programs, earlier intervention (we started at three months), more money, a more energetic and more dutiful father—so I told myself—but for being born five years too soon, Walker might today be as fortunate as Daniel. What if one of us had chosen not to work at all, had stayed home to be a full-time parent and disability warrior?

Every parent of a compromised child knows this secret envy, mines its thick seam of guilt. It's no more reasonable (or logical) to say that one parent has an obligation to stay home than it would be to insist that Amy Hess had an obligation to go to work. My wife and I did everything every doctor and medical report ever suggested, and then some; we had the ready advice of Toronto's Hospital for Sick Children and Bloorview Kids Rehab, two of the best pediatric institutions in the world. We enrolled Walker in early intervention programs when he was three months old, began using sign language at six months. None of it had any effect. Nature—the state in which he had been born—was stronger.

Kate Rauen's identification of the CFC gene means, technically, that a fetus could be tested for CFC in utero and aborted. All this pain could be avoided. (The disease is so rare, however, that routine testing is financially unfeasible.) Amy Hess won't even think about that. "I wouldn't change having Daniel," she insists. But when pressed, she admits she also wouldn't choose to have more children who suffer. She may adopt another special-needs child, "because at least then you don't have that guilt component, of bringing such a child into the world." She still blames herself for her son. She does not blame the world for the way it treats him.

Daniel, though, is freer. He often approaches strangers on the street. "Hi," he says. "Do you like me?"

That's the real question.

***

Eventually, having met Emily Santa Cruz and Daniel Hess and others through Brenda Conger's CFC website, I had the opportunity to meet Brenda Conger herself. When I arrived in Vestal, New York, where Conger and her family live, her son Cliffie was waiting at the door. He looked like a more urbane, less afflicted version of Walker—curly hair and glasses, but slimmer and taller, CFC's Noel Coward. The family's Labradors, Henry and Jackson, walloped into the door as I knocked.

"Those dogs'll wreck you," Cliffie said, and laughed.

This was my first conversation with someone who had CFC.

Before anything else Cliffie wanted to see photographs of Walker. Then he swayed over to help his mother tenderize the chicken she was cooking for dinner. Mr. Rogers, the host of the famous, glacially paced children's television show, was on the wide-screen TV in the living room. Cliffie was fifteen at the time—a teenager watching Mr. Rogers. There were little signs like that, just hints. Cliffie was good for ten smacks on the chicken, then had to stop, exhausted. That was when I noticed how slim his arms were, how glancing his attention could be.

He gave me a tour of the house; he seemed to prefer the second floor.

"This is Mummy's *offish*," he said of the landing nook where Brenda Conger had changed the CFC landscape.

"This is the new room"—the office his father was adding.

He showed me the bathroom, and the shower, and the shower curtain most of all. "Keep that closed," he said.

We continued down the hall.

"This is my daughter's room," Cliffie said, gesturing.

"Your daughter? You mean your sister."

"Right."

He has trouble with his "r"s, and his language did have that occasional pasted-on quality, as if he were reciting from memory, or from a list of possibilities in his head. Parts of his mind were his own; other pieces seemed as if he'd bought them pre-assembled off the showroom floor. Neurologists have described the same feature in the normal mind, the clip-in societal set piece—but in Cliffie it was slowed down and you could see how it operated.

His bedroom, his private sanctuary, was festooned with graphics of John Deere tractors, his great obsession: neat, useful, powerful. There was a John Deere tractor rug on the floor, tractor wallpaper, tractor curtains, a tractor bedspread. There were JD tractors on the light switch, his Kleenex box, his wastebasket; a JD tractor at the end of the chain on his ceiling fan.

We walked outside. While Brenda finished making dinner and his father, Cliff, talked to me about the wilderness days of CFC, before anyone knew anything, and about how he taught Cliffie to ski by walking the bunny hill in ski boots for two years before Cliffie felt comfortable enough to try it on skis—while we adults were occupied, Cliffie climbed onto his John Deere tractor, a sit-down, yard-work model. He started the motor. Then he drove the tractor out of its shed and around the yard. When he was done, he backed it, and its hitch-mounted trailer, into the shed. He did this perfectly.

"*I* couldn't do that," I said to his father. I suddenly had a mental picture of Walker picking grapes. Maybe Walker could pick grapes!

"He's a better parallel parker that any eighteen-year-old with a licence," Cliff said. It had taken him four years to teach his son to drive the tractor. Cliff started by cutting the grass with the boy in his arms.

At 10:47 that night, Brenda roused Cliffie from the TV. "Cliffie, time to go to bed."

"Mom," he said. Nothing delayed about that tone. "Why can't I stay up? I'm a teenager."

He had the routines of normal life down. Between what he felt and what he had been told to feel was the real boy, still forming. Was that the gift of the CFC child—to be always forming and never formed?

When I came down for breakfast the next morning, Cliff and Cliffie had been up since 7 a.m., making their Sunday omelettes. Cliffie was wearing his SpongeBob SquarePants pyjamas. He shuffled over. Wan wet light was filtering through the window.

"Mr. Bwown, you want mushwooms in yoh omelette?"

"Ian," I said. "Call me Ian."

"Ian." Perfunctory. Names, irrelevant. The moment was all. "You want mushwooms?"

"Are you a mushroom eater?" I asked.

"Yeah."

"Me too!"

"Yeah!" he fairly shouted. I knew that bang of glee from Walker. "He's a mushwoom eater!" he called to his father.

Cliffie paused. "What about pickles?"

"No," I said, "no pickles."

"Whoa!" He looked at me with new respect, the kind you accord a fellow who stands against the orthodoxies of the age.

"You a pickle man?" I asked.

"Yeah!" Again the grunt of enthusiasm.

Maybe that was why Walker did it too—when he felt we were equals, or at least on the same page.

All we had needed was an interpreter, a boy who spoke both our languages.

———

A lot of CFC parents, I discovered, lived a lot of their lives on the Internet. They met through CFC International, Brenda Conger's online chat room, or listserv. Parents with a new CFC baby burst into the chat room like travellers staggering into an oasis after years in the desert. They signed off as if they were saying goodbye to longlost siblings:

> *All our love*
> *Wife to Malcolm Mam to Lewis 9 James 7 Amy 4*
> *CFC confirmed*

And they always signed off the same way. "Confirmed" meant confirmed genetically, the *ne plus ultra* of CFC status. If you were confirmed—a genetic test for CFC had become available after the spring of 2006—your DNA could be included in research studies. Parents longed for the confirmation. Some children had been clinically diagnosed as having the similar-featured Costello syndrome or Noonan syndrome, but were then revealed, genetically, to be CFC; others who had been clinically diagnosed as CFC were re-diagnosed as having Noonan or Costello syndromes. (There is a faction of geneticists who believe that CFC and Costello syndromes are not separate syndromes at all, but merely variants of Noonan syndrome, which is more widespread.) Conger never kicked any of the children who were re-diagnosed as non-CFC out of her network, but the news was often devastating to their parents.

Walker was five before CFC International existed online. By the time he was ten, parents of children with CFC had created an online community. Monitoring letters on the CFC listserv over the course of several years was like watching a small town coalesce out of a galaxy of darkness—a light would blink on, and then another and another, and slowly, very slowly, the lights became a village. Cases of CFC began to turn up in other parts of the world—in Australia and Lebanon and Holland, a second case in British Columbia, even a second in Toronto.

The CFC listserv read like a vast epistolary novel. Newcomers would burst on the scene, teeming with intimacies and information; the old-timers welcomed them with reassuring arms. What no one mentioned was how similar the stories sounded, and how the complaints had remained the same for years, without remedy—the troubling quirks that new parents had been assured by doctors would go away, but which the rest of us knew likely would not. I remember a woman named Kate describing with passion the attributes of her little boy, an eight-year-old who had only just been confirmed with CFC. "He cannot talk and I have no idea if he will but he does get across in his own way what he wants," she wrote. "He gets very frustrated sometimes and bites his hands or bangs his head. He is such a character and has brought such joy into our lives. But to be honest there are times I so wish I could just be his mummy and not a nurse/carer as well, I don't begrudge anything that will help his life be easier but it has been hard sometimes."

The problem, as any experienced CFC parent reading her letter knew, was that there wasn't anything that could make his life much easier.

Reading the listserv inevitably led to comparisons, and comparisons were never a good idea. Sara and Chris, a couple in Massachusetts, had a daughter named Regan. She was two and a half years old.

Regan signs and speaks. I think she said "ice cream" tonight, although she would never try to eat it. She is a picky eater but is slowly broadening her tastes. She points to our plates and says "MMMMMM" but refuses most of what we offer her. . . . Regan is developmentally delayed and her gross motor skills are much more behind than her communication and fine motor skills. She cannot walk or get into a sitting position yet but she tolerates standing, scoots on her behind and just recently can pull herself from a sit to stand position

Was it better to be Regan, who is a better communicator, or Walker, who is a better mover? It was impossible not to ask yourself that question, and impossible to answer. The United States was pushing hard to establish compulsory state early intervention programs for any child as young as three months old who displayed a need for them. No such program had existed when Walker was a baby, and they are still rare in many parts of Canada. British Columbia was ahead of the game where custom-designed living arrangements were concerned; Ontario was very good about providing respite care. What did not exist was a consistent, reliable, guaranteed, easily accessed program of help and care for congenitally disabled children. It was hard not to conclude that the non-disabled world wanted to forget about these children, or at least not be reminded of them.

Some parents came late to CFC International after years of thinking their children suffered from other syndromes. They were often the most complicated cases, with cross-indicating symptoms. As a result, reading the listserv you never knew when you'd happen upon something completely new to worry about. There were dramas within dramas. A woman named Renée was caught in a hurricane in New Orleans in the fall of 2008 while her daughter Harley, who had CFC, fought for her life in hospital. Renée sent updates over the Web as if Harley belonged to everyone:

Hey my family. I have a few minutes to type this time. I am not for sure if i mentioned it, but the nurses from our hospice came out and in Harley's left lung, the only air being exchanged is what the bipap machine is pushing in. . . . The hospice nurses said she could go tonight, it could be 4 or 5 days, and then again Harley could do like all the other times and beat this, but they don't seem to think she will. Harley is in really bad shape. Keep her and us in y'all's thoughts and prayers. God Bless!!!!

Harley eventually died, in March of 2009. Parents of other CFC children wrote in to Conger's website for weeks afterwards, to praise her struggle and honour her memory. Like them, I never met Harley, but I knew a lot about her. She was another member of my son's other family.

Then there was the daily bread of the listserv, the habitual discussions of ear canals and earwax, feeding issues, sodium levels, seizure medications, the trials of puberty and the pros and cons of delaying it through hormone therapy, the prevalence of complicating autism within the CFC spectrum (low, but increasing), G-tubes, who could walk and who couldn't and what could be done about it, who could speak and who couldn't (ditto), who had hair and who didn't, who liked to be naked and who didn't, how to keep the kids occupied, and what might possibly make them sleep. Some mothers, such as Amy Hess, knew more than any doctor, and were widely consulted for medical and technical help. Hirschsprung's disease, a congenital condition of the bowel, made infrequent but harrowing appearances: a section of the large bowel was aganglionic (that is, the bowel lacked the normal enteric nerves that help a bowel movement along), which in turn resulted in a bowel obstruction, which in turn created a permanently swollen bowel known as megacolon. It sounded like an amusement ride and shared some of its terrifying qualities. Word for word, bowel movements and eating disorders were the most frequently discussed topics, along with the names of anti-constipation remedies, MiraLAX and Kristalose and Dulcolax, their brand names light and wondrous, like a family of famous singing sisters.

Occasionally there were bright bursts of insight. When a mother named Roseanna in Colorado admitted to despair and shame over wishing her child was normal, another mother, Stacey, replied with clarity and compassion:

> *I understand, as all CFC parents do, the challenges of our special kids. I think the hardest thing for me was giving up the dream of the typical family. Logan wasn't diagnosed until he was 5 and for the first 2 years I kept thinking "well after we fix THIS he'll be normal, after we fix THIS he'll be normal" and kept clinging to the hope that he was going to be like everyone else's children. It would upset me when I heard other new moms complaining about things I could only dream and hope for (eating everything in site, being fat babies, starting to run everywhere etc.). And I was OBSESSED when figuring out what was wrong with him on my own. I had a child that needed multiple surgeries, wouldn't eat, threw up EVERYTHING up to five times a day,*

*and no doctor would really listen to me or understand what
I was going through. At first they felt I wasn't trying hard
enough. Then, one day when he was 2 years old I realized I
was so obsessed with finding his problem and fighting this
battle myself that I wasn't enjoying him . . . because I was so
heartbroken over my dream of "normal" [being] crushed. So,
from that point on I accepted Logan as Logan, and I didn't
think about what he should or could be doing but what he
WAS doing. Though there are hard days and challenges,
there are many GOOD days and now this life for me is
normal. I promise it will get easier.*

*Good luck and I will be thinking of you and your family,
Stacey*

Regular contributors came and went as the health of their
children fluctuated—and it fluctuated with alarming frequency, in everyone's case. Some letters foamed over with
bossiness and displaced panic. There was a generally observed
reluctance to complain or despair—the "woe-is-me school,"
as hardline CFC moms called habitual complainers, rejecting
complaining as futile and self-indulgent. At the same time
there was a lot of religion in the mix: a day rarely passed
without someone thanking the Lord for the hidden "blessings"
of having a CFC "angel," without someone else insisting that
God "gives special children to special parents."

I understood that impulse: Walker had given my life
shape, possibly even meaning. But Walker had also made our
lives hell. On the hellish days the mawkish sermonizing
about angels and specialness felt like rank self-delusion, the
work of anxious cheerleaders desperate to justify themselves

to a cynical high school. Disability is no different from politics or even college football: it divides and politicizes people
according to their need, simplifying dark and unanswerable
experience into a dependable, reassuring stance. But the
details of Walker's life belied any certain path.

Johanna had been in touch with Brenda Conger's CFC
network early on, before the Internet existed. But she was
impatient then for specific advice, for skin creams and therapies that would help right away. "It seemed to be a lot about
Jesus and angels and thinking of the kids as gifts from God,"
she told me years later. It was hard to think of Walker as a
gift from God, unless God was a sadist who bore a little boy
a grudge. After that Johanna stayed away from the network,
and we coped on our own.

———

Lana Phillips was the mother of Jaime Phillips, one of the
first five people identified as having CFC back in 1986. By
then Jaime was ten years old. Lana dealt with Jaime's bent
and broken self for nearly twenty-five years before there was
an Internet, or any CFC network of any real note—and that
was near Wendell, Idaho, which is not exactly the centre of
the medical universe.

I met Lana over the telephone: she had a clean, clear
voice like something outdoors on a fresh day. Lana was
grateful that Jaime was even alive. The doctors realized
something was wrong from the moment the child was born,
but no one knew what. She wouldn't eat. A neighbour suggested goat's milk and yams—both easily digested by finicky
children, or so the neighbour said—so Lana bought a goat
and milked it and boiled up massive batches of yams. To her

surprise, the diet worked, and Jaime grew stronger. Getting Jaime to talk was less successful. Lana and her husband Mike, who owned his own insurance agency, drove to Los Angeles to have Jaime examined at one of UCLA's medical centres; the doctors there suggested they take her to see Dr. John Opitz, the famous geneticist from Wisconsin. When he examined Jaime a few months later, he told the other doctors present they would likely never see another case like Jaime's in their lives.

Two years passed before Opitz and his team of colleagues published their groundbreaking scientific paper naming CFC as a new and distinct syndrome. The day Lana read that paper was the first time she had ever seen a picture of another child with CFC. Lana had the idea that the publication of the scientific paper would unleash a flood of undocumented cases of CFC, and that the scientists would put her in touch with other CFC parents, and vice versa. She even gave them written consent to share her name and address. But nothing happened. The geneticists kept the information to themselves—for reasons of patient confidentiality. When you have a child with something as rare and unknown as CFC, the *last* thing you want is confidentiality. You want all the help you can get. But this is a measure of how segregated life with a rare syndrome can make you.

For four years, Lana heard nothing. It was as if the syndrome had been named and then dropped down a mine shaft. So she did the only thing she could do: she spent hours rereading the published report and inspecting the same pictures over and over again. Her own daughter seemed to have the severest symptoms, and Lana worried that she hadn't heard from anyone because no one wanted to meet Jaime.

By the time Jaime turned fourteen, Lana had gone to work for Head Start, a national education program for children from unstable and underprivileged backgrounds. She worked out of the local public school. One day word came down from the office that a new child would be joining her class. The new kid hadn't started walking until she was four—just like Jaime.

A couple of days later, Lana met the new girl. "When that child walked into our classroom I could not believe my eyes," Lana told me. "I immediately thought to myself, if I were a geneticist, I would say that this child has Jaime's syndrome, this child has CFC." As soon as she could, Lana contacted the girl's mother, and sure enough, she too had been diagnosed with CFC—by the same pediatrician who had diagnosed Jaime. He just hadn't thought to pass the information along to Lana. Instead, in a fluke of unimaginable proportions (there is no statistically significant geographic pattern to the occurrence of CFC), in as close to a geographically remote place as you can get in the United States, a CFC child walked into the classroom of a woman who had the only other CFC child for thousands of miles. Lana figured that had to be something like a miracle, statistical or otherwise.

For Lana the encounter was a huge relief. "There is something powerful and satisfying about knowing why your child is the way they are and being connected with other families who have a child like yours," Lana explained. Still, the new child was much more developmentally advanced than Jaime, and Lana was afraid her mother would be upset meeting Jaime, a much older and more severely challenged person, a portent of the future.

As it turned out, the other CFC mother never expressed any desire to stay in touch, and the family soon moved away. "But I got to work with the child," Lana told me, "and I thought, this is a real syndrome."

By the time Jaime was eleven, she was too much for Lana and her husband to look after (especially alongside their three other children), and she went to live in one of the top group homes in the United States, in Idaho. "That was the most dramatic, the most difficult thing I have ever done," Lana said. "There was this hole in my heart. And I think that was part of the difficulty I had when I thought about reconnecting with the CFC community." It was a steady reminder that other parents lived with their CFC children, could handle their CFC traits.

Jaime lived in the group home for nineteen years, until she turned thirty. She saw her parents every weekend, though they lived a three-hour drive away. A year before I spoke to Lana, however, Jaime became sick—a complicated mix of septic pneumonia and lymphoedema that left her close to death for four months in an intensive care unit. When she finally recovered, Lana and Mike—by then sixty-one and sixty-two years old respectively—took her out of the group home and brought her back home to live with them, with the help of a pair of full-time caregivers paid for by the state and proceeds from Mike's insurance business. "In the intensive care ward, it was almost like looking at a stranger, and I guess I didn't like that feeling," Lana explained. She wanted to protect her daughter. In the ICU Jaime was fed enough metabolized morphine to put a 225-pound man under for an entire day—except that in Jaime it wore off in two hours, whereupon she'd rip her IV lines out. She was four foot nine and weighed ninety-six pounds. She couldn't speak and she was only half trained on the toilet, but she had a will of granite.

Jaime's return after almost two decades in a group home had given Lana a new outlook. "I live my life less from fear now," she told me. Now that Jaime is home day and night, Mike and Lana have realized that she understands more than they thought she did. She has favourite signs for her favourite words, *shoes* and *more*. No one knows why: those just seem to be the most rewarding concepts in her unusual life, something she puts on every day, something she desires. "She got so many results from that sign, *more!*" Lana said. Jaime—who has the "mentality," as Lana calls it, of someone eighteen months to two years old—loves men. "At church she'll see some good-looking young man she likes, or some older man, and she'll run up to him and grab his arm and giggle." Jaime was thirty-three years old when her mother told me that story.

But Lana doesn't mind. "I just feel that I am becoming the person I've always wanted to be in life," she said. "I work with small children, I have learned patience, and empathy, to reach out for people no matter what they look like. And that has all been because of Jaime." She thought for a bit then, and went on. She's a devout Mormon, and had been talking about what Mormons call "the eternities," about heaven and God's justice. "Someday she's going to have a perfect body and a perfect mind."

Who wouldn't want to believe that? Jaime, a grown woman with an infant's mind, had changed Lana's life even as she went on blithely living her own. And that change had started, Lana remembered, the day another child with CFC walked into her classroom. "For me," she insisted, "that meeting filled a void."

As a fairly conventional atheist, I wasn't comfortable with the idea of eternity and words such as *miracle*. But they seemed to perform an important role in the lives of a lot of people who cared for children with disabilities. The possibility that their lives had been touched by God's grace was at least one way to make sense of the otherwise senseless burden they carried.

THE BOY IN THE MOON

nine

I tended to phone parents who had CFC children in the afternoon: I needed to work up to it as the day wore on, to shore up my courage. I was afraid of what I would learn—that this child was luckier than Walker; that these parents had been more dedicated. And yet that never happened. No one was luckier. If someone had an advantage in this strange world of the severely disabled, they had lost something somewhere else. Delusions were rare: these parents' circumstances were stark, but they were clear, and clear had a rare attraction.

So I phoned them, or sometimes travelled to meet them, and they would tell me the story of their lives. They told me the most remarkable things.

———

Shelly Greenhaw lived in Oklahoma City, and had one of those great wide-open Oklahoma accents. She was the mother of a five-year-old girl with CFC, Kinley, and a four-year-old, Kamden, who had what looked to Shelly to be an autism spectrum disorder. The thought of having two disabled children staggered me, but Shelly was a surprising person in a lot of ways. She'd played varsity softball in college ("I started out in left field, but by junior year I was a catcher"), and had also been Miss Congeniality in the 1995 Miss Teen America pageant, which she'd entered as a lark. After college she went to work for a pharmaceutical supply company, for whom she was still working as a salesperson. She wasn't the sort of person I expected to find as the mother of a disabled child.

"How do you do it?" I asked. "With two girls like this?"

"I guess sometimes I don't feel like I have a choice." She'd seen kids in worse shape, too, and felt she was lucky that she had "a walker and a talker." She was a Christian and that helped, she said. Then she admitted she had her dark days too; that they were inseparable from the good ones.

"I do know they have brought a lot of joy into our lives," she said. "I do know they're complete little people inside. I really believe that they're not a genetic mistake. Maybe they are mistakes in our minds, sometimes, because of the artificial boundaries we human beings create. But I believe that we all have genetic mutations, they're just not obvious in our clinical presentation. Having the girls has changed the way I live my life. Changed the way I communicate, changed the way I treat people." She appreciated these changes. "Life doesn't scare me any more," she said. "I don't fear the unknown." She told me that when she met someone in a wheelchair in a mall now, she wanted to run up and embrace them. "I know I'm in this for the long haul. It really is a value that a lot of people don't get to appreciate."

She paused for a moment, and then said she didn't really know why she still had moments of despair. "My little girls are the greatest example of selflessness and good nature that I know. And yet at the same time I feel a deep sense of loss for them. I can't separate it from my own sense of loss. That some of their hopes may be crushed. That they won't experience the same kind of acceptance as I have."

The light her children threw on her life, and the darkness that hovered around them and their future, went hand in hand, she said; one was not possible without the existence of the other. The most difficult part to accept was not just the hardship her children would face, but that she herself had not realized, until she had a handicapped child, how complex life was, how bleak and at the same time how rich. Kinley's mere existence (Walker's as well, I realized) was a form of remonstration, a reminder to look deeper, or at least to be alert.

"I look at the girls, and I think, Who's to say they're not happier in their world than I am in mine? And here I am feeling sorry for them because I'm trying to judge them by the standards of the world they aren't part of." She'd spent some time crying the night before, talking to her husband about having another child. "I had one of my good cries. I don't have 'em often, but when I do, look out. There are days when I say absolutely not. Are you out of your mind? When I think about the possibilities of having another special-needs child. But then I think, I've been so honoured to have these two daughters, maybe another would be even more remarkable. Maybe I'm being called to a higher calling. And then there are days when I think, my God, it's like playing roulette.

"Right now, I think Kinley has—oh boy—without trying,

taught me how to live with joy, despite tough circumstances. And to use my time wisely. Not to worry about tomorrow too much, but to enjoy today. She's taught me to laugh at the little things. She's helped me with my vision of life. Boy, she's helped me see that each person has something to contribute, and to learn from as many people as we can. No matter their ability, their ethnicity, their religion. She's taught me to look away from the mirror, to see that life's more than about me. I think I've learned, too, that we're very interdependent. I need those girls as much as they need me."

———

Diana Zeunen lived in Willmington, North Carolina. Her son Ronnie was thirteen, and one of the more profoundly delayed children in the CFC network: his goal these days was to eat on his own. Ronnie's life had taken the form of an extraordinary request, but this—to be able to feed himself— seemed such a simple thing to ask. Diana's husband, an auto mechanic, already had two children of his own when Diana married him; Ronnie was to be the child they shared. "He was the product of a reversed vasectomy," Diana told me, "so he was really wanted."

She'd had a typical pregnancy, but when Ronnie was born, his limbs alternated between being tight and still, or like Jell-O. The doctors diagnosed cerebral palsy. Diana never bought it. "Yes, he wasn't rolling over or making eye contact, like the other kids with cerebral palsy, but he wasn't the same as them. And of course there was no genetic test." Meanwhile he had countless medical issues: "Why did he scream? Why did he cry? We went to gastroenterologists, we went to skin doctors." He beat himself all the time, as if he were autistic. When Ronnie turned four, Diana read a scientific paper with pictures of children who looked just like him: that was how she determined, on her own, that Ronnie had CFC. "We still spoon-feed him," Diana told me, and I knew what that entailed. "He'll still hit himself. To me, that's communicating." (Ditto.) "People say he's got a contagious laugh. People say to me, he recognizes you, but I don't know. It makes me sad to think that he doesn't." (Check.) "You always want that 'Momma'." (Check.)

———

Talking to parents of other children with CFC was reassuring—there was someone else out there who knew what it was like—but it was discouraging too, to see your own anxiety transposed, ounce for ounce, into someone else. A net of loneliness and exile had been pulled tight over all of us.

Fergus and Bernice McCann lived in Burnaby, British Columbia, on the fringe of Vancouver, with their daughter Melissa. Melissa was born in 1985, before any scientific papers on the syndrome had been published. In the known CFC community, at the age of twenty-two, she was one of the ancients. She'd spent forty-seven days in a special-care nursery as a newborn before they let her come home: forty-seven days to prove that she could survive before the hospital handed her back to her parents, along with the grinding mystery of how to keep her alive on their own. There was no precedent for Melissa in the highly bureaucratized medical system in her home province, with the result that at first, she didn't qualify for occupational therapy or physical therapy.

"We saw a lot of that lack of values," Fergus said, "and a lot of being denied medical care. At that time, CFC was just a description. You know, 'Oh well, it involves this and that.'"

Melissa was an adult, but she functioned at the level of a smart two- or three-year-old; she could fetch a glass of milk from the fridge, she could eat, but she couldn't dress herself and she nipped at her hands when she was frustrated. She could tell her mother where the portable phone had been abandoned, but she couldn't possibly survive on her own. Outsiders were often afraid of Melissa: she was almost bald and had hemangiomas—wine-stained vascular skin growths— between her eyes. (Some doctors told her parents to have them removed, while others insisted they be left alone.)

We were speaking on the phone; Bernice was in what sounded like the kitchen with Melissa, on the speakerphone, while Fergus was on an extension in another room. "I think we would be quite critical of the medical care that was available for someone like Melissa," Bernice said. Her voice sounded heavy, as if it were wearing an overcoat. "Our pediatrician just couldn't get on board. He didn't think there was much point. He kept asking the same question: did anything change Melissa's life in the short term, in the long term? No. But he was certainly curious and interested. Medical people, to us, it seemed that they were satisfying their curiosity." Melissa was a specimen. But she had a personality, a noticeable presence as well as an astonishing memory: she still used the thirty signs she had been taught as a child. She could make choices, and had clear likes and dislikes, especially in what she wore. "She doesn't even appear to have looked at something," her mother said, "but she won't put it on." In this she was no different from many other teenage girls.

"Melissa's incredibly empathetic to people, and to dogs and animals," Fergus said then, on the extension, and I reeled again, in a way that has become familiar to me: crushing to hear a man speak about his daughter that way, reaching for nice things to say and coming up with her empathy for pets in his hand, like a fish he had to his own astonishment pulled from a fast river. I understood, believe me I understood, but it depressed me anyway. Every conversation I had with other CFC parents was like that.

What drove Fergus especially crazy was that because of Melissa, he wasn't allowed to have the same impulses and desires the rest of the world had—because to have regular ambitions for your own life meant you were putting yourself first, or even momentarily ahead of your all-consuming child.

"What has the toll been on both of you?" I asked.

"Go ahead, honey," Bernice said. This was obviously a well-travelled conversation.

"I guess there's a toll in terms of career," Fergus said. "Neither of us could change careers, get more education. I certainly have chased after career advancement. But I couldn't work a seventy-hour week. "

"And there's little laughter in this house," Bernice joined in. "Our boys laugh, but they're not carefree. They're twenty and twenty-two. When they were eighteen, they were changing Melissa's menstrual pads. What eighteen-year-old boy should be doing that?" At least one of her brothers had declared openly that he had no plans to have children: he had already put in his time that way, with his sister.

In the background I heard Melissa moan a little. I wondered if she was embarrassed.

"Yeah, they're not here," Bernice said to her daughter, referring to her brothers. "They're not coming."

"Our provincial system believes, when you have a disabled child, that your family should step in," Fergus said then. "They make money hard to get. Parents or children with disabilities are always asking for things, and the government says, 'Well, we can't give everything to everybody.' In my opinion, the whole support system is enmeshed with the welfare system." Melissa's disability was caused by a chain of miscommunicating genes. But Fergus believed that people were as suspicious of the cost of caring for the disabled as they were of providing welfare for the unemployed and the indigent. It was as if some people, the government included (in that it made money hard to obtain), believed that Fergus might actually have time or even the desire, in the midst of the hell of looking after a disabled child, to try to use that disability to scam the government and its taxpayers.

The provincial government's alternative—relying on extended families to care for a disabled child—didn't work anyway. The McCann clan was an extensive one—forty-four people on Bernice's side, another eight on Fergus's. None of them had ever offered to take Melissa for a weekend. Regardless of how one felt about that (and Bernice sounded slightly pissed: "They haven't stretched themselves in twenty-one years"), it was no basis for public policy. "The government should be giving you what your family needs," Fergus insisted. "Fair is not equal. Each person has different needs."

Still, the delicate balance between what you could ask for and what you deserved, and how much you deserved it, was always topmost in the minds of the McCanns. It was only after Fergus and Bernice begged and cajoled for years that the British Columbia government agreed to pay for a pair of day workers to live with the McCanns. They tried that for a while.

But one day Bernice arrived home to find her furniture rearranged. Another afternoon she discovered the fuzz had been shaved off Melissa's head by the workers in order to make her less noticeable. When Bernice told me these stories, even I wondered if she wasn't asking too much. She had a severely handicapped child, and the government was willing to pay for an outside helper to live in her house to help take care of that child: it was better than nothing. Perhaps some gratitude was in order. But the more I thought about it, the more flawed that argument seemed. Under what other circumstance would anyone consider it a boon that the government would pay for a bossy stranger to live in your house?

Melissa was an anomaly, and an upsetting one at that, and upsetting anomalies are not what political bureaucracies do best. The disabled are a challenge to everyone's established sense of order: they frighten us, if not with their faces, then with their obvious need. They call us to be more than we ever thought we would have to be. The very nature of Melissa's disability was an incurable problem, a sign of a flaw and a failure: there was no permanent one-size-fits-all solution, no matter how practical and generous the bureaucracy tried to be. Day workers! Funding by square footage per institution! Group homes! All good ideas, and all doomed to fail as well, eventually, for someone. And of course we all wanted solutions, bureaucracies and parents alike: we all wanted to free ourselves from having to face the darker truth that each disability is personal, unique, and possibly *unsolvable*.

Walker is a fact. He will be the way he is all his life. He is many things to me, not least a reminder of my own fragility and fear. I can afford to admit these failures, in the privacy of

my own mind, but no bureaucracy can. And so the bureaucratic solution instead becomes the Grand Solution, applied
indiscriminately. This is the unavoidable history of mental
retardation and mental illness alike. Fifty years after Philippe
Pinel wrote *A Treatise on Insanity* in 1801, thereby kicking off
the era of asylums, one in ten Parisians had spent some time
in one. Asylums were the one-size-fits-all solution of their day.

But what Fergus and Bernice McCann missed most of all
was not money or help, but privacy. Melissa had thrust them
into the public care system, had forced them to fight for
everything she needed. Melissa was disabled, but looking
after her had disabled Bernice and Fergus in turn. "If you
have a disabled child," Fergus said, "you can't just watch
the world go by, the way you would if you had a typical
child. You fight for things, put yourself in these awkward
positions, and you lose a lot. We've lost the right to just
have a family and be left alone."

Inevitably, Fergus and Bernice worried about what would
happen to Melissa when they were gone. They had devised
a plan whereby Melissa could live in her own home with
three young women to help her. They'd bought her a pretty
house, roughly twice the size of their own, which cost
$573,000. ("That's twenty-five years of my go-to-hell
money," Fergus said.) The government had programs that
would help pay for Melissa's companions; the operation of
the house would be overseen by a board of directors that
included Melissa's brothers.

When I spoke to Bernice and Fergus, they were "transi-
tioning" Melissa into her new home, into her own life. She
seemed to be enjoying the prospect. Their sons were moving
out too, and Bernice and Fergus were suddenly looking at

an empty house. "This is happening much sooner that we would choose to have any of our children leave home," Fergus said, "but they decided to do it all at once." After years of longing to be alone when he couldn't be, soon he would be. He felt surprisingly desolate.

There was a part of me that wanted to say to Fergus, *Well, you got what you asked for*. I wouldn't say that to an average father of normal children who despaired for years of having a moment to himself, and then missed his kids when they began to move away. But Fergus and Bernice McCann decided to make the world take notice of the plight of their daughter. Even I, who knew better, wanted to see them suffer for making me feel their agonies.

There was always another story to top the last one. However difficult someone's life had been—and I often had to coax people into complaining, so strong was the impulse to appear unaffected—there was always someone else who had it harder.

Angie Lydicksen still lived in the town where she grew up in Connecticut. She was forty-two years old and worked as the manager of a dental office. She had two boys, Eric, who was ten, and Luke, who was eight and had CFC. Before giving birth to her first son, she had been "desperate" to have a family; she had three miscarriages and finally resorted to fertility drugs. But with Luke she became pregnant quickly and just when she wanted. "I wanted to have them close together," she told me. Her pregnancy with Luke was "more than perfect," and even when she went into labour two weeks early the doctors considered her full-term. "My problem with pregnancies was always getting to the end of them," she said, "so when I got to the end with Luke, I never imagined a whole other life would start." A strange reward for persistence.

Her life changed in an instant. "From the second he came out, all hell broke loose. As soon as he came out, and they placed him in my arms, both my husband and I knew something was wrong. He wasn't connecting with us." He was moved quickly to the newborn intensive care unit. Meanwhile his mother began to hemorrhage in her hospital room and passed out. When the nurse found her, she passed out too. All in all, a day of note. Luke stymied his doctors; no one could diagnose his ailment. Angie carted him to Children's Hospital Boston and to countless Connecticut health care complexes for three years before someone suggested Costello syndrome. She accepted the diagnosis with reservations—she didn't think Luke looked entirely like other Costello kids. Then she read an article in *Rosie* magazine. The article, as it happened, was written by my wife. When Angie read Johanna's descriptions of Walker, she immediately took Luke and the magazine to her pediatrician and asked it if was possible that Luke had CFC instead. The pediatrician couldn't have cared less. "He told me to take him home and love him. 'You got what you got,' he said. So I got rid of that doctor."

She embarked on a long and frustrating search for a more precise diagnosis. She tried to see John Opitz, but Opitz was busy and couldn't see Luke for a year. *A year.* She eventually met the geneticist in Salt Lake City, but Opitz didn't think Luke was CFC: the boy's features were "softer" than those of a typical CFC child (Angie had noticed that herself), and "he didn't like the fact that Luke had eyebrows": 95 percent of the children with CFC symptoms who had eyebrows turned out to be Costello kids. To Lydicksen, such judgments seemed like guesses.

She carted her boy to the annual conference of Costello children, but she still didn't think he fit. On a second visit, in 2005, she met a researcher from the Comprehensive Cancer Lab in San Francisco who was trying to isolate the genes responsible for both CFC and Costello syndromes. Luke took the test for Costello syndrome: he didn't have it. Lydicksen "was just devastated. We wanted so badly to fit somewhere. Instead, we were thrown back into the unknown again." A few months later, as part of California geneticist Kate Rauen's pioneering research, Luke was confirmed as having CFC. But he was much worse off than most of the other CFC kids. He didn't speak (though "his hearing is very good," Lydicksen insisted); she wasn't sure about his vision (he watched pre-school shows on TV from inches away); to this day he requires a walker to get around, and prefers crawling; at three, he began to grow suddenly as he went into precocious puberty (a rare but noted feature of CFC; as if the regular features of the syndrome weren't taxing enough, Luke has had to submit to a pituitary shot every three weeks, to hold his hormones in check until he's older). Unlike most CFCers, Luke is tall: at nine years old, he's five foot eleven. His cardiac issues have diminished (like Walker's), but (like Walker) as he grew older, he began to have seizures. Luke recognized his mother and father, his brothers, his grandmother; he was very affectionate, though (like Walker) that didn't begin until he was five. Before that (like Walker) he preferred his own company. "I'd say that he's anywhere from fifteen to eighteen months old," Angie said. "He's definitely under two years old. He definitely has no verbal communication. He laughs, he plays—but he doesn't play with too many toys." Like Walker, he loved to pull his hat off again and again, to stymie whoever was trying to make him wear it. "I think Luke, for the most part, he's happy," Angie said. "When he does cry, he usually cries for a reason. I think his quality of life is good, for the most part—I think he's happy in his own little world. And for the most part I'm happy that he's happy. Sometimes it breaks your heart, because he's stuck in his own little world. But sometimes I wonder if it's not better there. Sometimes— because he goes to bed with a smile and wakes up with a smile—I like to think that he's happy all the time. I like to think he is."

This was a common sentiment among parents of CFC children; what made it more remarkable in Angie Lydicksen was that six months before she expressed that thought to me in May 2007, she had been diagnosed with lung cancer. But her health was less on her mind than her son's value to the world.

"Oh God, he's given us so much," she told me that day, when she already knew she was dying. "He's taught us how to accept life for what it is, to deal with it as it comes up. You can be either stuck in a bad rut, or you pick up the pieces and go on the best we can. Right then and there [after Luke was born], we just changed our ways. We bought a camper and went camping, because he likes that. One of the biggest things Luke has taught us is to accept being different, not to be afraid of him. It's just so different from when we were kids. We always stayed away from disabled kids. But nowa- days everybody plays with them." Luke is known as the

Mayor at his school. "The whole entire time I thought, if he can do what he did then I can do this." She meant deal with her own cancer. Luke seemed to put things into perspective. When other mothers complained about a child who hadn't slept through the night, she tried not to laugh. "Sleeping through the night! Oh my God! I haven't slept through the night in nine years."

She wanted to be around forever for him, and when she got sick became afraid that no one would be able to replace her in Luke's life. But of late she had begun to think otherwise. "In the long run he's very adaptable." Her own grave illness only reinforced what Luke's disability had already revealed. "Without him, I would have been more interested in material things," Angie said. "Stuff. And now, it's just like, you know, I can do without it. I don't need it. Just having your health and people that you love and a family that's strong . . ."

Talking to Angie Lydicksen was like talking to any parent who had experienced the ups and downs of raising a child— the steady low-key anxiety punctuated by explosions of fear and concern, the pride and frustration, the exhaustion and pleasure. The difference was that Lydicksen could not afford to succumb to the hyperbolic sense of isolation that can make a father or mother believe he or she is the only one to whom this or that is happening. "I don't get the complaining thing," Angie Lydicksen told me that day on the phone.

The following spring, she died of lung cancer. She was forty-two years old. Luke still lives with his father.

I was always looking for a context in which to make sense of Walker, in which his disorganized life (and my unavoidable devotion to it) might take on more meaning and purpose. I thought I might find it in the lives of other children with CFC, and in the example of their parents. To my surprise, while it was sometimes reassuring to know he was part of a larger community, and that I was not alone, the nature of that community—a hundred children and their parents, invisible in the greater world, desperately trying to quell their pain and rescue some semblance of normal life from an abnormal circumstance—was more complicated than it looked, sometimes as upsetting as it was reassuring. I now knew that "Walker and his ways," as Johanna described them, were not unique. What I had yet to find out was *why* he was the way he was. And so I turned to science, to see if the laboratory could explain my boy Walker.

ten

These are the glossary terms that "help with understanding cardiofaciocutaneous syndrome," as listed on the Genetics Home Reference page of the United States National Library of Medicine:

apoptosis; atrial; autosomal; autosomal dominant; cancer; cardio; cardiomyopathy; cell; cutaneous; differentiation; failure to thrive; gene; heart valve; hypertelorism; hypertrophic; hypotonia; ichthyosis; incidence; keratosis; macrocephaly; malformation; mental retardation; muscle tone; mutation; new gene mutation; nucleus; ocular hypertelorism; palpebral fissure; proliferation; protein; ptosis; pulmonic stenosis; RAS; seizure; septal defect; short stature; sign; stature; stenosis; symptom; syndrome; tissue.

The language of Walker's strangeness held me captive. New words had been invented for a new creation, infused with the pretend exactitude of scientific nomenclature, as if all the labels said something helpful and useful, which of course in any comparative sense they did. The alluring multisyllabic complexity necessary to describe a simpleton, to use the old, once-scientific word for such a boy. Everything about Walker was complicated by something else, and there were many days when I appreciated that, when it deepened him, and gave me more to think about. Sometimes it was all there was to think about.

———

I was sitting at my desk at the *Globe and Mail*, the large daily newspaper where I work, the morning I read the scientific paper announcing that a geneticist named Kate Rauen had found a mutation in three genes associated with CFC. It was a Tuesday in April 2007. My desk sits out in the open: it's a congenial place to write, as abattoirs go. But that morning I had to get up and walk outside. I couldn't catch my breath. A gene that caused CFC: after eleven years of living with the mystery of Walker, the notion was exciting, but also terrifying. My relationship with Walker, after all, had been personal, and private; we operated by our own standards, by what worked between us. I "spoke" to him and he "spoke" to me, clicking our tongues back and forth to one another to let each other know that we were paying attention, that we knew the other was there, and listening. Now there was a gene, an impersonal scientific cause, at the root of his affliction. What would it tell me? And would it prevent me from believing any longer in what I told myself were my son's secret capacities? Would I still be able to take comfort in our private language of click—to offer just one example—if the gene said it was pointless, that such a connection was beyond his capacities? So far I had already had to share my son with his other home. Would I now have to share him with the lab?

Not to say there wasn't huge hope in the discovery. If I knew what genetic misstep had caused Walker's troubles, I would have a hook to hang those troubles on. I might even have a cure for them. There would be a firm and unassailable cause, something to blame and something to fix—a shrimpette of concrete fact in the sea of speculation and vagueness that constituted his life, and ours.

Two weeks later I flew out to San Francisco to interview Dr. Rauen. At the airport, I rented a car with a GPS unit. It was my first time. Until then, I'd always used maps. I liked maps, liked the way they let you get used to the overview of somewhere new and unfamiliar, in plan form, before the place became details, close up and unavoidable.

With GPS, I could fly into a vast complicated confusing city after dark, rent a car and plug in the address of where I was supposed to end up. The GPS unit told me to turn left out of the rental lot and spat me instantly onto a chain of highways, a speedy tube of lights that ran for a long time until finally the tube dumped me out into a hotel parking lot. GPS made me feel like I was getting somewhere fast. The downside was that I never knew where I was in the bigger picture. GPS took you right where you already knew you wanted to go, and cut out the less efficient side trips. Just like a CFC gene, it turned out.

The genetic research labs at the Comprehensive Cancer Center in San Francisco, where Kate Rauen worked, were lit like the inside of a refrigerator and cluttered with textbooks and tubes and stoppers and scales and micro-array scanners.

The scientific papers the geneticists wrote—largely for one another—had titles that were incomprehensible to a layman, such as "Keratosis pilaris/ulerythema ophryogenes and 18p deletion: Is it possible that the LAMA1 gene is involved?" The geneticists themselves bore the slightly startled air of soldiers who had just emerged from the deep jungle, only to be told that the war they had been fighting had been over for twenty years. They were fond of unusual, non-human screen savers: a photograph of a cat, say, asleep in a tiny log-cabin cathouse. (I once stepped into an elevator full of young geneticists leaving work. It was Hallowe'en. Two of the female geneticists in the elevator were wearing devil horns on their heads. "Going out tonight?" one of the guys ventured. The women shook their heads. I can't say I was surprised.)

The morning I showed up at Rauen's lab, her colleague, Anne Estep, was feeding liquid medium into Petri dishes. The Petri dishes contained clones of twenty-nine different mutations of one gene that Estep and Rauen had isolated in the DNA of people with CFC. Rauen had yet to show up for work, so Estep, a personable, blond-haired woman in her thirties who openly admitted her love of lab work, undertook the challenge of explaining the complicated genetics of CFC to me.

She saw the entire process from a scientific height, as evidence of the elegance of human biology. "There are just so many things that can go wrong in conception," she said. "The majority of pregnancies are spontaneously aborted, or miscarried very, very early in the pregnancy—it's just nature's way of allowing only the right combination to come to term. Even to be born, you are already one of a minority of conceptions—so much has had to go right to get to that point."

This was a new way of understanding Walker—instead of broken, he was simply slightly flawed, like a discounted but perfectly wearable pair of shoes at an outlet mall. He was still "a genetic configuration," as Estep put it, "that is compatible with life, is a living, breathing human being. So there's a wide variance. They all have two arms, two legs. Most of the children have a range of emotions. They're human." Two weeks before I met her, Estep had been introduced to Emily Santa Cruz—her first encounter with a breathing embodiment of the CFC genes she had been studying in a dish in the lab for eight months. She found the encounter "very moving," although she had been surprised, she said quietly, "by how severe her delays were." Even for a dedicated scientist such as Estep, there was a gap between the life she studied in the lab, and the life itself.

Kate Rauen was in her early forties, short, blonde, vastly energetic. She kept an office at UCSF Children's Hospital across the city, where she ran a clinic, as well as another at the Comprehensive Cancer Center. She was good at clarifying complicated genetic processes. "Here's your chromosome," she told me later that afternoon, as she drew circles on a piece of paper to explain how a cell operates. "On this chromosome, here's your DNA. On this DNA are genes, kind of, maybe, next to one another. That gene makes an RNA, and then that RNA makes a protein. And proteins actually are the ones that float around in the cell and do the work." There are roughly 25,000 protein-making genes in the human genome, and another 35,000 regulatory genes. Some proteins fold up in complex patterns (again, according to instructions from the genetic code) and form cells, which in turn form human tissue. Other proteins operate as group managers, controlling other enzymes. (Bureaucracy is everywhere.) The RAS family of proteins and enzymes (for *rat sarcoma* virus, which was involved in its discovery) are managers— specifically, molecular on–off switches for a group of signalling pathways that communicate between a cell's membrane and its nucleus, to control cell growth. "The nucleus is the brains of your cell and the only way it gets instructions is from outside of the cell," is how Rauen put it. "And the instructions come in the form of signal trans- duction, or molecules talking to one another, which will actually end up telling the nucleus what to do." The entire process operates like a game of telephone. An enzyme or protein sidles up to the outside wall of a cell, and tells it to do something; an enzyme on the other side of the cell wall passes the instructions along to another series of enzyme systems within the cell, and so on through the body of the cell until the message reaches the nucleus—which does what it thinks it has been told.

RAS in turn activates other "downstream" signalling systems, such as the mitogen-activated protein kinases (the MAPK pathway) that control even more specific cell functions. RAS is an infamous route among medical researchers: 30 percent of cancer tumours display some form of RAS deregulation, where either cell growth has run out of control or cell death has stopped, because of an incorrect instruction, or signal transduction.

"I'm just a dumb old medical geneticist," Rauen told me. "I just see patients and try to diagnose what they have. Meanwhile I'm with all these smart biochemists that studied signal transduction. And I just remember looking at these pathways and thinking, oh my gosh, one of these days they're going to find genetic syndromes that are involved in these signal transduction pathways, part of this alphabet soup."

One of the genes associated with Noonan syndrome had already been found to have a role in the RAS pathway. So had a gene for neurofibromatosis. The physical traits of both syndromes, give or take a few details, were remarkably similar to the symptoms of Costello syndrome and CFC. It made sense that genes responsible for CFC's genetic mutations might lurk in the RAS pathway as well.

To fund a study of a syndrome that might affect three hundred people worldwide, however, was another matter. Fortunately—at least for Rauen's purposes—the RAS pathway had a known role in producing cancerous tumours, which are themselves the result of unstoppable cell growth. Costello, Noonan and neurofibromatosis all produced tumours, whereas CFC did not. To Rauen, those known facts looked like a research opportunity. Three out of the four syndromes found in the same cellular pathway produced cancer; the fourth did not. What made them different genetically? Would that knowledge provide clues to why tumours formed? By way of analogy, say 100 kids grow up on the same street, but only 75 of them get the same kind of cancer. It follows that if you can figure out what was different about the 25 who don't get cancer, you might have a clue as to its cause and cure.

"That," Rauen continued, wrapping up the tour of her logic, "was the basis of a National Institute of Health grant." Rauen was no longer investigating a mutation that afflicted a mere three hundred unfortunate kids. She was investigating a potential cause of cancer, via their handy DNA markers. "We are going to learn so much from these kids," she told me. "We are going to learn how to treat them better from knowing their genes. . . . We are going to learn so much about cancer treatment from these children that this is a huge discovery on multiple levels."

That, at any rate, was the theory. The practice was another matter. Rauen was working simultaneously on both Costello and CFC, trying to find the genes responsible. She needed thirty subjects with each syndrome, their consent and their DNA. Rounding up thirty Costello subjects took five years. By the time she completed her research—and the Costello gene was right where she predicted, in the RAS pathway—a team of Japanese researchers led by Yoko Aoki at Tohoku University in Sendai, Japan, had beaten her to it by a month.

She had better luck with CFC, thanks to the blood samples Brenda Conger and Molly Santa Cruz had been gathering at their CFC conferences since 2000. What had taken five years to find for the Costello experiments took mere weeks for CFC. "I was handed a cohort of CFC subjects in days—in *days*. I had DNA within that week. It was amazing."

In January 2006, three decades after cardiofaciocutaneous syndrome was first described, Kate Rauen published her findings. The mutations associated with CFC occurred in at least three genes: BRAF, MEK1, MEK2. Independent research in Japan had added another gene. Costello syndrome showed mutations in the HRAS gene, whereas Noonan syndrome showed up in the PTPN11 gene. All of them were found in the RAS pathway, and all of them influenced cell growth and cell death.

The genes and their complicated acronyms (most of which related to their chemical composition) sounded like newly discovered planets to me, as baffling and rarefied as genetics itself. But I didn't have any trouble following Rauen when she gave me her best guess of what had gone wrong in Walker. The dinner hour was approaching, and outside the windows of her office, San Francisco was washed in its standard impossible end-of-day gold.

The sequence of four paired nucleotides that, combined and recombined, make up the genes of a human being is three billion base pairs long. Each nucleotide is represented by a letter. "This mutation," Rauen said, referring to the one that caused CFC, "is one letter change in the entire gene. Yup. One letter in the entire gene, which causes one amino acid to change—one amino acid, one tiny building block of the entire protein. That's what causes CFC." That in turn had caused the snaggle of Walker's life.

"Does anyone know why that letter changes?" I asked.

"DNA replicates, right? DNA replicates, but it doesn't replicate with extremely high fidelity. If it replicated and never made a mistake, we would all look the same, right? The good news and the bad news is if it does make a mistake, it makes a mistake about once every million times. One in every one million base pairs has got a mistake in it. Now, you've got all kinds of proteins and enzymes and stuff that go back and try to find this mistake and correct it. So a lot of mistakes you never know about. But sometimes the mistake's not corrected. And when that mistake's not corrected, it causes a change in protein. And that protein behaviour might make our immune system better. It might make our muscles stronger. It could have beneficial effects called evolution. You know, survival of the fittest. But you can also have a genetic change that makes a deleterious effect, where it causes a hole in the heart, it causes your immune system to be weak. It might be a beneficial effect, it might be a deleterious effect."

I thanked Kate Rauen shortly after that, left her office, crossed the street outside her building, and sat down on a bench to think about what she had said. The scientific definition of evolutionary success, of a successful random mutation, is one that allows the organism to survive and reproduce. Nature alone would not have allowed my son to survive.

By the judgment of a geneticist, Walker was a *deleterious effect* of nature.

But he wasn't a product of nature alone. He had survived, and his survival was also a product of medical technology and human concern—the result of a G-tube and drugs and the steady attention of teams of people who believed their interaction with him was worth his and their while, even if the results were hard to measure. Walker wasn't much to brag about, intellectually or physically. But like many other CFC children, he had changed lives, mine as much as anyone's—deepened and broadened me, made me more tolerant and durable, more ethically dependable. He had given me a longer view. That felt like some form of evolution too, a positive ethical evolution, albeit not the kind modern genomic science tends to measure.

I looked up then, and discovered I was sitting in front of a street sculpture, "Regardless of History," created by an Englishman named Bill Woodrow. It was seven feet high, and bronze—a thin tree, blighted and leafless, stunted and growing out of a rock. But growing.

I flew back to Toronto. The summer became the fall. Our search for some insight into Walker's condition resumed.

On a Wednesday morning in October, I met Tyna Kasapakis, the manager of Walker's other home, at the genetics clinic of the Hospital for Sick Children. Walker was there too. The genetics clinic occupied a corner of the fifth floor of a downtown Toronto office building. From the front, the building looked like a giant tube of lipstick. It had once housed the corporate headquarters of a Swiss bank. The security guard behind the desk in the lobby nodded good morning to me. He had to have seen some sights. I took the elevator up and got off at the fifth floor and walked down the hall to the genetics clinic and sat in the same spotless waiting room in which I had cooled my heels nearly twelve years earlier, when Walker was diagnosed with CFC. I'd arrived early, before Tyna and Walker, and had to wait, as I had back then, for someone to arrive at the front desk. I didn't mind. I loved the optimistic calm of the office before 9 a.m. I sighed and breathed in, once more, the odourless still air of the empty hallways, under the usual fleeting illusion that we were the only people who ever came here, a rare breed that had strayed into a pristine, otherwise mutant-free world. (Appointments in the genetics clinic were spaced out, to guarantee a minimum of interaction between the aberrations.)

After living for eleven years with a clinical diagnosis of CFC, Walker was now to be tested genetically. Under the Canadian system of publicly funded medicine, a genetic test

THE BOY IN THE MOON

for CFC entailed a six-month wait: three months for the provincial health-care bureaucracy to approve the cost of the test, and another three months to organize a sample of Walker's DNA, fill in the paperwork, send the sample to the testing lab, have it tested and get the results back.

The usual routine ensued. While Walker threw toys around the playroom and moved onto and off my lap, a genetic counsellor (and sometimes two) ran through the standard disclaimers. There was no guarantee they would find an aberration in his genes, but that didn't mean he didn't have CFC. If these tests of three genes returned negative, we would look further afield, at rarer (and more expensively tested-for) genes. Even so, a diagnosis wasn't a cure. The state of genetic research was proceeding rapidly, but the technology was more advanced than any scientific understanding of what the technology revealed. A genetic diagnosis might or might not confirm that Walker was CFC, but even if it didn't he was still Walker, the same boy. Did we have any questions . . . ? I was close to being able to recite this entire spiel from memory, like a soliloquy out of Shakespeare. To test, or not to test: that is the question. Whether 'tis calmer in the mind to ignore the touts and dreams of genetic research, or to scan each cracked gene known to man, and by testing think we have an answer. To test and test and test some more, and by this test pretend it ends the heartache and the thousand natural shocks his small flesh is heir to. 'Tis a consummation devoutly to be wished!

Then the hard part: collecting the genetic material. Walker's DNA had been taken and sorted for a chromosome test when he was an infant (unbelievably, it showed no aberrations), and was still on file. But this morning the clinicians would take a new sample, just in case. I knew my part. Even doctors were afraid of how Walker might react; they couldn't tell the difference between what hurt him and what merely upset him because it wasn't part of his usual routine. I held him tight in my arms, my left hand across his chest to control his head, to keep it pointed in the same direction and keep his mouth open while the doctor stood back like the great white safari hunter, waiting to take a shot. I knew to hold him firmly, that control was the answer, but my thorough grip startled most doctors we saw, as much as they appreciated it. It made me feel useful, and it made me feel closer to my boy; his trusted handler, a strong man who still would never hurt him. And then the opening—*now!*—and the doctor swabbed the inside of his mouth with what looked like an extra-long Q-Tip. The Q-Tip went into a plastic tube. Done.

Winter came. It was a cold one, with lots of snow. Walker developed the habit of crooning along with me as we drove back and forth to the group home to Ray Charles singing "What Kind of Man Are You?" and "I Had a Dream." Sometimes the moist air in the car condensed on the inside of the windows; I could hear Walker's fingers squeaking on the glass as he rubbed the fog away, as we drove north and east, singing the blues, Olga laughing with Walker in the back seat. Some days, to give Olga a break, I took him back by myself, but it was tricky: he relished the chance to sit in the front seat, liked to lower the windows in order to throw my maps out into the rushing highway air. Now, that was a metaphor. He was a ball of writhing glee in the front seat, but he loved to chat—or to have me chat at him—as we sped up the fine wide highway. Christ it makes me ache to think of how much I adored him on those funny rides. Dad and boy, driving—how much more obvious does it get? But they were lonely rides, too, because I was often faintly, subliminally panicked when Johanna wasn't with us. But of course we were efficient: she and I took turns driving him because there was no point in two people spending two hours in the car, not with everything else there was to do.

Spring arrived. The trilliums I planted came up in the front garden. Then a young genetic counsellor named Jessica Hartley telephoned with some unusual news. None of the genes commonly associated with CFC—BRAF, MEK1 and MEK2—were mutated in Walker's DNA.

I made another appointment, and Walker and Tyna and I headed back to the building shaped like a lipstick. The genetic testing was my idea, hence my duty, not Johanna's.

Hartley seemed impossibly young to be so knowledgeable. She had black hair and a mild Goth style. She was joined at our appointment by one of her superiors, a slim, middle-aged scientist named David Chitayat, a senior genetic scientist at the Hospital for Sick Children. The fact that Walker had shown no mutations in three genes commonly associated with CFC, the counsellors were keen to assure us, didn't mean much. "If we don't find something, that doesn't necessarily mean he doesn't have CFC," Hartley said in an apologetic tone. "If everything comes back negative, we can revisit the test. CFC is definitely the most likely possibility." She suggested retesting, this time looking for other mutations too, notably Noonan and Costello syndromes.

As their understanding of CFC and its sister syndromes evolved, more and more researchers were once again thinking of CFC, Noonan and Costello as related syndromes— "RAS pathway disorders" or "Noonan spectrum disorders."

The genome was slowly yielding its arcane secrets, and scientists were beginning to attribute a wider and wider array of mental retardations—particularly if accompanied by facial disfiguration and heart conditions—to disruptions in intracellular signalling pathways. The bodies of these children couldn't seem to figure out when to build cells, and when to stop.

Chitayat was a widely respected geneticist with a long history in the field. The mutation would have occurred, he said, in the first two weeks of Walker's life in his mother's womb. Each of the different genes associated with CFC was supposed to perform its on/off signalling job at a different stage in the "cascade" of communication that occurred within a cell: the mutated BRAF gene came into play (or "phosphorylated") earlier, and therefore corrupted the cell's message at a more fundamental level than the MEK genes did. But the pathways fed back into themselves as well, with the (possible) effect that MEK-mutated CFC kids seemed to have frailer physical selves but milder cognitive problems. That was one theory, in any event—and it was *all* theoretical. Geneticists had uncovered a vast realm of human physiology, but it often seemed that the more they uncovered, the less they understood about the ways the details fit together.

Jessica Hartley and David Chitayat and Kate Rauen worked on the genuine frontiers of science, and based their hypotheses on known and testable biochemical interactions, but there were days when their speculations didn't seem to me much different from the medical purification rituals of seventeenth- and eighteenth-century France, when coffee and chimney soot were confidently prescribed for madness, and melancholia was considered curable by drawing ten ounces of a man's blood and replacing it with the blood of a calf. In any event, Chitayat added, "The important thing for us to find is a diagnosis for what he has. But jumping to the cause of what he has is not so easy."

After an hour of talking, the next steps became clear. We would retest for CFC, to make sure we hadn't been dealt a false result. We would test for Noonan and Costello mutations, as well as for several other RAS-pathway cousins. If those tests also came back negative, we'd step back, and run a microarray of Walker's chromosomal DNA. Microarray scanning of chromosomes was infinitely more sensitive than the chromosome screen that had been conducted when Walker was a baby. "The microarray is looking for missing or extra bits in the chromosomes," Dr. Chitayat explained— missing words in the genetic sentence of his life—"whereas the gene testing is looking for spelling mistakes as well." If Walker had a mutation in an as yet undiscovered gene that led to a chromosomal disorder, the microarray might reveal where in the genome his abnormality was. We knew I had parked the car in Ontario, I just didn't remember what city— that was the gist of it.

Some of the new tests (the microarray, for one) could be conducted in Canada, but others were possible only at certain approved labs in the United States. If Walker turned out to be positive for CFC, and his DNA was to be available for scientific studies, the result had to come from an approved lab. The tests cost $1,500 to $2,000 each; all required provincial approval if they were to be covered by the provincial health plan; the U.S. tests cost more, and required even more rigorous review and approval if my provincial health plan was to pay for them. The doctors submitted formal reasons for the tests, which were based on the need to find a genetic diagnosis for what Walker had—a reasonable enough request, given that a proper diagnosis might lead to a more complete understanding of his needs, and better treatments. This time around we could expect results in seven to nine months.

In the meantime all we could do was wait. It was as if a small part of Walker's body had been mailed out into the world, and was trying to mail itself back again. Not that anyone felt any need to rush. Whatever the diagnosis, it wouldn't change Walker.

The results finally arrived in the fall of 2008. I headed back to the lipstick clinic. Jessica was there again, and this time so was Dr. Grace Yoon, a Toronto neurogeneticist whose work on the neurological effects of CFC had led to an association with Kate Rauen's research team. She was a beautiful woman in her thirties, recently married, with a precise and careful way of speaking.

The latest round of genetic tests, alas, had only deepened Walker's mystery. He was still negative for BRAF, MEK1 and MEK2, the standard CFC genes. Nor did he test positive for KRAS, the gene for Costello syndrome, or for Noonan syndrome. His PTPN11 gene, associated with neurofibromatosis, showed no mutation, and neither did SOS1 and BRAF1, two newly unearthed genes thought to have a connection to CFC.

"It does not mean that he doesn't have CFC. There are always genes that we don't know of yet," Dr. Yoon explained in one of the tiny consulting rooms at the clinic. "There's no question in my mind that he has something genetic. But at the moment I don't know what it is. CFC is the diagnosis made by earlier doctors, and I think that's still the best guess." Only 65 percent of people thought to have Noonan syndrome, for instance, display the "correct" gene.

Yoon added that researchers in the United States and Japan had more recently linked the SPRED1 gene to neurofibromatosis. "But to be honest the patients who have that kind of genetic disorder are much milder," Yoon admitted. CFC, she repeated, "is the perfectly reasonable conclusion." Walker might have a more severe manifestation, and thus a rare mutational version, of CFC. But she wanted to consult her colleagues. She took some photographs of his face and feet and hands, conducted a physical exam, measured the space between his eyes (they are wider apart than those of most CFC kids), noted his coarser features as well as his more familiar epicanthal folds and the thickened skin over his ears. The familiar chant of symptoms. She would e-mail the photographs and the data to her international team, to canvas their opinion.

In the meantime we would wait some more. I felt the same way I did when I woke from a dream that at first I didn't remember having: something had happened, but all I could recall was a mild, faintly disturbing residue.

"Our knowledge is way behind the genetic-testing technology's capabilities," Yoon said, sensing my bewilderment. Her area of expertise was the effects of genetic mutation on cognition—an explorer at the far edge of not one but two frontiers of medical research, the barely known genes and the still unknown brain. Out where she worked, researchers didn't so much make discoveries as discover how much they didn't understand. "There are only three things in medicine that have made any real difference to the quality of human life," Yoon said, as our meeting ended. "Clean water, vaccinations and antibiotics." Genes don't yet make the list.

———

Memories of my many meetings in the well-swept clinic lingered like a mild virus. I didn't resent the geneticists: they were the first to admit how little they knew, and at the same time they were obviously the promise of the future. Kate Rauen's isolation of the main mutating CFC genes has already contributed significantly to the welfare of the syndrome's children by making the condition easier to diagnose. Early diagnosis in turn permitted early enrolment in a raft of therapies to diminish the syndrome's effects. The identification of the RAS pathway as a prominent culprit responsible for a wide array of developmental delays, to say nothing of an entire family of mental retardations, is an enormous finding.

There was lots of promising research that buoyed my spirits—at least until the research amounted to nothing, and my spirits sank again. Two years after Rauen published her findings, for instance, researchers based in Rotterdam discovered that simvastatin—a common cholesterol-lowering drug—can reverse the cognitive deficits caused by neurofibromatosis in rats, especially spatial learning deficits and attention disorders. (I learned about the study when I was contacted out of the blue by Dr. Paul Wang, the developmental pediatrician who had assessed Walker at the age of two in Philadelphia—the doctor who told me that, as far as knowing how to be in the world, Walker was miles ahead of the rest of us.) Unfortunately, the astonishing results demonstrated in rats weren't replicated in humans. The halting progress of genetic research was a given, and hardly cause for discouragement. What *was* discouraging was that to a laboratory geneticist who studied CFC as a genetic disorder, the syndrome was always *only* that: a disorder, an unfixable spelling mistake in the grammar of humanness. I understood that stance, and also hated it. Seeing Walker only as a genetic disorder was a guaranteed way for me to remember that there is such a thing as genetic *order*; that for each Walker, there are millions of genetically complete children. In a genetics lab, Walker would always be a deleterious effect of nature and evolution, and little more.

As Walker's test results wandered back to the lab in the fall of 2008, the genetic testing industry was gearing up for a major burst of hyperbole. In December, Sequenom, Inc., a biotechnology firm in San Diego, announced a new non-invasive prenatal genetic test, to be sold online starting in June 2009. The test licensed procedures developed at Oxford and Stanford universities.

Until Sequenom came along, there was one medical option available to a pregnant woman who had reason to be worried she might give birth to a child with a defect or syndrome: she could submit to a standard blood serum screening test. The blood test was (and is) famously unreliable, and given to false positives: in one study, 136 out of 199 women tested positive for Down syndrome, but only six had a Down baby. Roughly 2 percent of women who test positive at that stage abort the fetus; the rest move on to amniocentesis, a much more accurate but invasive procedure that draws fluid from the amniotic sac, with occasional complications.

Sequenom's new test measured fetal cells in the mother's blood—a non-invasive blood test that was as accurate as amniocentesis and that could be administered a mere ten weeks into pregnancy. So far the test can determine the sex of the baby and screen for Down syndrome and two other conditions, trisonomy 13 (extra material in the thirteenth chromosome, associated with Patau syndrome, which can create "events" such as cleft palate, extra fingers, severe retardation, heart defects and cryptorchidism) and trisonomy 18 (clenched hands, heart defects, low birth weight, retardation, undescended testicles, a short breastbone and related muscular deformities in the abdominal wall.*) The company plans to widen the test's capacities to include other disorders such as cystic fibrosis, sickle cell anemia and Tay-Sachs disease. All

---

* Notice how many of these symptoms are shared with CFC, Costello and Noonan syndromes (to name just a few candidates), despite the fact that they are associated with radically different genetic and chromosomal causes. Thinking about these similarities often drove me to distraction. According to the popular model propounded by geneticists, each gene leads to a different effect—that's how geneticists can associate different diseases with different genes. But all sorts of different genetic syndromes share a number of effects, heart problems, mental retardation and facial disfiguration being common to many. How can distant locales in the human genome produce the same effects? (And I am more and more astonished by how similar children with genetic defects are, especially when mental retardation is a symptom.) Obviously the model that genetic science uses to announce its discoveries—gene A causes condition B!— is much too simple to explain how complicated genetic interactions really are. My concern was this: Does an oversimplified model of how a human being comes to be result in an oversimplified model of what a human being is?

of which promises less anxiety for pregnant women, especially older ones (or women with older husbands) whose unborn children are at higher risk for genetic disorders.

The test is by no means comprehensive or subtle: it doesn't pick up rarer conditions such as Walker's, whose affliction is far worse than that of the majority of Down children, many of whom live normal, reasonably productive lives. Nor can it measure the severity of a syndrome. Even within the range of CFC children, for instance, there are vast differences in capacity. Walker can't talk or communicate, but Cliffie Conger can, and will very likely live a close-to-normal existence. And yet if Sequenom had a CFC test, it is Cliffie who would show the mutation and pop up on a prenatal CFC test—not Walker. It is Cliffie, the more capable, self-sustaining kid, who would be a candidate for termination. This is a subtlety genetic testing companies do not emphasize in their sales literature.

Nevertheless, the decision to avoid creating such a life in the first place can now be made at ten weeks of pregnancy.* Already in the United States, between 80 and 95 percent of women who receive a prenatal diagnosis of Down syndrome end their pregnancies. The new more accurate blood test will undoubtedly increase that percentage. Result? Down syndrome is en route to endangered status. Meanwhile there are

---

* On April 29, 2009, Sequenom announced that the launch of its Down test would be delayed due to "employee mishandling of data and results." The price of the company's shares nosedived from $14.91 a share to $4.69. Five days later, on May 4, 2009, a class action shareholder lawsuit was launched in California district court against the company and its officers for "false and misleading statements." There are other companies, however, that claim to be developing similar tests.

seventy thousand people in the world with cystic fibrosis, and someone with sickle cell anemia—a third of sub-Saharan Africa has the gene—can live to be nearly fifty. Sequenom has both diseases in its pre-emptive sights. Genetic tests are a way to eliminate the imperfect, and all the pain and agony that comes with that imperfection. When Walker was an infant, before he lodged himself in my heart and mind and memory, I spent part of every day furiously wishing that a test had been available, wishing that we had had a choice in the matter of his existence, for his sake and our own as well. Now that I know Walker, I am relieved there was no such test, that I didn't have to face the ethical dilemma it may soon present. Because on his good days, Walker is proof of what the imperfect and the fragile have to offer; a reminder that there are many ways to be human; a concentrator of joy; an insistent nudge to pay attention to every passing mote of daily life that otherwise slips by uncounted.

A test avoids all that, for better and for worse.

But if there were a more adequate system of caring for the disabled, if we were less frightened of them, if the prospect of looking after a disabled child did not threaten to destroy the lives of those doing the caring—if we had such alternatives, would we need a test at all?

———

I finished reading the newspaper story about the new test and got up to do the dishes. Johanna was making a Cobb salad. "What do you think of a test like that?" I said.

She took a long time to answer. "If there'd been a test when I was pregnant that revealed what Walker's life would have been like, I would have had the abortion."

I didn't say anything. I'd made a chocolate cake earlier that morning, and was now trying to scrape the hardened chocolate off the beaters I'd used.

"We were young, we got pregnant right away," she continued. "There was every chance we could have had another, normal child." A normal sibling for Hayley, an ally against us when our daughter needed one.

"But then you wouldn't have had Walker," I said.

Johanna began to move around the kitchen faster. She was stalling, that was obvious. Finally she said, " You can't say, after I've known Walker, would I have done something to get rid of him? It's one thing to abort an anonymous fetus. It's another to murder Walker. A fetus wouldn't be Walker."

"What do you think the world would be like without people like Walker—without kids like him, I mean, kids who have real setbacks?" This is not so unreal a possibility, given the sophistication of prenatal testing.

"A world where there were only masters of the universe would be like Sparta. It would not be a kind country. It would be a cruel place."

"So he has taught you something."

"He made me realize how good we have it, most of us, most of the time—how we think we have problems, but we really don't, compared to him."

More scrubbing, chopping. "But I'm not the person to ask," she said. "I don't think I'm a very good person."

"What do you mean? You're a perfectly fine person."

"I couldn't cope with being with him. I still have mixed feelings about everything I've done and everything I haven't done."

She was his mother, after all, but she had not saved him. Nor had she become one of the full-time disability moms who never stopped researching and defending their disabled child. Did she have more of an obligation to stay at home with a retarded child than a woman who stayed at home had an obligation to work and be part of "normal" society? I didn't think so. Johanna had been a superb mother, had done everything there was to do and had done it well, but she was convinced it was not enough. Certainly the world had ignored her plight, but it never let her believe she was guilt-less either. A lot of CFC mothers felt the same way. Amy Hess and Molly Santa Cruz did, for instance, and they had stayed home to boot, had become the most proactive super disability-moms I knew. But there was no escaping their guilt: it lived deep in them, deep in the germline of the maternal. Johanna was Walker's mother, the human being out of whom his flawed and aching body had emerged. She could not think about his brokenness, it called that yelping sadness up from within her, and yet she could not ignore him either. The best she could do was to stay calm, keep busy and moving, keep caring without asking herself too many ques-tions. It was a delicate trick. Like trying to walk in high heels over a grate in the sidewalk, except that the grate passed over hell and eternal damnation.

When she spoke again she said, "I don't know what Walker's value is to the world. I'm not sure that I agree that his lasting value is to have touched people. That his whole life has to be this fucking Gandhi thing, making people feel better about themselves. I don't think his life should only have value because he makes other people feel more contented with their own lives. I think his life should have a value of its own."

"No, I'm not suggesting that either," I said. "He might make some people think that way, but his life is a life. Regardless."

"I don't have any problem with group homes or with him living as he does," Johanna said, speaking faster now. "The only problem I ever had with his life was when he was in pain. I couldn't stand it, it was unbearable. Unbearable pain, and not sleeping."

"You know," I said then, "there was no way we could do it alone."

"Emotionally, I still think if I was any kind of a mother he would still be at home." She paused, and then the snap happened, as I knew it would. "I don't feel like his mummy any more. I'm not the person he turns to now." She was crying, I could tell without looking. I could feel her start to go, as if the floor of the house were falling away.

"He turns to others." It was the best I could do.

Yes, yes, she was nodding, there was that. "As long as someone loves him every day, I don't care who it is." Sobbing now, one of her fast, efficient sobs.

He was an emptiness, a hole in our lives that would always be there. He was here with us and now he wasn't. Did facing the wound every day make us better people? No. Did we have a choice? No. Did it make us remember the wound? Yes. Does that change anything? I don't know.

eleven

As long as someone loves him every day.

Who will that be? That is the question.

Like Molly and Eddie Santa Cruz as they tentatively entertained the frightening idea of a group home, like Brenda and Cliff Conger as they argued with Brenda's stepmother to secure Brenda's father's home for Cliffie, like Fergus and Bernice McCann as they looked at the large house they had finally bought for their Melissa and wondered where they would find someone to share it with her—like all of them, as much as I think about getting through the days with Walker, I think more about the future. Who will care for Walker after we are dead?

Johanna and I never entertained the idea that Hayley would "inherit" Walker. This was no reflection on Hayley. I had no doubt she would take a lifelong interest in her brother. Her affection for him guaranteed that, and she wasn't one to walk away from an obligation. If anything she was too dutiful, a serious person made more grave by years of living in the often lonely shadow of Walker's need. (At fifteen, she wanted to work in Africa, building houses for orphans.)

But I knew how much work Walker required, and how impossible it was for one or two or three or even four people to care for him adequately, to do everything that needed to be done, and still live productive, engaged lives in any other way. Hayley's life was her own; that, at least, was a gift we would give her. I refused to cover her with the thick, wet cloak of guilt under which many families of disabled children operate—a swamp of irrationality that has afflicted social thinking about disability for millennia. My wife and I often discussed having more children (definitely one, occasionally two)—brothers and sisters for Hayley and Walker—allies to insulate him from the world, but also to dispel our guilt. There are political factions and even entire governments that tap into this guilt and suggest that family is the only real solution to the problem of caring for the disabled.

But families, like disabilities, are not uniform or consistent. They're anything but perfect. No one asks to join them, and more than half the time they don't last. As a result—this was my thinking—the nuclear family is no model for a system to care for the severely disabled. Even if I did decide to provide lifelong care for Walker through the vehicle of a large primary family—and I'd need at least six kids living all their lives in the same place to take care of him properly—is that a responsible (never mind realistic) choice, in an overburdened, overpopulated world?

My mind raced around these ideas like a Jeep circling a minefield.

The truth is, even the best care available left me riddled with doubt. Walker's group home was and is the best of its kind. But what if its funding failed? And was it the best of all possible places for Walker to be? The fact that Walker had a second home where he was cared for in ways we couldn't manage didn't stop me from wanting to improve it (as wary as I am of even mentioning the fact, for fear that what he has will somehow be taken away from him—a special brand of anxiety that plagues every parent who has a disabled child in care). Walker's home is run by an organization that offers assisted living at a thoroughly professional level. But how does one make a professional operation a home as well—a place full of compassion where people are forgiven endlessly, to use Mother Teresa's definition? Walker had a home where he was taken care of, but was it also a family? Would the place he was cared for after we died also feel like *his* home, occupied by a group of friends and measured by the collective inner life created by its residents?

That was the kind of home I wanted for Walker. There was a group of forward-thinkers in British Columbia known as the Planned Lifetime Advocacy Initiative, which developed networks of contacts and friends around pods of disabled individuals. It was a newfangled notion, however, and far away, and still required, from what I could see, a battle for money that I didn't know how to win. More to the point, I had to contend with my own skepticism. I found it hard to believe a place existed that would let my son live his life as he could, and regard him well for it.

But in the spring of 2008, after I published a story about Walker, I received a letter from a man named Jean-Louis Munn. He was the communications director of the

Canadian branch of L'Arche, an organization based in France that operated a string of 135 communities for the intellectually disabled that stretched from Toronto to Kuwait. They weren't an option for Walker: the waiting list was twenty years long and they accepted only adults. But Munn wanted me to visit him in Montreal. There, in a former church hall in Verdun, a working-class community on the southern edge of the city, I saw for the first time the outline of the unthinkable community I was looking for. In that community, *I* was the stranger.

The church hall was the administrative centre of the Verdun branch of L'Arche. L'Arche had been founded in a single house in France in 1964 by Jean Vanier, the son of Georges Vanier, a famous Canadian diplomat. A lifelong student of philosophy and Catholic theology, Jean Vanier still lived in the village of Trosly-Breuil, where he ate lunch most days with his disabled companions.

That was in France. In Montreal, mass was being served in the basement of the church hall when I arrived. L'Arche had been founded on Catholic precepts (another reason I had avoided L'Arche as a possibility for Walker, though the organization has since widened its spiritual foundation). But the mass in the church basement was unlike any I'd ever seen—more along the lines of a village meeting, held in a pub over a raucous meal, with a satire of a church service thrown in for entertainment.

The altar was tucked into a corner where a stairway met a wall; the equivalent of the vestry was simply a space cordoned off by office dividers. A tall black priest in white vestments and a coloured scarf was administering the Host in a loose approximation of the liturgy. The service didn't seem to have a strict beginning or end. The priest was alternating between French and English, and talking about Jesus and his flock. Every once in a while he asked a question, and someone called out an answer.

"Why do we say Jesus is a shepherd?" the priest asked.

"Jesus has people who follow him, like sheep, right?" This from a thirtyish man standing halfway back in the congregation. He was wearing a black hockey jersey with *Canada* across the back in red script. Several jokes about sheep ensued.

There were twenty-one people in the corner of the church basement, all adults, most of them evidently handicapped. Three spun around to examine me as I walked in; two immediately reached out to shake or hold my hand. I didn't know what they expected of me.

"Where else have we heard these words, about Jesus being a shepherd?" the priest asked.

"Bap-bap-baptism with Jesus?" someone stuttered.

"Oh!" the priest said. More applause, then acknowledgment of that applause with even more applause.

A band—two guitarists and a drummer—began to play, accompanied by a steady chorus of coughing and airway-clearing; the service might as well have been held in a tubercular ward. A woman in front of me—short, stooped, in her sixties, her mouth permanently open—looked at my tie and whooped, loudly. Another man walked back to me and said, "I'm praying for you." I have to say I felt I could use the help. "What's your name?" he added in French, as an afterthought. We stood for the interdiction and the tie-whooper reached back for my hand; she did not want to let it go. I worried about germs, briefly. They wanted to be friends.

In front of me, the man in the hockey jersey (I later learned his name was Ricky) reached his arm around Richard, an older, balder man standing beside him. Richard was wearing a black sweater and checked shirt and a thick strap of black elastic to hold his glasses on. Ricky squeezed his pal, and whispered something in his ear. The older man sighed and said, "Ohhh! I like you too."

There were seven L'Arche assistants in the group, one for every two residents, and that seemed to be sufficient. One of the assistants, a First Nations woman in her twenties, put her face down to the face of the man with Down syndrome beside her, and then touched his forehead with her finger. Every so often, Jean-Louis Munn, my host, recognized someone in the crowd and gave me a nudge and an update. "When he came twenty years ago," he said, gesturing with his head to a tall, still man in a green shirt, "he was so nervous his hands were always curled up into fists." Now the man seemed content to dispel his anxieties with only a little lip-licking.

Just as suddenly, the service was over. People began pulling on their hats, an astonishing array of classic Canadian winter headgear, caps with vast bills and peaks and ear coverings like mud flaps and hoods that dwarfed their heads.

Ricky stepped up to me with his arm linked in Richard's; Richard was making a farting noise with his lips. "This is Richard," Ricky said to me. "He was in my *foyer*. We used to sleep together." He meant in the same room in their L'Arche residence. L'Arche calls its houses *foyers*, after the French word for "hearth."

It was like being in a novel by Balzac or even Hugo, with outlandish, unforgettable characters everywhere. Surrounded for the first time in my life by intellectually disabled adults I had only just met, I suddenly realized I didn't feel nervous.

———

My anxieties resurfaced as Jean-Louis Munn led me through the streets of Verdun, in south Montreal: we had been invited to dinner at one of the five homes, L'Arche maintains for the disabled in the area. A huge blizzard had engulfed the city the day before, and the evening streets were full of people digging out their driveways. I had no idea where we were going, what to expect, what was expected of me. Eventually we pulled up in front of a tidy two-storey house. Jimmy Davidson greeted us at the door—a stocky guy with red hair and Down syndrome. He had his pajamas on—blue flannel Power Rangers bottoms and a matching T-shirt top, and slippers. "I'm so totally relaxed," Jimmy said, and then he shook my hand. He was forty-five years old.

There was a picture of the Last Supper on the wall, the sort of icon that always gets my guard up, as well as a bulletin board, yellow cupboards, plants—it was a lived-in place. In addition to the house's three assistants (caregivers in L'Arche homes are always called assistants) and Jimmy, four other residents (as the disabled are known in L'Arche homes) sat down with us for dinner at the pine kitchen table: Marc, a middle-aged man who smiled a lot but said nothing; Sylvie, who also never spoke; Jadwega, a woman in her sixties who had cooked the meal and who could remember numbers, but not many faces; and Isabelle, a calm young woman in a wheelchair with what was clearly a form of cerebral palsy. Isabelle sat at the end of the table. She couldn't move her arms or legs or change the angle of her head, or speak—but she followed everything, including the conversations, with her eyes, and often smiled benignly on the proceedings.

A tide of awkwardness rose around me, but I didn't have much time to think about it, because Jimmy, who was sitting beside me—I had the place of honour at the head of the table—was peppering me with questions about which Power Rangers I liked and did not like, and I was peppering him with questions in return. I asked him how long he had lived in the house.

"Two years in the house," he said.

"Where did you live before?"

Jimmy couldn't remember. "With, um," he said. And then: "With my mother." His mother came to visit every week. He got serious when he talked about her.

We were making our way through various details of his life—Jimmy was a Toronto Maple Leafs fan, also considered a disability in Montreal—when Natalie arrived. She was a tall woman in her thirties with a three-hundred-watt smile, and a stylish scarf twirled around her neck in the style of Montrealers. Natalie was head of the home, its manager: she'd been visiting Madeleine, yet another resident of the house, who was in hospital with a broken leg.

Jimmy jumped up and fetched Natalie a chair, and held it for her. I must have been in homes where the return of someone at the end of the day was greeted with as much pleasure, but not often. "Madeleine says hi to everyone, especially to Jimmy," Natalie said, in French.

Isabelle, the young woman in the wheelchair, smiled broadly.

"Bad girl, Daff," Jimmy said, adding by way of explanation to me, "That's the first name of Daffy Duck."

Then we held hands, and said grace, and tucked into a delicious bouillabaisse, though some of the residents seemed to have special meals of their own.

There were three other guests—Alain, a psychologist from France who was working in the house for a few months; Katie, an assistant from Palestine; and Segolène, a nun from France who was working at the house while she considered her future.

"This has been my first home," Natalie said. "My first family." She had started out as a teacher in the public school system, but working at L'Arche had changed her. She'd been there now for eleven years. "The first time I ever worked with handicapped people, it was the first time I felt comfortable with myself," she said. I was surprised to hear her say that: she was an attractive, outgoing woman, articulate, confident. "I was shy. But with them, I was the leader. I came out of myself." There was a religious aspect to her work, she felt: it offered her a chance "to recognize God in my life. And God in the life of others. And to name it, too." But religion was a personal thing, nothing she pushed on anyone else. "The biggest challenge for me is to be with people who *aren't* handicapped," she said. "It's more difficult for me to accept them. It's easier with Isabelle. In my head, when Isabelle or Jimmy or Madeleine make things strange, I think, oh, that's just because they have a handicap. But I can't use that excuse with normal people who don't have disabilities, when they make things strange."

"People make things strange? You mean this guy here?" Jean-Louis said, nodding at Jimmy.

"Some days yes, some days no." It was a joke. "You know, Jimmy, Jean-Louis knows Isabelle's mother."

"Isabel doesn't know that," Jimmy replied.

"No. But *you* know that."

"Yes."

"Mmm," Natalie said.

Isabelle, immobile at the end of the table, shone like a benign star, watching. She had only two ways of communicating: eyes rolled up, for yes, and down, for no; sometimes she did one when she meant the other, just to play a joke on people. It was one of the few jokes she could make, but she made it. She was pinned on her wheelchair like a lepidopterist's specimen, but like a butterfly she was never ungraceful. Segolène, the visiting nun, told me it was looking after Isabelle, caring for her and dressing her and bathing her and keeping her company, that made her understand how much she loved her. An intent, dark-haired woman in her early thirties, Segolène was a sister in the Jerusalem Order in Paris. Working with Isabelle at L'Arche had made her wonder whether she wanted to return to her order, whether she could better use her time on earth. "Sometimes when I see Isabelle," she said, "I want to care for Isabelle, love Isabelle. And I want to do it for Isabelle, because it's almost counterproductive to do it for any other reason. But my faith says I should do it for Christ. And I don't want to love Isabelle behind the image of Christ." Isabelle had shaken Segolène's faith and what she thought was important. Segolène had left the safe confines of the church to join the outside world because of a young woman who couldn't move or speak.

"The first time I met someone with a disability," she went on, "was in a psychiatric hospital. And it was someone very fragile. It called up a tenderness in me that surprised me, that came out of me through that person. And I interpret that tenderness, which was so immense, as coming from something bigger than me. And that's what makes me stay here, that moment, that tenderness. Isabelle needs that. And that's why she's here. It was her who showed me the difference between we who choose and a person who can't choose. I think for me she is already a saint. Isabelle teaches us to be ourselves because Isabelle is just herself. And she's at peace with that."

As a newspaper reporter, I spend most of my life talking to people who have made a claim on my attention. Once in a while, a claim turns out to be justified, and at those moments a stillness surrounds the conversation, and I have no desire to be anywhere but there, where I am, in the company of the person I'm talking with. The remarkable thing about that house in Verdun was that the calm descended upon me again and again in a single evening. For a long time I didn't want to leave.

But eventually we had to, and Jean-Louis and I said goodbye. It was snowing again outside in the streets of Verdun, wiping out the day's shovelling. I couldn't forget what Segolène had said. I kept thinking: could Walker be someone's Isabelle? Could he be mine? Walker was himself; he had no choice. If I could let him be the boy he was, and let go of the boy he might have been—maybe I could do the same.

Rogue thoughts at night in the snow.

Six weeks later, in Cuise-la-Motte, a village ninety kilometres northeast of Paris, I saw an even more precise version of a possible future for Walker.

Cuise-la-Motte is one of four villages with L'Arche communities that form a tight knot in Picardie—Pierrefonds, Trosly-Breuil, and Compiègne, which is large enough to have a university, being the other three. A 36,000-acre forest—one of France's famous hunting preserves, a former forest of the king—sits in their midst. Joan of Arc hid in these woods before her capture in Compiègne in 1430. The same forest was where Marshal Ferdinand Foch signed an armistice with the Germans on behalf of the Allies on November 11, 1918, and where, twenty-two years later, Adolf Hitler forced France formally to surrender to the Nazis. There are two grand châteaux in the region, one of which is said to be the inspiration for the castle in Walt Disney's *Sleeping Beauty*. But no tourist plaques mention the L'Arche communities, though the people who live in them walk the streets like ordinary citizens.

The most critically disabled residents, both intellectually and physically, lived in a *maison d'acceuil spécialisé* called La Forestière, in Trosly-Breuil. La Semence—the seed, in French—where I was planted, was home to people mostly incapable of speech, but mobile, after a fashion; conscious, and capable of registering their consciousness, but incapable of doing so alone. Walker would have fit in here, at the bottom end of the range. I was staying in the guest room, the sole person in a room that accommodated four. Outside my window a magnolia tree was flowering. Rosemary and lavender bushes were in bloom. It was April.

My flight had arrived that morning in Paris, and I'd arrived in Cuise-la-Motte just before lunch. My plan was to stay a few days, see how L'Arche worked, talk to Jean Vanier. He was one of the world's foremost thinkers on the subject of disability, and I wanted to know what he thought would comprise a satisfying, decent, just life for Walker. I had read some of Vanier's books, and found them radical. Vanier believed the disabled deserved a place of their own, that they often wanted to live apart from their families and parents if they could find a sufficiently supportive environment. That was an idea I thought I could get behind. He also insisted that the disabled were capable of teaching the able-bodied more than the able-bodied could ever teach them. If Vanier was right, I didn't have to feel so bad about letting Walker live his life at least to some degree on his own. In some way I was there to find out if I was letting my son down. I unpacked my bags and sat down at the table in my room's small kitchenette to look over the questions I planned to ask Vanier that afternoon. I had a page or two of notes prepared when there was a knock on the door. I opened it to a tall man wearing a beard and a red sweater. He immediately offered me some water. I said yes, invited him in, and offered him a seat at the kitchenette table.

He was sixty-four years old, but he looked fifty. His name was Garry Webb and while he wasn't disabled, he too lived at Semance. Webb was L'Arche's director of special projects: he'd just returned from taking fifteen L'Arche residents on a trip to Portugal. He'd grown up in Vancouver, but left home at eighteen. "It wasn't my culture," he said matter-of-factly. I asked him how he came to work at L'Arche, but that didn't work, because he refused to classify what he did as work. "It's living. Being. Working is only part of it. Everyone who comes here is transformed by it. Relationship is our priority. And then we tell people about it just by being who we are." All of which was interesting, free, spirited, and made me extremely nervous. But that was often the way conversations with people at L'Arche began. They didn't seem to suffer from the self-consciousness the rest of us do: disabled or not, they launched forthwith into the act of "relationship" with whomever they met, whenever they met them. I found their enthusiasm alarming. Were they high? Had they been smoking kindness? What the hell were they up to, anyway! I admired their openness, but being a city boy, had no desire to emulate it; I appreciated their generosity, but as a product of twentieth-century capitalism, doubted its sincerity. If Walker ever lived in such a place, would he be surrounded by people who cared for him for his own sake or by people who cared for him because they were in a cult? I didn't want Walker in a cult.

Webb had trained as a Jesuit and spent seven years in a Trappist monastery when he took a leave of absence to reassess his life. He had a lot of options. He'd studied philosophy and theology and psychology at university; his parents had been artists, and Webb was himself a part-time sculptor and sometime actor. He had strict requirements for his new path. It had to unfold in a new community; it had to be responsible work, with the poor or their equivalent; it had to be non-exclusive, nothing that shut out the rest of life (he didn't want to be locked away in a monastery again); it had to be a long-term commitment; it had to be holistic; and, most importantly, had to occur in a community that respected "the spirituality of each person." The first time he visited L'Arche, "I asked to stay for three days. But then I asked to stay for three weeks, then three months, then for a year."

I was about to ask if living at L'Arche ever got boring, but at that moment Webb explained he was only popping in to say hello on his way to the nearby village of Trosly-Breuil, to visit Jean Vanier at his home. They met every other week.

"What do you talk about?"

"Us," Webb said.

"Not the business of L'Arche?"

"Oh God, no. Us. My stuff. Why I'm still shitting my pants, figuratively speaking, in my dealings with the world. Why he's still running around like a rooster with his head cut off."

As he got up to leave, I confessed I was a little nervous at the prospect of talking to people who couldn't talk. Webb scoffed and waved his hand. "I think the core members of L'Arche are our teachers," he said. "And if you communicate with them, you'll be okay. Lunch is at twelve-thirty." Then he left.

An hour later, in the dining room, I met the people I was to live with for the next three days.

Gérard was in his fifties. He could speak, after a fashion, but made whinnying noises as he did. He liked to tell stories, and was known to go into town for a beer. Laurent (also known as Lorenzo, because he was born in Italy) was trim and well dressed; he made a soft moaning noise as he ate, and liked to walk into a room and then stand stock-still for long stretches. Lydie, a young woman from the south of France who was Laurent's assistant, said, "Laurent loves trains. He has all sorts of books about trains."

"*Train!*" Laurent said, in French. It was the only word I ever heard him speak.

"*C'est ça,*" Lydie replied.

Several of the residents wore large neckerchiefs, bib fashion, in preparation for lunch. Francine was in a wheelchair; thanks to cerebral palsy she never spoke, though she could make noises, and was keenly interested in those around her. Another resident, Jean-Claude, could power himself in a wheelchair, liked cognac, could hear what people said, could not respond, and carried his favourite object, a stuffed raccoon, wherever he went. He was my age. Sabina appeared to have a severe form of Down syndrome, and spent all her time silently in her wheelchair.

The person who captured my interest most was a small, stooped, watchful man named Gégé. He was forty-six years old and he reminded me of Walker. The similarity smacked me like a blow: I could see Gégé's ceaseless curiosity, and his permanent loneliness. He never spoke, but observed the action around him intently and slyly, with his head tilted. Singing made him smile. He made popping noises with his mouth, and walked in a crabbed forward crouch, half bent over. He had a habit of staring at his hands as if they belonged to someone else, the way Walker did.

No one at L'Arche talked about integration, the way staff sometimes do at conventional homes for the disabled: this community existed for the disabled and made no pretense that residents eventually would be part of the "normal" community. People like me were the outsiders here. There was a routine, a structure, a community of individuals, and their lives counted for what they were, no added value required. The table was set, grace was sung. Red leather pill-wallets were set out carefully at the head of each resident's place setting, alongside any required digestive powders—a small neat pharmacy of remedies next to each water glass. Some of the residents could eat on their own, but just as many needed their food spooned into their mouths. As we ate, the assistants talked to their wards, and the wards grunted or laughed or moaned or peeped in reply. Gerard was the only resident at the table who could initiate what someone on the outside would recognize as conversation, but that didn't stop everyone from interacting. It was a form of speaking, but you had to let it lead you.

After lunch, the residents who worked in L'Arche's workshops making trinkets and jewellery returned to their labours; the others went for a walk. It was a community for the disabled, there was no question of that, but because the disabled were considered, and considered themselves, equals, none of it felt like a "special" arrangement. This was their world, not ours; these were their standards, not ours. The pace of life was slower, life itself was simpler; there were delays and problems, but no one took them seriously. It was a pleasant place to be, and conveyed no sense that life ought to be otherwise.

A couple of months after I visited L'Arche, at a party in Toronto, a friend scoffed at Jean Vanier's saintliness. "It's just so hard to accept that a guy with his intelligence and his opportunities would want to live with those people," my friend said. "But maybe he just always wanted to make sure he was the smartest guy in the room." Which he conceded was a terrible joke almost as quickly as Vanier would have laughed at it.

But there was something to the joke. Vanier had an imposing reputation, the result of a life dedicated to accomplishment. He had founded L'Arche. He was a perennial candidate for the Nobel Peace Prize, and had written dozens of pamphlets and books, including the international bestseller *Becoming Human.*

But in person, Vanier was anything but intimidating. His house—the house he lives in when he isn't travelling the world for L'Arche—was a tiny stone cottage that backed onto the main street of Trosly-Breuil. Inside, in a cramped study off a modest kitchen, I found a tall, shy, unassuming white-haired man in a pale blue sweater.

Jean Vanier was born in Geneva, Switzerland, on September 10, 1929, while his father, Georges Philias Vanier, a retired general in the Canadian army, was stationed there on a diplomatic mission. Vanier attended school in England, but at the outset of the Second World War went to live, for reasons of safety like many other English children, with his brothers in Canada.

Late in 1941, he approached his father for a meeting. As his father was Canada's special envoy to half a dozen European countries and the Free French government-in-exile (he was later Canada's nineteenth governor general), this required making an appointment. Jean wanted to join the British Navy, by way of the Royal Naval College in England. He had to cross the dangerous waters of the Atlantic, an idea his mother strongly opposed. But his father held a different view. "If that is what you really want to do," Georges Vanier said to his son, "then go. I trust you." Vanier later remembered the conversation as a formative moment of his life.

He was too young to see active service, but did witness the liberation of Paris, and in the years that followed helped process the return of survivors from the concentration camps at Dachau and elsewhere. By 1950 he was assigned to Canada's largest aircraft carrier.

At sea, Vanier began to wonder if he really wanted to be in the navy. He had begun to pray, for starters. He later wrote in *Toute personne est une histoire sacrée*, his account of his spiritual call to arms, that he had begun to feel "called to work in a different way for peace and freedom." He was more attentive to reciting the Divine Office than he was to night watch. He felt he was being called to God, and within a few years had resigned his naval commission and enrolled as a student of philosophy and divinity at Paris's L'Institut Catholique. He also joined L'Eau Vive, a small community of students devoted to prayer and metaphysics under the direction of a French Dominican priest, Père Thomas Philippe. Shortly after Vanier's arrival, Père Thomas fell ill. Vanier was asked to run the community, which he did for six years.

"I suppose I had been hopping around," Vanier told me that afternoon over a cup of tea. "I'd been a naval officer, I'd left the navy, I'd come to a community near Paris. I was searching. I didn't know quite what to do. Later I got a letter from St. Michael's College in Toronto: will you come and teach? And it was interesting." By 1963, at the age of thirty-four, Vanier had defended his doctoral dissertation at the University of Toronto (*Happiness: Principles and Goals of Aristotelian Morality*) and was a popular lecturer with a scholarly interest in the ethics of friendship. "But I knew that teaching wasn't my thing. There was something in me that wanted a commitment to people, and not ideas." He spent a lot of time visiting the edges of society—notably prisons near Ottawa, where he took to praying with the inmates, guards, wardens and in-house psychologists alike. "After a while, no one knew [during the prayer sessions] who was a prisoner or who was a guardian," he later wrote. It was his first experience of non-hierarchical life—an early model for what L'Arche would later become, with its residents and assistants living side by side, as equals. Raised as he had been in the protocol-encrusted diplomatic community and in military college, casteless society was a revelation to him.

During the summer of 1963, after the school year finished in Toronto, Vanier visited his old spiritual mentor, Père Thomas. Thomas had retired from teaching following a disagreement with the Vatican, and was by then serving as chaplain at Le Val Fleuri, a small institution for men with developmental disabilities in the tiny village of Trosly-Brueil. "I was a bit scared," Vanier said of his first visit, "because—well, how do you share with people who don't speak, or speak badly?"

But his encounters with the intellectually frail men of Trosly were the opposite of frightening. "What touched me was that everyone, in one way or another, said, 'Do you love me? And, will you be my friend?' I found them so different from my students at the university. My students wanted my head, and then to leave, to get a position, get money, found a family. But here was something else. I think their cry—'Will you be my friend?'—triggered off things within me. I think I was searching for a place of commitment.

"These were the years of Martin Luther King," Vanier explained. "He wanted to liberate those who were oppressed. I think my impression of people with disabilities was that they were among the most oppressed people of this world. I suppose that somewhere at the heart of the beginning of L'Arche was a desire for liberation, to liberate them.

"It seemed obvious. That was the period in Canada where there were twenty institutions for the handicapped just in Ontario; here in France it was the same type of thing. And I had visited institutions where there were a thousand people with disabilities all cluttered together. And I thought: what is the meaning of this? And so my sense was just, why not get a house? And why not welcome two people? And see what happens? In a way, I'm quite naive. I think I like risk. And if you put naïveté and risk together, then you start L'Arche."*

A small house was available in the centre of Trosly-Breuil. Vanier bought it. The house was so primitive it had no indoor toilet. On August 6, 1964, he moved in with three intellectually disabled men (one of whom quickly proved beyond his capabilities and moved out again). Neither of the remaining men, Raphael and Phillippe, could speak. Vanier's only other asset was an unreliable Renault, in which he and his companions roamed the countryside.

"I can say that as soon as I began, I think I became a child. I could laugh, we could have fun. We'd sit around the table

---

* I'm always surprised by the range of people I meet who have experienced the energy of the handicapped, however difficult and even embarrassing that energy can be. Not long ago, for instance, at a Christmas solstice party, I found myself at the cheese tray, standing next to John Ralston Saul, the writer and public intellectual, and his wife, Adrienne Clarkson, the former governor general of Canada. I had only just learned that Saul had written about disability. I asked him what had drawn him to the subject. Saul—a fairly intimidating figure at the best of times—revealed that he had an intellectually disabled brother. "He was certainly the most influential person in my life," Saul told me, reaching for the Havarti.

"Why?" I asked. But he only looked at me, thinking, until Clarkson answered for him.

"Because John and his brothers were always trying to communicate with him. All the brothers, they wanted to include him. And they couldn't. And so that left them always wanting to get through to him. Everything else in John's life has flowed from that." The process can work the other way, as well. The playwright Arthur Miller renounced his own Down syndrome son, and even denied he existed; a number of critics maintain this is when Miller's decline as a writer began.

and fool around. I had been quite serious up to that time. As a naval officer you're quite serious. You know how to command people. Then when I started teaching, I was quite serious: you have to give the impression that you know something when you teach.

"But here it was something else. We could fool around. Because the language of people with disabilities is the language of fun. But you know that with Walker. Don't be too serious. Celebrate life, have fun." A profound three-way ritual of acceptance developed: Vanier's acceptance of his two new disabled companions, their acceptance of him, and perhaps most significant of all, Vanier's acceptance of himself in his new, less ambitious, countercultural role.

He called the house L'Arche, after the French word for ark, as in Noah's ark. To his surprise, the venture attracted attention over the ensuing years, and eventually donations and public funding that allowed it to expand.

"In the beginning Jean was still in the very traditional thing of doing good for the poor," Jean-Louis Munn had told me when we met. "But then it switched: he realized *he* was benefiting. After that Jean wanted to be a voice for people who had no voice. He quickly discovered that the simple life, living with Raphael and Phillippe, was satisfying." Gradually, lured by Vanier and word of mouth, young people from around the world began to show up at L'Arche to do a year or two or more of service. (Jean-Louis Munn and Garry Webb were two of them, as were many of the people who still work for the organization thirty years later.) By 1971, as L'Arche expanded internationally, demand for places was overwhelming, especially from parents who could no longer look after their adult children. L'Arche couldn't build homes and communities to serve them all, but that year, with the help of a colleague, Marie-Hélène Mathieu, Vanier created Faith and Light, a net of extended support groups for people who have no recourse to a full-service L'Arche residence. Today there are nearly fifteen hundred Faith and Light networks in seventy-eight countries that cater as much to the parents of the disabled as to the disabled themselves—an evolution with which Vanier did not feel comfortable at first. "At the beginning my concern was not with them: it took me a long time to really listen to parents," he said, leaning back in his seat in his study. "Because most of the people we brought in to begin with, their parents were either dead or had abandoned their children young. And so there was inside of me to begin with a little bit of upsetness with parents." I understood that feeling: I had a little bit of upsetness with myself for letting Walker live somewhere else, however necessary it was. But as Vanier met more parents who had not abandoned their children but who never-theless couldn't care for them, his strict views began to moderate. He was struck more and more by the immense lake of pain and guilt in which many parents of disabled children tried to stay afloat.

"The guilt. The guilt. The parents of the disabled were as a group the most pained people, because many of them feel guilty. They ask that terrible question, why has it happened to me? You find in the Knights chapter of St. John, when Jesus and his disciples meet a man born blind. And their immediate question is, why? Whose fault is it? Did he commit a sin, or did the parents commit a sin? Why do you have a son like that and why does someone else not have a son like that? Wracking your brains about that sort of stuff—we can spend a lot of time asking the wrong questions. The right question is, how can I help my son, to be happier? The wrong question is, is it my fault?"

"But the social disapproval is still intense," I said. "People don't like to be reminded of the disabled. Why is that?"

"I think people are frightened at seeing people with disability," Vanier replied. "It might say to them, one day, you might have an accident and you will be disabled. You know, we are frightened of death. And the disabled are a sign of death." He then embarked upon a story about the first person who ever died in a L'Arche home in Trosly, an assistant named François. As the word got around among the residents, two of them decided they wanted to see François. Another assistant led them into the visitation room where François's body was lying in an open coffin. One of the men, Jean-Louis, asked the assistant if he might kiss François goodbye. The assistant said sure. And so Jean-Louis kissed dead François. "Oh shit!," he exclaimed. "He's cold!" Then he left. On his way out the assistant heard Jean-Louis say, "Everyone's going to be so surprised I kissed a dead person!"

Vanier stopped speaking, looked at me and shrugged his shoulders. "What is happening?" he said then. To my relief I wasn't supposed to have an answer: Vanier was going to tell me. "My belief," he said, "is that he's kissing his own handicap. And so accepting people with disabilities is some way of accepting one's own death."

I suddenly found myself telling Vanier the story of Walker's bath—how when I felt out of sorts, when nothing helped, I could feel better if I gave Walker a bath, because it made him feel better too.

"You see?" Vanier said. "You are bathing your own handicap."

It was a point of view I'd never encountered before, I can say that for it.

"What is it that makes you open your heart to someone else?" Vanier asked.

I stared at him. I had no answer.

"A weak person," Vanier said. "Someone who is saying, 'I need you.'" If the need of the person is too great to be satisfied, as is often the case with parents looking after a severely disabled child on their own, the result is guilt and disaster. "But parents in a village where there are young people who are going to come and sit by Walker and take him for a walk, and all that sort of thing, then life changes. But alone, it's death.

"I mean, it's crazy. We all know we're going to die. Some of us will die at the age of ten. Some of us will die at eighty-five. We begin in fragility, we grow up, we are fragile and strong at the same time, and then we go into the process of weakening. So the whole question of the human process is how to integrate strength and weakness. You talk about your vulnerability with Walker. Something happened to you, which people who haven't lived what you've lived will never be able fully to understand—you have been able to become human by accepting your own vulnerability. Because you were able to say, I didn't know what to do.

"We're in a society where we have to know what to do all the time. But if we move instead from the place of our weakness, what happens? We say to people, I need your help. And then you create community. And that's what happened here."

We talked on for an hour and a half. By mid-afternoon the light outside was a burnished yellow. "Unless we move from a society based on competition to a society based on welcoming people back to the village," Vanier said, "we will never get away from our obsession with strength. In a way, that's all that L'Arche is: it's a village where we meet each other. We celebrate life. And that's what these people do. They celebrate around the weak. When you're strong, the way you celebrate is with whisky."

Vanier paused, and laced his hands behind his head. "In 1960, the big question in France was, what sort of a society do we want? Was it the society of Mao Zedong? Was it the society of Russia? Was it a slightly different form of communism? Nowadays, nobody's asking what sort of society we want. They're just asking the question, how can I be a success in this society? Everyone, they're on their own. Do the best you can, make the most money you can. So what sort of vision have we? Somewhere in L'Arche, there is a desire to be a symbol—a symbol that another vision is possible. We're not the only ones who are doing this sort of thing, of course. There are lots of little communities."

A community of the disabled as a model of how the world might co-exist more effectively: I have to say, that struck me as a radical idea, even a gorgeous one. It also struck me as hopelessly unrealistic—the sort of idea that is beautiful in repose, that an idealist would love, Vanier included.

So I said, "I think that's a beautiful idea, but the world doesn't work that way. People don't work that way. It takes a massacre of 800,000 people in Rwanda before we try to stop it. We can't seem to act to prevent the most obvious tragedies—never mind the small, individual ones. So how can I hope to convince the world that Walker ought to be seen as a human being—not just as a disabled human being, because he is that, but also as a human being, who may have talents—just not the talents we expect to find?" What I meant was that I wished the world might see Walker not just as a boy without many common qualities, but as a boy with uncommon qualities as well. But it was too much to think that might be possible. "The truth is," I said, "the world isn't that kind of place."

"There's a beautiful text of Martin Luther King's," Vanier said, without hesitation. "Someone said to him, will it always be like this—that someone will always despise people and want to get rid of others? And he said yes, until we have all learned to recognize, accept and love what is despicable in all of us. And what is that despicability? That we are born to die. That we have not full control of our lives. And that's part of our makeup. But we need to discover that we are built for something else, too, which is togetherness, and that we have to try and stop this need to be the best. Only then can we build something where there are fewer of these things that are going on in Rwanda and elsewhere."

I left Vanier soon after that. We were done for the day, and he was preparing to depart for Kenya soon. I ducked out of the cramped stone house in Trosly, walked down the street and up a lane and across a field. I couldn't decide if I was defeated or enthralled. Vanier's ideas appealed to people: two of his books had been best-sellers, and several had been translated into nearly thirty languages. He had been awarded the Légion d'Honneur in France and had been made a Companion of the Order of Canada. He had radical ideas: frailty was strength, peace no longer lay in the tolerance of difference, but in the bridging of it through a mutual concession of weakness. I wondered how that would go over in the Middle East—if Israel, say, confessed its fears and weaknesses to Hezbollah, and asked for the Palestinians' help, instead of vowing to annihilate the source of any threat to Israel's security. In Vanier's world, Walker was not a weak link, but an extra-strong one.

Look: I wanted to believe it. Every ounce of me knows my odd little boy can teach everyone something about themselves. Whether that will ever happen is another story.

twelve

In my room before dinner, Walker was suddenly there. He often steps into my mind the way a long-unseen but suddenly remembered friend can, opening the door of my memory. I wondered what he was up to, thousands of miles across the sea.

For his twelfth Christmas I bought him a Magic Ball—a "decorative light for tomorrow" that looked like a crystal ball and responded to touch and voice and music. You plugged it in and fingered the glass and tiny lightning bolts raced around the inside of the ball, thick and white and almost molten where your fingers were touching, mingling with pink and purple streaks that emanated out of the centre of the ball. I knew Walker would love it, and he did, once he lost interest in the red and green metal-scaled fish ornament he plucked off the Christmas tree and rolled in his hands for two days straight.

When Hayley finally redirected his focus to the Magic Ball, he stayed glued to it for two hours. (I began to worry it might induce a seizure.) He plunged his hands straight down onto the ball, leaning over his arm gaiters. He didn't move for five minutes at a time. He approached the zapping lights gravely, like a small Zeus trying to blow the earth below him apart with a single thickened beam.

Johanna went the other way that Christmas, picking up an array of small gizmos: a ball filled with sparkling liquid; a round, multi-striped wooden snowman top he might one day twirl in his hands for several hours on end. Her last gift was the really weird one. It was made of felt, and was six inches long: an orange triangle with a green pompom at one end, and four blue-green stalks protruding from its base for legs. A sober, unsmiling but abstract face had been stitched onto a smaller green triangle, which in turn had been sewn onto the larger orange one. The entire contraption was ostensibly a massive key chain, and looked like a cross between a carrot, a comb and an alien.

"What is it?" I said. She had plucked it out of its bag to show me as soon as she walked in the door.

"I don't know. I really have no idea. I said to the guy behind the counter, 'I have no idea why I'm buying this,' and he said, 'Everyone says that.' 'Really,' I said. 'Have you been selling many of them?' 'All day long!' he said." She was so pleased with the thing.

"It's fetching, but totally weird." I turned the thing over in my hand.

"I think that's why the people who made it thought people might buy it," she said. Then her face took on a new look, an emptied moment of cognition, a look I knew well.

"I guess I bought it because it reminded me of Walker. Fetching, but hard to figure out."

———————

Dinner was the centrepiece of the day at La Semence. My French was beyond rusty, but in that house it didn't matter: I was just one more semi-mute, often incapable of making myself understood.

Everyone at La Semence took dinner seriously. There were flowers on the table. The assistants, being French, took the food seriously; the stews and soups and salads arrived at the table in attractive serving dishes, and were uniformly delicious. Wine was always served, even to the residents, if their medications permitted; there were often guests (like me), and they were welcomed and toasted. The meals always began with ceremony: we held hands and sang grace. That act alone, grasping one another's fingers, was a prolonged moment of uneasiness—I felt awkward holding hands with someone I didn't know, and absurd for feeling awkward. And the hands! Whether they were stiff, crabbed, dry, moist, boneless, deep in the palm or fat as scallops, they all hung on; there was no self-consciousness there. Each hand was a world unto itself.

Gégé's hand was tight: I had to force my right-hand fingers into his small left grip. Jean-Claude held his hand open and then laughed as he took mine, and held on, but there was the limpness of his grasp to contend with, as if he had forgotten that his hands were attached to his arms. I tried to be light-hearted about it. Sometimes he forgot to let go too.

Once grace was finished, the assistants served bowls of green mush for those who couldn't eat easily, their nightly dose of fibre and vitamins. The rest of us had firmer vegetables. Everyone wore pyjamas: Jean-Claude in stripes, and a striped terry-cloth dressing gown over them; Francine in her wheelchair in a pink housecoat; Gégé in blue jersey Dr. Dentons, a smaller striped bathrobe over his bent body, but never done up, the belt trailing him like a forgotten task; and of course Lorenzo, the speechless Italian train-lover, in a magnificent dressing gown with silk piping and frogging on the sleeves, a gift of breathtaking luxury for a man with a beggared mind, who stood still in the middle of the room, motionless, arms extended, waiting, expectant as always. But waiting for what? The unknowable thing. He was no different from any of us, I suppose. In this fashion the residents transformed life in the house into theatre. All you had to do, to appreciate the depth of the performance, was watch carefully, and think about what you saw.

The conversation rotated around the table: when Jean-Claude burped, which he did frequently, Garry Webb made a face and a joke, or at least a parallel noise. Jean-Claude seemed to appreciate this. Garry improvised in the moment, drawing on his training as an actor. At dessert—ice cream and chocolate sauce—Gégé ended up with a chocolate moustache. Garry immediately started in. "Ah, you have a moustache! Hello, sir. Are you—a crow? Are you Corneille?" (He meant Pierre Corneille, the seventeenth-century French playwright, who had a distinctive dark moustache and soul patch.) "Perhaps you are a Mexican bandit! Yes—Sancho! Draw!" Garry made his fingers into guns, and mimed shooting Gégé. By now the entire table was laughing, watching Gégé, the butt of the joke. He was gazing at Garry, his face unmoved. And then very quietly he began to make a noise that sounded like gas escaping in bursts from a balloon. He was laughing.

The way Garry teased Gégé was no different from what any pair of able-minded pals would get up to if one of them burped or smeared his face with chocolate. Garry had a connection with Gégé: he tied his bib, fed him his medicine and his dinner, joked, always sat next to him, bathed him and helped him to bed. Some assistants worried that making gentle fun of the habits of the residents was incorrect, but the residents enjoyed it most of all. They liked being the object of attention and of fun: they had no illusions about the way they looked, about what they couldn't do. "I give it everything I have," Garry said.

Jean-Claude, my dinner companion, was sixty-one. Sitting with him, I began to imagine this life for Walker after I was gone; I could imagine much worse ones. But the waiting list to get into L'Arche in Canada—where there were far fewer outposts than in France—was indeed twenty years long. I sketched a picture of Jean-Claude in my notebook; he saw me, so I showed it to him. He erupted in pleasure. It seemed I'd found a way into his trust and his company—into his world. It was easier to do this with the residents than I had imagined. There were no rules, no prescribed routes: you went with what was available, with the most human thing you could catch on to.*

And this is the strangest thing: even in the three and half

---

* There were even couples at L'Arche, not just among the young assistants, who often went dancing in town after a long day's work, but also among the residents. Some were even married. In Holland, some communities for the disabled are particularly progressive: professional sexual masseuses are hired by homes on a regular basis. That is not the practice at L'Arche or in France. "Here," Garry said, "if you're physically handicapped, your physical and sexual

days I stayed at Trosly-Breuil, those broken men and women taught me things.

An example. There was an artisanal bakery in the village, a *boulangerie* some five minutes walk from where I was staying. I set out two mornings in a row to buy a baguette and have a coffee but I chickened out before going in. It is hard to describe how much mental agony this small failure caused me. My French was inept, they would laugh at me: the entire prospect intimidated me. I realized I was afraid of everything: afraid to take a shower, for fear of waking everyone up; afraid to come down to breakfast. (By nine in the morning the house was alive with noise—long high moans, train hoots, *ays* and *oohs* and clapping.)

But something about the unassuming nature of life in the *foyer* fixed that. My third morning at La Semence, I woke early and snatched a shower down the hall from my room. It was the first shower I'd had in three days—in a stall that took up a closet, the spray far from ideal—and it seemed like the height of luxury. I understood then how much a shower or a bath must mean to Jean-Claude and Gérard and Laurent and Gégé, and to Walker—a steady dose of pleasure, the sense, in their disorganized bodies, that for the moment they had a physical outline.

After the shower I dressed and walked into the village, through a small construction site: L'Arche was building two

---

needs don't exist. Instead you're an angel." He wanted the French system to be more lenient. I admit I was shocked at first, but then, I often am: the first time someone suggested to me that Walker might one day marry, I reeled. But why shouldn't he marry? His condition deprives him of so many pleasures already; why should he be deprived of the pleasures of a steady companion, if there is a steady companion who wants to share a life with him?

new *foyers*, transforming old buildings into new residences. (The French government had recently recodified housing requirements for the handicapped, and the retrofit had already become a serious financial challenge.) It was early spring—there were buds the size of peewee footballs on the trees. An owl was hooting. The best routine, Garry had explained, was to buy something to eat at the boulangerie, and then take it next door to the hotel for *un café*. There was only one thing to remember. "When you go in, say *'monsieurs, mesdames'*—that way at least they won't think you're some completely rude tourist." I sat in the square, working up my nerve. Some teenagers were hanging out at the bus stop next to me, smoking. How did I get so frightened of everything? To take a shower, to buy bread in French, to step into a tiny country hotel—afraid to *be*. Retarded, incapable of language, afraid of what others would think.

Walker never worries about any of that.

I stepped into the boulangerie. One of L'Arche's residents was there already, a young thin girl with a high, stalling voice, a stammer—as if her body would never be quite ready for her mind. She, however, managed to buy breakfast for her entire house. I leapt into the fray. Thanks to my French, I ended by buying twice as much bread as I could ever eat—the woman thought I wanted two baguettes, and I didn't know how to dissuade her. But at least I had breakfast. I moved with my armful of bread down the street to the hotel. *"Bonjours, mesdames, messieurs,"* I sang as I crossed the threshold. Two large French gentlemen in leather jackets sat at the bar. They looked at me as if I were a visiting madman.

But now it was done, and it was nothing.

I understand how insubstantial this seems, how minor: man buys a coffee in French! But it was Gégé and Jean-Claude, and my own Walker, who reminded me how to do that simplest thing. They reminded me not to be ashamed. That is never a small accomplishment. The essayist Wendell Berry even thought to write a poem about it:

> *You will be walking some night*
> *in the comfortable dark of your yard*
> *and suddenly a great light will shine*
> *round about you, and behind you*
> *will be a wall you never saw before.*
> *It will be clear to you suddenly*
> *that you were about to escape,*
> *and that you are guilty: you misread*
> *the complex instructions, you are not*
> *a member, you lost your card*
> *or never had one. And you will know*
> *that they have been there all along,*
> *their eyes on your letters and books,*
> *their hands in your pockets,*
> *their ears wired to your bed.*
> *Though you have done nothing shameful,*
> *they will want you to be ashamed.*
> *They will want you to kneel and weep*
> *and say you should have been like them.*
> *And once you say you are ashamed,*
> *reading the page they hold out to you,*
> *then such light as you have made*
> *in your history will leave you.*
> *They will no longer need to pursue you.*

You will pursue them, begging forgiveness.
They will not forgive you.
There is no power against them.
It is only candor that is aloof from them,
only an inward clarity, unashamed,
that they cannot reach. Be ready.
When their light has picked you out
and their questions are asked, say to them:
"I am not ashamed." A sure horizon
will come around you. The heron will begin his evening flight
from the hilltop.

———

At eighty, Vanier was preparing for the end of his life. He was wary of public honours and awards, and didn't want to be cast as an expert. "I don't want to be more of an authority than I already am," he said to me the next morning. "I want to be less of one." He didn't want to be bitter, the way so many old people were, "upset at the grief of not having power." People keep thinking they are supposed to behave one way or another, think one thing or another, believe in one God or another, but "you don't have to do anything. You have to cross out 'have to.' Just be. And let it come. What is to come will come. The greatest fear of human beings is the fear of power, and the fear of failure, and the fear of guilt. That we are guilty. What of? Disobeying the law. But what law? We don't know."

"Oh," I said. "So the guilt is unavoidable."

"Yes. That's the problem. There's a really interesting text in Genesis, which is one of the oldest books we have about the beginnings of humanity. At one point Adam and Eve separate from God. And God runs after them. He says, 'Where are you, it's me, God. Where are you?' He doesn't say, 'You're no good.' He just says, 'Where are you?'

"And Adam responds, 'I was frightened because I was naked. And so I hid.' So: fear, nakedness and hiding. What is that nakedness? It's our mortality. Whether we like it or not, we are not in control. And so, the whole reality for human beings is to accept oneself as one is."

"Walker," I said, suddenly, "he can't speak. And I have a language with him where I connect with him by clicking. And he recognizes it, and sometimes responds." I did a little imitation of our clicking.

"He's clicking, and you're clicking, and I call that communion," Vanier said. "You're vulnerable to him, he's vulnerable to you. You're not doing something for him. You're just with him. Clicking. I like that expression. So when you're with Walker and you're clicking, you're grateful for one another. You can imagine how grateful he is, because this is Dad, looking at him. And you're grateful, because he's looking at you, at the child within you. Not looking at you as somebody who's written the best something or other. He's looking at you as you really are in the depths of your being."

I'm not suggesting this is the only way to understand a profoundly disabled boy. But Vanier said these things. Sometimes they made sense to me, and sometimes they seemed the exclusive thoughts of a man with a deep religious faith I did not share.

I took comfort in what Vanier said about Walker's value, and yet the effort of believing it was sometimes exhausting.

Later that day, the day of my bakery breakthrough, I came upon Francine, taking the sun in her wheelchair. She was parked on the path that led from La Semence out to the road; Lydie, the pretty assistant from the south of France, was fifteen feet away, raking the garden. *"Comment ça va?"* I said to Francine, and touched her shoulder. I was already moving away when she grabbed my hand, and then my arm. She was powerful; she pulled my face close to hers. She was spastic, palsied, but her mouth was open, making growling noises that got louder and louder. Her mouth was near my ear, her teeth a derangement of spaces: I thought she was going to bite me. I didn't know what to do, so I hugged her, gave her a kiss. I looked up, and Lydie was watching us. "I'm sorry," I said in my bad French. "I think I upset her."

"No, it is good," Lydie said. "She likes men." Then she turned back to raking the leaves.

———

By the time Walker was two, I seldom thought about him without also thinking about death—mine, mostly, but sometimes his. At night after he fell asleep, *if* he fell asleep, or in the middle of the night if I woke and he did not, I saw the years stretched out ahead of us, unchanging. I wondered if I would have an opportunity to do anything but care for him; wondered whether caring for Walker eventually would erode and erase my affection for my wife. I imagined where all my worry went, what abscesses and cankers it was breeding.

But mostly I worried about dying: about going too soon, before I had a chance to arrange the future, and what would happen to him afterwards. I wondered if it might be a relief if he died, and whether it might be a relief if I did too. Money was a constant worry, a canyon. Because I didn't want Johanna to be stuck with the double burden of looking after Walker alone and making the family's income by herself in the event of my predeceasing her (as my bank manager put it), I bought mortgage insurance. That was $500 a month. Olga's salary and Walker's formula sucked away more than $40,000 a year. (For many years Walker's formula bill was $800 a month, four times the cost of regular infant formula, and not covered by my benefits at work—food, after all, is not a deduction. I spent another $800 a month on groceries for the rest of the family, and we ate well for that; Walker's had to be some fantastic formula! These days it's $1,200 a month because it is, according to the manufacturer's description, "pre-digested" for children who suffer from reflux.) Prescription costs, medical devices, even the toll for parking at the Hospital for Sick Children (at least $9 every time we were there)—it all added to the usual wear and tear that a family puts on a health plan. It was always interesting to see when our benefits would top out: mid-August? Or would we make it to September this year? Three years after he moved into the home, I'm still paying off Walker-related debts.

On especially difficult nights, or if it rained hard, or most of all after the terrible arguments my wife and I sometimes had, strained by sleeplessness and ashamed of our failure with this strange boy, I asked myself if it might not be braver to take my life, and to take Walker with me. Suicide is not my default setting. But the hopelessness of life ahead, caring for Walker, could raise the spectre in me. There was chloral hydrate; there were pills. There was the car, there were places to drive the car off of, there were lakes to walk into.

One of my secret death fantasies was to pack Walker into a baby backpack I owned, a kind of Snugli, and take him high up into the mountains of western Canada in the winter, one of my favourite places on earth, and lie down in a snowbank, and end it there, quietly, hypothermically. I imagined the venture in complete detail, how I would pick a moment when Johanna was at a movie and Hayley was at school, how I would get him out of the house and to the airport, with all his gear and all the ski equipment. Unfortunately that alone derailed my death fantasy: if I could get through that fucking nightmare, the airport with Walker and skis, I could survive anything, and there was no need to kill myself. It wasn't quite what Nietzsche meant when he wrote that the thought of suicide has saved many a life, but it would do.

And anyway I couldn't do it—because of Hayley, because of Johanna, because of me, and because of Walker too. Because they expected me to keep going. Because they needed a good example—the standard chant of the well-meaning father.

Occasionally I had an even more radical thought: I could just fall into caring for Walker. That thought had some appeal too, a soft smothering fated feel. I suspect many mothers, and especially many single mothers, know it—neither optimistic nor pessimistic, merely resigned. At least that way I would avoid the resentment, the awful change-overs from my watch to my wife's and back again. One of us would at last be in charge. Taking care of Walker was so all-consuming that all the time you weren't caring for him, you had to spend catching up—on sleep, on work, on chores and tasks and taxes and returning phone calls, not to mention whatever exigencies and emergencies were waiting as far as his care was concerned. Whoever was caring for Walker, the other person was perforce catching up, and so it always felt as if you were doing it alone, on your own. You couldn't help but feel resentful.

Do you recognize any of this? I suspected on those dark nights that no one else did, that no one else knew what this was like; I was convinced we were alone. It's hard to explain how we felt for having failed to teach Walker to sleep or speak or eat or pee or even look at us—can you imagine the magnitude of that failure? I know it is not rational, but we felt responsible. You can't help what you feel, not in the middle of the night on the back porch of a little ramshackle house in the middle of the city, with the white fluorescent light from the kitchen of the Chinese family next door shining out over your backyard like a floodlight in a concentration camp, with Young Frankenstein himself asleep upstairs on the third floor, the third floor that is like Everest to reach some nights. There were nights I was so far gone, so tired, so spent and totalled, I would start to laugh as I plodded down the hall, and I would keep laughing for minutes at a time. A madman. I felt like a well-trained dog who realizes he cannot learn this last new trick. Christ, I was so tired: I can remember literally lifting my legs with my left hand, one after the other, as if they were logs, hefty stumps, up the stairs, and pulling on the banister with my right hand for leverage. I can remember thinking: *I can't do much more of this.* I was forty-four years old at the time.

One evening I was so exhausted I fell down the stairs with Walker in my arms: my heel slipped on the lip of the step, I fell backwards, the familiar bolt of terror sucking my breath out of my throat, that thought, *Walker*, flashing through my whole body, whereupon I curled my arms around him and made a sled of myself, and we shot down, Walkie on my chest, until we bumped to a stop at the bottom. He laughed. Loved it. And so, I did too. He took me into darkness but he was often the way out of it as well.

After three and a half days, L'Arche started to feel normal. Everyday life there had a natural rhythm and sense of purpose, however unconventional it was. I had a lot of time to think.

I went to France because I wanted to see if there was a graceful, meaningful way for Walker to live in this world—to see for myself if it was possible to create not just a roof over his head for when I was gone, not just an ad hoc solution to his needs, but a community and family he might call his own, even—this was the most radical notion—a liberty and a freedom he could claim.

And if that kind of community was possible, how could the cost be justified? Compassion wasn't a good enough reason, historically. Could creating and sustaining that sort of community also provide a substantial, concrete benefit for the rest of us, the non-disabled? I wanted to know if Walker's life had some value. It seemed to me it did. Vanier said it did.

Gilles Le Cardinal had gone one step further. He had proof.

Le Cardinal is professor emeritus of communication and information studies at Compiègne University of Technology, and the author of several respected management books in

France. But he began his professional life as a computer engineer in artificial intelligence, designing decision-making robot programs for the oil exploration industry. Every Wednesday, he accompanied his wife to lunch at one of the L'Arche *foyers* in Compiègne where she worked.

"I was incompetent as an assistant," Le Cardinal told me one night over dinner at his house, "but I was a good listener." The apparent effortlessness of the L'Arche community impressed Le Cardinal—the way it satisfied the ambitions of a diverse group of people with a smorgasbord of capabilities. Le Cardinal believes that everything he has since accomplished as a writer and systems analyst fetches back to "things I learned at L'Arche."

Predictably for someone whose job it is to break down a complex process into its component parts and then train a machine to replicate those actions, Le Cardinal began to analyze L'Arche. He made a list of all the "shareholders" in a *foyer*—the residents, assistants, managers and parents who had an influence on quality of life and a stake in the outcome. He then sorted their needs and inputs into distinct points of view and subdivided them by the intersections between those points of view. He overlaid that schematic understanding with what he could discern of everyone's hopes, fears, expectations and any temptations they had to subvert the system. Then he studied his findings.

Le Cardinal's conclusion surprised him. L'Arche produced a collective intelligence that was greater than the sum of its parts; interaction between the able and the disabled produced points of view that were more sophisticated than either group reported on its own. Looking back on my own brief stay at La Semence, I could see this dynamic had been in play: Gégé seemed more or less insensate until I discovered him laughing at Garry's performances, and his response clearly thrilled Garry, and drove him to try harder to reach the residents. When I encountered Francine in her wheelchair and she grabbed my arm and pulled my face close to hers, I responded with an embrace and a kiss, and beheld that Francine liked men. I had assumed Francine had no needs; I was shown otherwise. I could satisfy her with simple affection. Francine discovered she could have comfort when she needed it, if she made that clear. Only by encountering each other as equals in the moment did we make these discoveries.

"What I found fascinating was the paradigm of complexity," Le Cardinal told me. "I'm sure that mind, energizing mind, is part of the complexity—it's a new, unplanned quality that comes out of the complexity. The intelligence of the system is not in the neurons. It's in the complexity itself, in the process by which people interact. Similarly, a community at L'Arche produces new qualities that are not in the independent parts, such as reciprocity and total equality. And one of those new qualities is this total respect between the most brilliant person and the most handicapped person."

"Can you really have complexity in a handicapped mind?" I asked. "It seems counterintuitive."

"You can, if you have a community," Le Cardinal replied. He picked up a piece of flatbread, and some butter on a knife. "If you want to spread butter, it breaks." He demonstrated, and the flatbread broke on cue. "But if you use two crackers to reinforce each other, they don't. I discovered the difference between weakness and fragility. The contrary of weakness is power. The contrary of fragility is strength.

Weakness is not the issue with the handicapped—they are anything but weak. Fragility is another matter, but one that can be solved by co-operation."

Le Cardinal realized he had a radical new theory of management on his hands—one that has since become the basis of several popular books. In *The Dynamics of Confidence*, Le Cardinal applies the lessons he learned at the feet of the disabled to theorize about why some people are more confident than others and about how confidence can be created. The book has helped establish the scientific study of confidence. One of leaders of the new discipline is Martin Seligman, a California psychologist who first came to prominence with his studies of learned helplessness in the 1970s.

"This was absolutely new, what we were learning," Le Cardinal said. "The handicapped are always saying: 'Can I trust you as much as I need to?' It's their central question. Once the trust question is solved, it becomes easier to enter the world of the handicapped and find out what they can learn and accomplish."

Le Cardinal has since applied his L'Arche-rooted discoveries about assessing risk and creating trust in a group—his notion that confidence and learning spring from a mutual admission of mutual need—to other problems. For six years he worked in Belarus, where he was asked to find the fastest and most effective way to teach women near Chernobyl not to serve radioactive milk to their families. It was harder than it sounds: how do you stop people from imbibing an essential food—especially one they produce themselves at no cost on their own farms—because of a disaster that happened thirty years ago? The Belarusian government had tried banning the drinking of milk, but that hadn't worked.

Beginning with a single woman, Le Cardinal set out to create a "culture of care" that would develop its own "self-generated awareness of risk." He then employed L'Arche-based confidence-building techniques to extend the influence of his chosen woman over other mothers in the community. When Le Cardinal began the project, in a town of 1,200 people and 350 children, a child consuming a container of milk averaged 2,000 bequerels of radioactive contamination. (A level of 100 bequerels is considered acceptable, or at least non-damaging.) Six years later, Le Cardinal and his team had reduced the average intake to 50 bequerels per child. The program has since been expanded to protect more than 600,000 people.

But Le Cardinal hadn't invited me to dinner to praise himself. He wanted to tell me I could use the same principles on Walker. "For Walker, for someone with his profound intellectual disability, the difficulty is to find the 'proximal zone of learning.' In some zones, we are comfortable learning new things. Then there's a nearby zone where you can learn, with effort. And there is another zone, where you can't learn. It's hard to find the proximal zone between the second and third areas, but if you ask the right question, it can be identified." If I could find that zone, maybe I could teach Walker some crucial skills.

The trick, Le Cardinal said, was to find something Walker cared about—say, going outside, which he loves more than anything—and then give him the tools to convey that desire. We needed a sign, a symbol. "With the identification of a precise symbol, even if it conveys the simplest concept, it is possible for the handicapped to express themselves on matters that are important to them. So suddenly with one word or sign, you and Walker can be synchronized—heart to heart, hand to hand. Whereas perhaps with a thousand words, he can't be synchronized, because there are too many choices."

Walker already trusted me, so we had met the first requirement. The next step was to find his zone of proximal learning by teaching him to indicate yes or no—something he can't yet do.

Learning "no" might be easiest for him, I explained. "He used to shake his head, and still turns his face away. But yes"— the nod to agreement, to be included—"still eludes him."

"You must find it," Le Cardinal said, and his tone was insistent. "It is difficult, but it is always possible. It could take as long as a year, but it's essential. It's fundamental. And it must be a strong sign that everyone can read, not just you or your wife. Because it's his first chance to express his preference. Not even, do you want apple or orange? Just: do you want orange? No. Apple? Yes. It's liberty. It's the first step for him to be free. The first step for him is to choose: that's the key for him to meet his intelligence, even if his intelligence is very small. It is the door to his future, essential."

Le Cardinal has conducted experiments in which he asked handicapped boys who couldn't speak what piece of technology they wanted most. The most common answer, by overwhelming majority? Not a computer, not an iPod. The gizmo the boys wanted was an electric wheelchair. Why? "'Because then I can go near people I love and away from people I dislike,'" Le Cardinal reported them saying. Trust breeds desire; desire breeds discernment; discernment breeds dignity. Because if Walker chooses something, he can assume some responsibility for himself, can try to control a slice of his fate. He can be more human. It didn't even have to be much of a choice: it just had to look and feel like one.

"You have to give Walker his liberty," Le Cardinal said. "And when he learns the sign, if you will let me know, I will be very pleased. Very pleased. I will give you my e-mail address so you can let me know."

I've been trying to teach Walker the sign for yes since that day, more than a year ago. Sometimes I even think he's getting there.

———

I will remember, for a long time, sitting and talking in Gilles Le Cardinal's house in Compiègne, eating the simple but delicious cassoulet his wife Dominique had kindly prepared for us. It was as if we were sitting in a secret clubhouse, passing around a treasure map that so far no one else knew about. His ideas were memorable enough on their own. That they had been inspired by people like Walker made them unforgettable, even "revolutionary. Because it is about how our weaknesses can be fecund and fruitful. Especially for handicapped people, but also for others. And that was something I discovered from handicapped people, when they said you do not have to hide what is imperfect in you.

"And this changed me," Le Cardinal said, after a pause. "Because in a competitive world, you must hide what is weak or wrong. Someone will try to beat you when they discover a weakness, try to take advantage of the weakness. When two players on different teams play, they try to defeat each other. And that is exactly where the handicapped disagree. They respect our mutual weakness." One is revealed by one's need. There is no need for posturing.

Another of Le Cardinal's heroes, Jacques de Bourbon-Busset, the French diplomat and president of the French Academy who renounced politics to become a writer, said it famously: "The enemy of love is self-esteem." De Bourbon-Busset was a friend of Charles de Gaulle, as was Georges Vanier, Jean Vanier's father. Both men knew de Gaulle's handicapped daughter, Anne, who was born with Down syndrome. De Gaulle was a famously undemonstrative man, except to Anne. She died in 1948 at the age of twenty. After her funeral, the president comforted his wife as they walked away from Anne's grave by saying, *"Maintenant, elle est comme les autres"*—now she is like everyone else. De Gaulle carried a picture of Anne wherever he went after that: he claimed the bullet fired at him in an unsuccessful assassination attempt in 1962 was stopped by the frame of the photograph, which that day happened to be propped up on the back window shelf of his car. Twenty-two years later, de Gaulle was buried beside his daughter, a detail I find crushingly sad.

Though *sad* is not the right word, or not enough of a word. Still-making, at the very least: the thought of his long unrequited desire to reach her, finally and unavoidably granted; the gaunt, spare shape of our human loneliness and longing clarified by his simplified child.

All of this was passed on to me, via Gilles Le Cardinal, via Jean Vanier, from the source of Walker.

So you can perhaps forgive me for thinking, some days, that Walker has a purpose in our evolutionary project, that he is something more than an unsuccessful attempt at mutation and variation. For thinking, probably vainly, that if his example is noted and copied and "selected," he might be one (very small) step towards the *evolution* of a more varied and resilient ethical sense in a few members of the human species. The purpose of intellectually disabled people like Walker might be to free us from the stark emptiness of the survival of the fittest.

thirteen

From my notebook, December 8, 1999, when Walker was three:

Staying at the Yacht Club Hotel, a Disney resort, here in Disneyville, Disneyworld, the Disney Universe. Care of Johanna's stepfather, Jake, and her mother, Joanne. Her sister and brother and their spouses and children are here as well.

So many, many strange, strange things. First, Walker, who is in agony, whacking his head constantly, crying, snotting, freaking—in pain, cause unknown. I suspect toothache or overstimulation. My fear—unsubstantiated, but convincing anyway—is that he hurts himself intentionally, that he knows there's something wrong with him.

Then there's Jake, who is dying, slowly, from bone cancer—impossibly sad, but no one mentions it. He has a scooter to ride around on; the kids join him. Sometimes after a few drinks we all do.

Then of course there is Disneyworld itself. The great American oasis of sameness. I wonder how archaeologists will interpret Disneyworld thousands of years from now—as a religious shrine, I imagine, and quite accurately. Disney tunes leak out of the bushes here, and make me jump. The employees are instructed to be nice to guests, to inquire first as to their well-being, no matter what: even the guys repairing ductwork in the hallways of the hotel, having covered endless runways of carpet with RugWrap, an impermeable dirt-stopping Saran Wrap, halt all work and say "Hi there! How you doing today?" as Walker and I cruise by on a hall stroll. It makes me long for some scrofulous shitsack to tell me to drop dead, just to bring me back to reality.

I am in a Bad Mood. I have been in a Bad Mood since I got here. Walker keeps reminding me that life does not have a theme.

Except at Disneyworld, where if you're going to do something, you have to do it within a theme, and preferably on a scooter. No wonder Hayley said to me this morning, "Mickey's real, Dad." And you're not, Dad, she might have added. No one uses money: our expenses are simply deducted from our life total on the Disney card, which of course can be used everywhere, because everything is owned by Disney. There's a water park called Blizzard Mountain, the conceit of which is that a giant glacier is melting in the middle of Florida, but instead of skiing down runs, you slide down slides in your bathing suit. And that's the best of the theme parks. Today we are doing Epcot, yesterday was the water park and the Magic Kingdom for the Christmas party, tomorrow, who knows, maybe the Kingdom of Surgical Brain Replacement. This is what is making me grouchy: there is no room for any deviance, for any divergence from the norm, from the package, from the oneness of Mousedom. You are not an individual here, you are a member of the extended and mechanized Mouse Family. Walker too. I guess you could call that a form of inclusion. But that's the problem with an official policy of inclusion: you can never be who you really are. I suspect I feel in Disneyworld the way Walker feels in the real world: it has its charms, but mostly we don't quite fit.

The all-inclusive version of life comes with an all-inclusive morality too. On the flight here I sat next to a woman of sixty-two. She was flying for the first time in her life. True. And the first time she boards a plane, she flies to Disneyworld! She had the flat, platter-like accent of upstate New York. "My son," she said as I tried to read my book, "he really believes in family. The other night, I said to him and my daughter-in-law that I'd take the kids one night and they could go to dinner. And he said, 'No, this is the kids' holiday.' And my daughter-in-law, she goes, 'Well, it's my holiday too.' And my son, he said, 'No, honey, our holiday will come when the kids are grown up.'" I wanted to find her son on the plane and say, "Here, take Hell Boy for a few hours, see how willing you are then to sacrifice your life and your wife's." He is the sort of asshole that makes me feel like a failure as a father, because sometimes the only thing that gets me through a day or a night with Walker is the possibility that I might be able to spend a few hours away from him, to read or go for a bike ride or cook something that doesn't have Pablum dust as the main ingredient. Last night after he dropped off I moved into the living room of our suite to read, but all I could do was listen for peeps and shifts and other signs that Walker was waking up. I don't have the sixty-two-year-old woman's son's selflessness, and I certainly don't have his single-mindedness. The world rebukes me for my inability to accept Walker's fate, and thus my own; rebukes me for my vanity and laziness.

And yet Walker is also the antidote to this self-recrimination. It happened again today, walking through Disneyworld's Plaza of the Nations or the Congress of the Universe, whatever the hell it *was—a flat, mysterious acreage studded with a forest of flagpoles of many nations. Walker was freaking out, screaming and bashing his ears (he's not a big fan of Florida's humidifier weather) and I was talking to him, muttering my steady chant to see if I could distract him, pushing the stroller with my hips while I held his hands above his head, to keep him from smashing. I'd been with him for three hours straight, after he woke up early and I took him for a walk outside so Johanna could sleep (Hayley is sleeping with her aunt, Anne, in the next room). I was near the end of my tether. His screaming had been non-stop for an hour, and under the relentless steamy Florida sun had expanded in my head to the point where the human agony it represented, the displacement and existential isolation it represented, were the only things I could hear or think about or even see: the white band of his noise became a strain of aural glaucoma, closing down all my other senses. I thought, "You know, my boy, there are times when I hate you"—which is not the attitude of the son of the first-time flier, but it was at least momentarily true, and Walker forced me, even allowed me, to admit it. He is the antidote to false consciousness. He will always remind me of where we truly are.*

And somehow—maybe because of the fierce light of his doggedness, or because we had survived another meltdown, another encounter with chaos—a force field of resilience formed around us, and gradually, with hiccupping tears and gulping breaths and finally sighs, he stopped crying, and sat back, and rode with me, with no strength left to do anything except take in the details of the passing world.

———

A white bungalow on the edge of the city is where my son lives now.

When I'm not there, I can see it in my mind. I think about it all the time since he moved, three years ago now.

A white ranch-style bungalow. Wider than it is long. Ramp to the door. Always at least two cars in the driveway. Sandbox and outdoor toys in the back. Strip mall on the corner, community centre on the other side of the intersection. Names of the kids painted on the glass of the patio door. Charts and medical histories in the kitchen. No carpets (they foul up the wheelchairs and walkers). A busy house.

It's first-rate as assisted-living homes go: well organized, well staffed (the twenty-four-hour care Walker needs, even asleep), stable. Clean—clean is important. He lives there with seven other handicapped children.

I know his bedroom by heart: blue-green walls, needs another window. But neat. Blond wood chest of drawers. Stickers of soccer balls on the walls. NASCAR bedspreads! Three of them share the room: Marcus (deaf, delayed, anxious, but lively); Yosuf (tall, skinny, delayed, decomposing skeletal strength, sweet and quiet—he always shakes my hand); Walker, the most intellectually delayed of the three.

Picture of Hayley on the wall. Picture of Olga. Picture of his ma. Picture of me.

The closet, military in its order. Bins, labelled: SHIRTS, PANTS, UNDERPANTS, SPARE ARM TUBES. A picture of a snowman and a pair of boxing gloves, traced out of purple paper. A boy who boxes his own ears, turned into a picture. He has always been that. A boxer, a tough guy: he may be tiny, but he is rugged, and has a bottomless capacity for pain. At his baby shower—held after he was born, because he arrived five weeks prematurely—a friend gave us a George Stubbs print of a famous small bulldog, *Billy Martin*: *a fighting dog*. How apt some gifts turn out to be.

I drove out there the other afternoon after school to fetch him home for a few days. (Did I tell you? He lives there now.) I go out often enough that I can recreate every foot of the route in my head. I tend to speed on the drive to get him; when I'm taking him back I am not so eager. Even after three years, the departures (kiss him goodbye more than once and give him a squeeze and kiss him a final time and then step quickly outside and pull the automatically locking front door of the house shut behind me and walk down the wheelchair ramp to the car) are like small deaths, as if the sun is slowly dimming. As if something wicked and deeply unnatural is occurring.

Today I arrived before Walker was back from school. I waited in the kitchen. The house was completely silent and overcast. Seven people in the living room, the residents of the house—Jasmine, Colin, Yosuf, Tharsika, Cindy and Karen, with Marcus (who reads lips) watching TV with the volume off—but not a sound to be heard. Of course not: none of them can speak. They were lost in their helmets and wheelchairs and their private minds. Scrabbling at the air with their hands. Jumping over and over again, face to the wall. It could have been performance art. Their lonely anxious agony.

Then I heard Walker's short yellow bus pull up in front of the driveway. I ran out to meet him. "Hello, Beagle!" I said. To my surprise, he jumped into my arms. For all the times I've picked him up here since he moved out, I'm never sure he'll remember me. He always does, but I'm never certain.

I gave him a hell of a squeeze back.

And then, while we gathered his pump and his formula

and his meds and his snowpants and his camouflage back-pack and his arm cans and his foam helmet (I forgot the stroller), he wandered into the living room.

None of the others said hello, but then, neither could he. He went straight to the Christmas tree instead, in his delib-erate way, to examine its ornaments. In that house of eternal silence, he alone was drawn to brightness. I haven't been able to forget that.

We left quickly. He loves the snow, the outdoors, the fresh air on his ears and his head. Everything he likes is so impor-tant to me. They feel like accomplishments.

When Hayley turned fourteen, I began to take her to the ballet. She has been a dancer herself since she was three and it's my favourite evening out: I wear a bow tie and she wears a dress, and she tells me which moves are difficult and which are not, and we discuss what a dance means, how the movement of the body can make the mind feel things. On those evenings with my graceful daughter, in our seats near the stage, I am grateful that my life has been touched by good fortune and grace.

One night we went to see the National Ballet of Canada performing *Glass Pieces*, originally choreographed by Jerome Robbins to the chanting instrumental music of Philip Glass. Row after row of evenly spaced dancers paced across the stage in identical time to Mr. Glass's rhythmic score. Occasionally a couple broke step to perform a *pas de deux*, only to be instantly reabsorbed into the rank and file.

A ballet about the life of a great city, in other words, with its armies of people doing the same things in the same impersonal place to the same rhythms, save when they break away from the pack and just as quickly conform and return to position, as we all must. A work of art that lets you see the crisp shape of your own existence, even while you are immersed in your repetitive, blinkered life. A generous, hopeful gesture, a gift of perspective. It brought thick tears to my eyes.

Walker makes people cry too. It can happen any time and eventually does to almost everyone who meets him. But they aren't tears of loss or pity. I have come to the conclusion that most of the time they're tears of gratitude.

The disabled, especially the severely disabled and the intellectually challenged, remind us how dark a life can get—every life, not just the handicapped ones. Born out of darkness to head immediately toward another darkness with only a blink of light between: that was Samuel Beckett's description of the human ride, after all. Most of Beckett's characters are legless, or confined, or without reason for hope—disabled.

So when Walker does anything to suggest there's a point to his life besides pain and isolation, it seems particularly brave. For a boy like Walker, an ornament on a Christmas tree could be the Ark of the Covenant: it glitters and snatches his attention, and the shred of care and detail and imagination that went into its making is refracted from its designer to me, or anyone else who can take the time to look at it, through Walker. If I pay attention long enough and sit still long enough to think about it, if I am daring enough not to scurry along to a more "productive" or distracting activity, the idea of hanging a trinket on a tree, a memory on a branch, an ancient pagan ritual, rises into fresh view again. Walker is a lens—one with an unusual shape, I admit— through which to see the world more sharply. Walker makes me see the ornament for what it is—better still, for what it could be, what it might be. *Look here, Pa,* he says, *see what you missed. All you have to do is slow down. Let me show you how.*

If my son is trying not to succumb to pain and suddenly finds it bigger than him and is stricken with grief at his defeat and a deeper, graver wave of crying erupts from within him—that too makes me cry. Why? Because it's painful to watch? No: his pain makes me angry. What makes me weep, I suspect, is the hidden optimism in even that crisis: at least he had hopes of beating that pain, was expecting that it might pass. A pal from Winnipeg put it well the other day, apropos of something else: at the end of the day, there's always a cup of grog for the undefeated.

I think that's what my steady weeping is about. Walker has the same effect as the ballet: they both can reveal the larger shape of the world. He is one of the pools where hope resides.

So to anyone who wonders about the potential value of a severely disabled child, and the possible meaning of a penumbral life passed mostly in pain, that's one possibility. What if Walker's life is a work of art in progress—possibly a collective work of art? Would that persuade you to take care of him for me?

I think about him for the first time each day before breakfast, at quarter to seven in the morning as I make my daughter's lunch for school and come upon his feeding paraphernalia in the back cupboard in the kitchen, or when I notice the still-mangled louvres in the blinds on the front door as I get the paper. There are the photographs of him on the fridge and on the cereal cupboard, and on my bureau as I get dressed; there are the magnets he's obsessed with on the fridge. His empty bedroom calls out from the top of the stairs. Every time he comes to mind I remember that we couldn't keep on with him, and my hands and chest go cold; think of how long it has been since I saw him last and when I will see him next; remind myself of what I have to do the next time (doctor? insurance? tests?); calculate the number of days he has been away, feel okay or reprobate about the number; think about the shape of his head; think about his eyes, if he might talk; calculate when in my week I will have time to drive out to get him, and what time of day the traffic will be least onerous; think about arranging Olga; think about Hayley, alone with him in the world. That's more or less every time I think about him. For a boy of so little purpose, he makes me think a lot.

———

But after Walker moves into his new home, I gradually forget the rhythms of his sleep. It makes me weep to say so: how did I let him down that much? And what will raise him up again? I forget about the way he insists on thumping his head, the wall, my head with his head, until he comes home for a visit and reminds me all over again. I forget how gradually and inexorably he wakes up, ever so slowly torturing whoever is lying with him with the prospect of his impending consciousness, repeating the same bonking of his head or the same scraping of his hand (hard, against something harder), the same murmur or moan, until finally he breaks through, often unhappily, into wakefulness. I forget how steadily he can hit the wall, four and five times a minute, for twenty minutes, without opening his eyes, and how quickly I leap into action, to keep him under, asleep. I forget how calm he can look nevertheless in the course of his surfacings, the seamlessness of his eyelids, the smoothness of his brow, how handsome and deeply calm even my small bent boy can look. How convincing his fake calm can be. I forget how infuriating he can be, when he resists my will. Last summer, at our friends' remote lakeside cottage, he stayed awake until quarter to three in the morning. I first tried to put him down at quarter to eleven, when Johanna said, "You need to take him off Olga's hands, she's had a long day."

I pushed the usual wave of resentment back into my chest. I removed his helmet, lifted the dead weight of him into the bed, collapsed beside him. I sang my store of songs to him—the only songs to which I can actually remember the words, "Amazing Grace" (four verses, one made up), "*Amore,*" "Are You Lonesome Tonight?," "Old Man River," plus a repeat of "Amazing Grace," this time to the tune of "The House of the Rising Sun," the way the Blind Boys of Alabama sing it. I did all that twice. That didn't work. I cajoled him, clicked, joked, laughed, held him down, whispered in his ear, rubbed his head, his back. I did everything I had ever invented before. In reply he attempted repeatedly, by which I mean three dozen times, and with pathological enthusiasm, to conk my head with his head, as hard as he could. He enjoyed a 40 percent success rate.

Finally, after four hours, getting up twice in the process to listen to the night and patrol the now-deserted screened-in porch with him, after a particularly mean-seeming crack to my nose, I gave him a medium-light smack on the backside, and swore at him. "All right, you little bastard, that's quite enough of that!" is what I growled. I knew I was in the danger zone where, as the advice books say, one must step away. I thought briefly about waking up one of the others,

Johanna or my host, and begging for help. (Never Olga: she worked hard enough during the day, the nights were ours to solve.) I didn't, of course, wake anyone. I hardly ever do. But the option was there. I had somewhere to turn. Alone, with no one to fall back on—I don't think about that alternative.

Instead, I gave him the whack and told him to behave himself. Whereupon he turned on his side, leaned up on his elbow, looked into my face as if he were Milton Berle, emitted a loud, cackling "HA!" *and rolled over and went to sleep.* He just wanted to show me that now he can outlast me, that he's up to whatever I can throw at him. I don't know how other, normal twelve-year-old boys reveal that moment to their fathers, but that is how Walker told me. He used what he had.

But how do you know that is what he is trying to tell you?, someone might ask. How do you know you aren't imagining all these messages between you? If he can't talk how do you know you aren't making this up? The answer is, I don't. But the average father doesn't know a lot of the time if he and his sons aren't making up their bond either. The frame of any human relationship exists behind a veil of words, and sometimes sounds like something other than it is. Only a fool, or someone intent on disappointment, pretends otherwise. Walker and I don't compound our confusion with words. We prefer noises.

After Walker had lived in his other house for two years, I had a dream about him. He was in his new house and I was visiting. He was very, very happy: he still couldn't speak, but he understood everything and could instantly convey all he wanted to say in murmurs. After our visit, he walked me to the door of his house to say goodbye, and stood there, beaming. His housemate Chantal, or his other friend Krista Lee or some combination of the two, was standing behind him. It was clear she was his girlfriend. That pleased me: I knew he had finally found someone to love and someone to love him, not just in the public way everyone loves Walker, but in a way only he could understand—his own private love, at last, to give and receive. And we both knew it. He smiled as I said goodbye, and looked directly into my eyes, and nodded, gave me his blessing. He had forgiven me for his life. But in the end it was just a dream.

He is becoming a different boy there, in his other house. He has a life of his own, something I thought he'd never experience. Intellectually, he's an infant, always will be; he reminds me what it's like to be with a baby. But while I think Walker will never change, he changes all the time.

On his last trip home he refused to do anything I asked, refused to pay attention to me for two days: banged the table, inspected the microwave, played with Olga. He was behaving like a teenager, holding out. On the evening of the second day, after I had asked him to come and see me thirty times, he tossed me a bone. He sat down on my knee; looked at me; and slowly, ever so slowly, gave me a half-grin, while peering off toward his next destination. I have to say the word *knowing* crossed my mind. He seemed to understand precisely what he was doing: *Time to placate the old man, who obviously needs placating—don't you, old man.*

I never expected to see him become independent, to have a life of his own, but he has and does. The latest development, the workers in the house tell me, is that he shouts "Bus bus bus!" when it arrives. I find that hard to believe. But there have been other shifts too, subtler changes in his current.

There was an evening in November, six months ago as I write this, that I remember a little too clearly. I arrived at six to pick Walker up and bring him home to us. As I pulled up into the driveway, Colin, the oldest boy in the house, was staring out his bedroom window, which was to the right of the locked front door. He was standing so close to the glass, his breath was condensing on the window, next to his Toronto Maple Leafs sticker. Colin was a shy guy: small, thin, twenty-five (that was a shock—he looked sixteen), permanently furrowed brow, misshapen face, bent body, understands but does not speak, devoted to video games, and very decent: he would let Walker stand between him and the TV screen where his video games were projected, waiting patiently until Walker moved away. I always said hello to Colin, walked over and rubbed his back, treated him as the oldest, the leader; it was the only thing I could think to do, the only way I could connect without feeling like an idiot. He seldom made eye contact and kept his head down, but I noticed he always smiled quietly if I said his name; and when I called his name as I left, which I always did, he smiled again, secretly glancing up. His shyness, his deep hiding, his shame, his pleasure, his gratitude, his solitude, his longing—all there in those moments.

A few weeks passed. Late on a Monday in December, Trish Pierson, Walker's night worker, telephoned my mobile. That was unusual. "I just thought you might want to know that Colin's near the end," she said. "Because you have a thing with him." He had only one lung—I hadn't been aware of that—and now it was failing. I didn't find words to say.

Colin lasted three days, and then he was gone. Now no one minds or doesn't mind if Walker blocks their view of the TV.

Walker came home to us a week later. I walked in the door after work and Olga told Walker I was home, and he came over to say hello—which was unusual; normally he doesn't do that, you have to call him. He seemed not sad, but expectant. If something could have been on his mind, it would have been, if you understand my meaning.

I didn't know whether to mention Colin. Had he noticed? Trish didn't think any of the residents were aware of Colin's death, but I wasn't sure.

I thought: I'll say something anyway. He was standing next to me, and he wasn't moving from my arms, from the basic comfort. "Hello, Beagle," I said, because that is what I always say, trying to be consistent, "how are you?" I rubbed his shoulders briskly as I always do, and put my head at his eye level, and (lightly) bonked his helmeted head with my unhelmeted head, and said, "*Alayalayalayalay*," which is what I always say, and then I pulled him closer and put my mouth beside his ear. It felt important, but also like I was talking to a brick. I said: *I was sorry to hear about Colin* and *Do you miss him by the TV, hunched on that little stool?* and *I know you were pals* and *He let you stand in the way. That's a nice thing to do for someone, you know, not to mind if you stand in the way* and *Colin never looked at anyone but he always knew when someone was there, right?* and *He always knew you were there.* Then I stopped, and waited. Walker was looking right at me. I said, a little louder, *It might be better for him now, he was in a lot of pain and very sick,* and *Remember how when we called his name or said hi he never looked up, but we always caught him looking afterwards, looking and smiling, how grateful he was?* and *He was a good guy,*

Walkie, and *He was glad you were his friend* and *You must miss him, I know it's sad, but don't worry, sometimes you have to feel sad.* I said other things, but I can't remember them now. Finally I said, *I don't know where he is now, but that doesn't mean you can't remember him. Anyway, Bubby, I'm sorry your friend died.* Then I rubbed his back again. He seemed—I admit this is highly subjective—somehow relieved. Something in his eyes softened. His breathing slowed. Could that be what he had meant to tell me?

I said all this quietly, so Olga wouldn't hear and think I'd lost my mind, but I'm pretty sure she heard me anyway. I still don't know why I said it, but I would rather have said it than not—in case he heard, and understood.

Two days later I took him back to the house. Tanya, a young woman from the Caribbean who looked after Walker from four in the afternoon until eleven in the evening, was waiting when we walked in the door; Trish, his night worker, was waiting too. Tanya had been with Walker six months, a long time: he had stretches of running through workers, two weeks at a time before they gave up in despair from too much crying or too many head butts. Trish was even more unusual: she'd been hired to look after Walker at night when he first moved into the group home, three years earlier. She knew Walker as well as a mother knows her own child. Each night Tanya put him into his Power Rangers pyjamas, whereupon Trish took over. In the morning Tyna, the manager of the house, would come in and do twenty minutes of signing with him while he sat on the toilet before school. She'd been trying to teach him the sign for "Play" (an outstretched hand). It wasn't going well, but she kept at it. At home I was trying to teach him modified signs for "Stop" (chopping motion of one hand on the other) and "Yes" (fist flicked up and down) and "No" (head shaking back and forth) and "Love" (hand over heart) and "Friend" (a touch to the chest). They seemed like words he might need to use. He wasn't very good at this, but neither was I. I'd make the sign and he'd laugh uproariously, and then proceed to ignore me. It was like working for a boss who always seems to have something more important on his mind. The only way to keep Walker's attention at all during the signing lessons was to *talk* while I flapped my arms and hands. He liked this for the same reason he gravitated to his workers more than he did to the other kids in the house: none of the residents spoke, and Walker was drawn to the sound of the human voice. He just couldn't master his own.

Why couldn't he learn sign? There are scientists who believe even severely delayed children like Walker set the pace of their own progress, that they have a sense of what they can and can't manage, and adjust accordingly. Darcy Fehlings, a developmental pediatrician at the respected Bloorview Kids Rehab centre in Toronto, had known Walker as a baby. "I do believe that the children as much as possible make sense in their own way of the environment around them," she told me one afternoon. "I think there are patterns that Walker would recognize, that give him comfort and structure." But he could only absorb what he was ready to absorb—and if he was easily overstimulated, and wasn't ready to make eye contact, then he wasn't ready for sign language: it was me who had the problem, not him. On the other hand, Dr. Fehlings remembered Walker going down a slide, as a little boy, with total enthusiasm. "That, the slide, was an iteration that made sense to him," she said.

Something else that clearly made sense to him was to stay awake as long as he could and be as physical as he could be while he still had an ounce of energy in him. He didn't want to miss *anything*. Even at the new house, as he slowly became a teenager, a full night's sleep was rare, and when he had one it made his handlers ecstatic, because then he was less temperamental. "On his happy days, he'll jump on the bed," Trish said to me one day, "and if you close the net"—the netting on his veil bed that kept him from falling out—"he'll run into the net and fall down. He thinks that's hilarious." On weekends after he went swimming at the community centre she took him for walks. "They know him at Sobeys," she said of the local grocery store. "They all say 'Hi, Walker.' And then we get coffee, and he tries to smash everything, and then we sit." He loved to pull bags of pasta and cans of soup off the shelves.

He tended to bop the female workers in the house with his arm cans, but not the men. "Just the girls," Tanya said, "because he gets a rise out of them. They say, 'Walker, don't smash my bum.' And he goes, heh, heh, heh." She looked at him. "Is that your mating dance?" she said, her soughing island accent softening the joke. Tone, inflection, implication: he got all that. He was a master of the unspoken.

———

After three years of nights with my son, Trish knows things about Walker that I don't know. She brings back nuggets from her explorations, lays them out for me to see and admire.

Let's say it's the day I am to meet Trish and Walker at the Toronto Hospital for Sick Children at 6:30 a.m., the prescribed check-in time for a 9 o'clock operation to have his teeth cleaned, his ears irrigated, and a hearing test for good measure. Nothing serious—but because it is Walker's ears and Walker's teeth, the procedure requires a general anaesthetic. Without a general anaesthetic none of it is possible: Walker is not going to sit still to have someone jam a probe down his ear, or even a toothbrush into his mouth. (The only person who can get his teeth brushed is Olga, his nanny. To her he submits, only emitting a quiet, steady moan like a sump pump.) There are the usual delays at the hospital: the standard one- to two-hour wait, plus the usual interview with the anaesthetist, today a young Indian who seems barely into his twenties and who wants to know of any allergies and where Walker's heart murmur is, exactly. I say, "It'll be in his chart," which is what I always say. But because the chart is six inches thick, no one ever seems to have read it. By now the young doctor is paging through: over his shoulder I can see letters from neurologists I have never read, but getting copies of them is like trying to lay my hands on classified government secrets. Walker sees many doctors many times a year: he is an ideal candidate for a universal online chart. The hospital has been talking about digitizing patient charts for years, and the government has spent nearly a billion dollars to that end. Diabetics will be the first group to have their records computerized, though concerns about confidentiality keep getting in the way, to say nothing of the cost. Still, if ever there was a child who had less need of confidentiality and more need of a universal medical record, it is Walker. I have such conversations many times in the course of a single visit to the hospital.

"How will you administer the anaesthetic?" I ask.

"Probably a mask. Or maybe an IV, but if he's reactive, probably the mask. Is he congested?"

I would have thought it was a little late to be asking, but out-patient medicine is practised this way, on a strict tell-me-what-I-need-to-know-and-no-more basis.

"He's often congested." This is Trish speaking. "It's allergies."

"Pneumonia? Allergies to azithromycin?"

I've asked for the anaesthesia details to put the doctor at ease, to reassure him that Walker is as tough as other kids, that his father is fully engaged in his health and welfare. The doc is surprised—most parents don't ask for details—but thrilled at the chance to talk about the heady tools of his trade: sevoflurane; fentanyl (a morphine-like sedative); propofol in the IV. "Maybe some rectal Tylenol when he comes out of it." Rectal Tylenol? Is there no end to the indignities the boy has to suffer? *Not tonight, dear, my ass hurts.* The jokes bubble away in my mind. It is not always so grave, the hospital. "He's fed by G-tube, right? Maybe we'll just do it there, forget the rectal Tylenol." We go back to waiting. To distract Walker, I sit in a wheelchair and lift him into my lap and tool around the ward and the floor. I try to wheel as fast as I can; it's not as easy as it looks. For twenty minutes the boy's in heaven, a new record for sustained mutual pleasure. He loves to cross the pedestrian bridge that spans the lobby and look out at the huge coloured mobiles of cows and pigs and moons hanging in the atrium. I'm surprised by his glee, and tell Trish.

"Oh, he loves to ride in the chair," she says, matter-of-factly. By now she has taken off her jacket, and I have to work not to stare at her cleavage. Staring at a woman's cleavage is not an act a man ever wants to be apprehended in the middle of, but it is especially not the sort of thing you want to be caught at while you are in pre-op at a children's hospital with your intellectually disabled son while you zoom around with him in a wheelchair. But Trish ignores me, or forgives me.

"He used to ride all the time with Krista Lee, on her lap."

Krista Lee, from his first group home, where most of the kids were medically immobile. Walker was King Rat in that place, its star boy: he could walk. Within weeks we noticed his confidence improving. Living with us, he was always the least capable one. There, he was a traveller, a cosmopolitan. Kenny, Walker's first roommate, had suffered brain damage in a near-drowning, and could no longer move easily on his own. But Walker's mobility made Kenny so excited he'd clap his hands and laugh. Kenny couldn't form words or fully control his body, but he could hear and understand and make himself understood in a flurry of gestures and noises, especially when he had visitors. He was a sweet kid. I never felt so loved as in that place, surrounded by those fallen children.

Krista Lee was a pretty girl with wheels. But her mind was unreliable. Walker adored her anyway. "Sometimes he'd get up and use the automatic lever on her chair and set her going," Trish said. "And Krista Lee'd be all 'Walker! What are you doing!' He loved that." I have no doubt. When he grew too big for the house, and moved on to the second place, a few miles away, the workers kept the news from Krista Lee until the last minute.

All these strangers were now a part of Walker's life, to which each of them brought their own story. Trish lived with her husband and daughter to the northeast of the city in a suburb called Ajax, a town that had sprung up like moss in the shadow of a munitions plant during the Second World War. Now it was a vast rolling suburban plain of bungalows and split-levels and malls and churches that advertised their sermons on sign boards by the road (FORBIDDEN FRUIT CREATES MANY JAMS). It was a place where you saw married women with cigarettes in the corner of their mouths hauling out the recycling and boys in helmets with hockey sticks riding home on skateboards, where the intersections were as wide as baseball diamonds.

Trish was married to a thin, wiry, older man named Cory. "He makes bouillon cubes," she told me one evening. I admit it came as a surprise: I had never considered that an individual might make bouillon cubes, though of course some individuals must and one of them is Trish's husband. He owned his own business, and worked long hours. He'd started out making gravy that he sold to chip wagons, and from there he moved into essences and sauces and spices. I had a lot of time for those bouillon stories.

Trish and Cory had a little girl, Hailey—so named after Trish met our daughter, Hayley, and admired the name—and they were into flipping houses and cottages, something they'd done twice, with some success. Trish didn't want a second child until they could move closer to Cory's business, so he could be home more. "Thank God. I feel like I have two, with Walker." It shocked me when she said that. She thought of Walker as her own, at least part of the time.

Trish grew up in Grand Falls, Newfoundland, where her father worked in the local mines and the paper mill. She was a tall, forthright, practical person with a pretty face and a square jaw, an extrovert and unselfconscious. She first looked after someone with a disability, a girl with cerebral palsy named Dylan, when she was sixteen. Trish taught Sunday school and spoke openly of her belief in God—another experience Walker might not have had if left solely to an upbringing in our staunchly secular household. She had a degree in early childhood education, but the specialty was too academic for her tastes: she preferred the rough-and-tumble of the kids themselves, the earthiness of their needs. She liked a practical challenge, liked to fix their problems. She'd been hired specifically by the organization that ran Walker's group home to look after Walker, and she took pride that she had done so well with a boy everyone acknowledged was a tough case. She worked nights, in seventy-two-hour stretches, three nights one week, four the next. It seemed like a gruelling schedule, but Trish welcomed it; that way she could be with her daughter before and after nursery school, and she had health care and benefits. I came to think of her as a sister, except for the cleavage.

Walker loved Trish almost as intensely as he loved Olga. Olga was Walker's second mother and father: he did anything for her, went anywhere with her. Olga could make Walker spin on the spot and smile like a madman just by singing "The Wheels on the Bus Go Round and Round," something she did dozens of times a day when she was with him. He was also fond of Will, his other night worker (who worked when Trish was off), a tall, gentle guy in his twenties. Will was as quiet as Trish was chatty, but Walker was devoted to him. And Walker adored Jermayne, his day worker for more than two years.

Jermayne was Jamaican, six-foot-four with braids and a voice so low it made my chest vibrate as if a train were passing a few blocks over. My wife had a slight crush on him. He liked kids: if you asked Jermayne how many children he had of his own, he'd say, "Two, at home." His daughter was ten: Walker would walk up to her and give her his hand to be led. "Jermayne treated Walker like a part of his family," Trish told me. "He got socialized with Jermayne. The first time they met, Walker wiped his nose on Jermayne's black pants. 'You're going to be best friends,' I told Jermayne, and they *were* best friends. They played basketball, after a fashion. They were bros. Jermayne'd say, 'Walker, let's go,' and Walker would go, 'Hunh!' These days Walker gravitates towards men.'"

I dressed Walker in the kind of clothes I wore—checked shirts and corduroy, jeans and a sweater. After Jermayne came into his life, Walker showed up back at our home with a skull-tight haircut, in silky basketball shorts and jerseys and baseball caps, DJ Head Thumper. Because of Jermayne he began to respond to reggae on the car radio; a strong backbeat always made him smile. It was as if he'd been away in a foreign country and was telling me what he'd seen and heard and tasted.

He wasn't just a different boy with Will and Trish and Tyna and Jermayne: he was their boy, just as he was my boy and Johanna's boy and Olga's boy; he belonged more and more to all of us, because he was the sort of boy no one person could manage alone. That was the price and the marvel of his life.

"All of his clothes folded in there, in his closet, that's all me," Trish said to me one afternoon. At home we woke him up; Trish let him rise on his own. "He likes to think it's his idea." For months the lot next door to the group home had been a building site. "He *loved* that," Trish said. "I say, 'Let's look at the trucks.' I'm very close to him. Very fond of him. They call me the Walker Whisperer at work. I find that when he's going down, he's tired, but he doesn't want to miss anything." The difference between Trish and us was that Trish wasn't Walker's mother: she could look after him, but she could also detach herself, see him clearly, less emotionally.

She claimed she never doubted our decision to move Walker to a group home. When she first met Walker, before he wore a helmet or arm cans (I was convinced the restraints would frustrate him to the point of madness), when he was still rubbing his skin raw with his fists, despite our constant efforts to prevent it, she said, "I knew you having put him there was a cry for help. I don't know how you did it for that long. And when I first went there, I didn't know if I could do it. You have to get it into your head that his obstinacy and hitting and crying are not malicious. That maybe when he thumps you, it's more 'I like the way it feels, and you should too.'" Trish was one of the women who had invented Walker's arm cans, fashioning the original pair out of recycled Pringles potato chip cans. The first time the workers slipped them onto Walker and he discovered he couldn't whack himself any more, she remembers, "He sighed. He sighed. And then he just picked up a toy and played with it." Trish rerouted his brain.

It was Trish who suggested he wear a helmet, Trish who suggested a weighted blanket (fabric with weights sewn into it), to give him a more reassuring awareness of his own physical outline. She had shifting ideas on why he hit himself. "Sometimes it's out of frustration. And sometimes it's out of loneliness. And sometimes I don't know. Or if he's hot—he's a hot kid. Or if he's dropped his toy and can't get it. Or if his meds are coming up—sometimes I can see it, and sometimes I can't. He's hard to figure out. Sometimes he'll just do the one punch. He'll be pouty, sad, and then he'll just do one. Get one in. Does it just knock his vision into place a bit?"

Described by others, Walker's life sounded more purposeful, more complete than it sometimes seemed to me, his father. "He loves the smell of my coffee," Trish informed me. "He's obsessed with my coffee. Caramel macchiatto. He could care less about flowers. He likes the harder stuff, pine and rosemary."

He could also be more difficult than anyone let on: he ripped through workers at a clip, at least twenty by Trish's count. "The new people come in and they'll last two weeks and they'll say, 'I can't do it.' He either likes you from the get-go, or he doesn't. Because he's like that." He was stubborn, and he had both a temper and a sense of humour, like his father and mother, respectively. "Sometimes someone will say a joke and I swear he'll laugh," Trish said. "Not a complex joke, but a joke. And I think he swears. When I tell him to do something, he throws his book at me. And I'll say, 'Walker, you don't throw your book at me, you go get that.' And he'll go 'Hunh!'. And I swear he's swearing. Like, 'Fuck you, lady.'" Of course, I have no idea where he gets that from. He didn't like being told what to do.

She figured he understood the words *pick up* and *come* and *stop* and *leave it*, which was more than I gave him most days. "I think Walker is much nicer than some kids I've been with," Trish told me. "But the unknown with Walker makes him more difficult. Walker can have a relationship—he can have a conversation of sorts, he has a sense of a person." He knew who to persist with, and who wouldn't respond. He was nice to people who were nice to him. "But with Walker, if something's wrong, you don't know how to fix it. "

Trish had a view of Walker's future as well, and to my relief it was tolerant, one that suggested others might see something in him. "Walker, I mean, he'll never have a job," Trish said one afternoon. We were sitting in the formal living room of her house in the suburbs: it didn't look like a room that was used much. "And he'll never have a paycheck. But things change for Walker. And without giving him the opportunity to see new things, he won't become who he is. He learns. He's learning. The sounds he makes tell you that. Now when you say, give me five, he gives you five. That's huge. I think it's huge. So I don't think he's done, developmentally. He's constantly listening. It just takes him longer to process it."

A few months later Trish dropped some bad news: she and Cory had found a farm north of the city, near his work. Now Cory could live and work in the same neighbourhood, which meant he'd be home more, and not commuting. They could get on with their own family, make a brother or sister for their daughter. After Christmas, Trish would no longer be working with Walker, except on special occasions. It was another loss, like Jermayne (whose back fell apart), like Tanya (who had a child of her own). But Will was still there, and someone new would be there, and we were there, the ongoing community of Walker.

Trish insisted he'd weather it well. "The other night I came in—Saturday—he was just kicking and screaming. But when he's happy, when he's content, he's the most beautiful child. His smile, when he smiles, he melts you. That goofy little grin, that sideways look. People stop me sometimes with him, they ask, 'Do you need help?' You get that pity look, you know? And it's not necessary. Because if you see his happy look, you don't pity him."

fourteen

Walker makes me live here and now; he leaves me no choice. But he is also a product of the past, like everyone else. The history of the care of the mentally retarded is the story of our discomfort with the irrational, our struggle with what frightens us, our longing to control what we encounter. There's archaeological evidence of Neanderthal man caring for his physically handicapped co-tribalists (intellectual delay wasn't so noticeable then, I suspect), but such moments are decidedly rare over the course of civilized human history. Our more usual motto has been "out of sight, out of mind." Infanticide of the disabled peaked when it least needed to, at the height of Athens's affluence and influence; it was Plato and Aristotle who both suggested (for different reasons) that the deformed be put away at birth. Meanwhile in Sparta a father had the right to terminate the life of a weak child. The mentally crippled were raised in the dark in Rome, as that was thought to be therapeutic, at least until the Roman surgeon Soranus (with a name like that, how could he not be a physician?), the father of gynecology and pediatrics, argued against the practice. He also insisted that rubbing the heads of the intellectually handicapped with oil of thyme and wild rose was not going to cure them.

In the original Greek, *idios* simply meant a private or unknowable person—thus the word *idiot*, which for roughly twenty centuries, and as late as the 1930s in North America, was still accepted terminology for someone with profound intellectual disabilities from birth, as opposed to an *imbecile*, someone who was born normal but later became mentally disabled, and who might recover. Walker would have qualified as an idiot: he is a public boy, raised almost by committee, but also intensely hidden and unknowable, hence private. Christianity introduced the idea that someone like Walker was closer to God ("for he that is least among you all, the same shall be great:" Luke 9:46), but the Christian church also encouraged the belief that the disabled and the insane were witches, possessed by the devil, or were a form of punishment for their parents' sins. Britain's Poor Laws of 1563 and 1601 required the state to care for the disabled, but until well into the nineteenth century a handicapped or retarded soul was much better off with a wealthy, loving family and a large home. Even in many parts of North America today, this is still the case.

A lot depended on where you lived. The nasty, aforementioned Martin Luther hated and denounced the disabled as possessions of the devil, but in Frankfurt the mentally challenged were assigned minders, and in Nuremberg (at least for a stretch) they were allowed to roam the streets unmolested, to be fed and comforted by neighbours. Tycho Brahe, the first modern astronomer (and Kepler's mentor), kept a retarded dwarf as a companion, and listened to his mutterings as if they were divine revelations. But in Prussia the mad were often burned or jailed. Society couldn't seem to make up its mind about intellectual disability (the distinction between madness and intellectual disability was first drawn in the 1500s, but only sporadically): the spectacle of human disarray was fascinating, but also too terrifying to watch for long. The result, as Michel Foucault insists in his magnificent and maddening *History of Madness*, was the suppression of not just madness, but the idea of madness, through the invention of confinement. Confinement is a way of containing the problem, keeping it within our grasp and out of sight. We have been organizing and categorizing and "solving" intellectual disability since at least the onset of the Age of Reason—when Descartes decided that he existed only because his brain was capable of thinking that he existed. But in the course of making the problem appear to disappear by appearing to contain and resolve it, society has also managed to contain, and box in, its own fear of disability, our terror at the prospect of physically engaging with it. Madness, profound retardation, and even blithe cretinism were once considered to be existential states. Madness was irrational, but it was not an affliction that needed to be cured; madness, Foucault notes, was "not about truth in the world but about man and the truth about himself that he can perceive." Walker showed me what I didn't want to see—his vast needs, the limits but also the potential of my capabilities and compassion—but also what I would never have seen without him—his capacity to make a passing moment memorable, and my capacity to appreciate its significance. No one wanted to be mad, but madness had its purposes, as a route into difficult self-contemplation. In the pre-scientific world of Shakespeare and Cervantes, where art and alchemy and logic and divine revelation and experience all enjoyed equal status, madness was a direct shaft into the darkness of human existence. Born into pain and sadness, only to face . . . death! What could the nightmare of existence possibly mean? Even to contemplate its purpose required a special vision and point of view. Madness and mental affliction were fast cars through that tunnel. Intellectual instability was an excuse to be unconventional, to think unconventionally. Shakespeare's fools, or lunatics on a ship of fools, are allowed to speak their minds and reveal the vanity of our daily goals and the outright denials by which we live our everyday lives—they can't help it, they're defectives. In medieval Europe, wandering madmen were forced to live just outside a city's gates, but were invited in on occasion to entertain the residents— to reveal the shape of the residents' lives. There are days when I contemplate Walker's home on the outskirts of the city where I live, and think: not so different.

But madmen and mental defectives challenged the social order, Foucault insists, and so were calibrated (which meant they could be "understood") and then suppressed ("treated" and confined). Foucault's vision of history and civilization as engines of human repression sometimes left me bewildered and often struck me as over the top, but I understood his point: if I get too much satisfaction out of simply being with Walker, out of being forced to be myself, I will contribute less to the keep-up-with-the-Joneses, get-ahead-at-all-costs, other-directed, results-oriented rat race of Western capitalism that produced, for instance, the global economic defrosting of 2008. We desire the status quo, Foucault claims, so we set out to "cure" or "solve" madness.

By the late 1500s intellectual deficiency had been quantified for the first time: a sot and idiot was someone who couldn't count twenty pence, couldn't say who his mother or father were, couldn't reason what was to his profit. By 1801, Philippe Pinel, the father of psychiatry, had laid down the rules: there wasn't much hope for educating mental defectives, but humane attention to their physical requirements was the least society could offer. (Of the 31,951 children admitted to the Paris Foundling Asylum between 1771 and 1777, nearly 25,000, or 80 percent, died within a year.) Pinel was unorthodox: he chose a career in medicine over one in the church, after a close friend went mad. But his desire to help mentally deficient human beings by rationalizing and organizing and controlling them also produced some of the most inhumane conditions in the history of Europe. In Salpâtrière, the famous Paris asylum Pinel directed, three thousand women were dressed in burlap sacks, and slept five to a bed; their daily rations were a mug of gruel, an ounce of meat and three slices of bread. Over a thousand people "deprived of reason" lived in one wing alone. In Bicâtre, another, even more atrocious Parisian asylum Pinel oversaw, criminals lived side by side with the mentally incapacitated, and food was often served, by necessity, on the point of a bayonet. And yet this vision of controlled madness caught on and reassured Europe's citizens, in the same way that the construction of prisons has reassured many American voters for the past thirty years that their society is ordered and safe and just. Confinement of the mentally disabled became the rage:

one out of every hundred residents of Paris spent time in an institution.

Nor did it stop with Pinel in France. By 1890 the number of people in European asylums had more than doubled. "A new dividing line has appeared," Foucault writes, "rendering the experience so familiar to the Renaissance—unreasonable reason, or reasoned Unreason—impossible." I have no interest in romanticizing mental disability, but I know what those oxymorons mean: they are a way to try to understand Walker and myself, by listening to a boy who cannot speak, by following a boy who has no known direction.

It was against the incarcerating, bureaucratizing, controlling impulse of the rational establishment that an alternative view of disability slowly flickered on. In Italy, Vincenzo Chiarugi banned the use of chains on asylum inmates nearly a decade before Pinel did. "It is a supreme moral duty and medical obligation to respect the insane individual as a person," Chiarugi wrote. The struggle to do that—to treat the intellectually disabled as individuals, as equal and contributing members of society, no matter how subtle or small their contribution is, and how reluctant we are to understand what it might be—is the unresolved struggle in the history of intellectual disability. No one can deny that huge progress has been made. The last 150 years alone have radically improved the physical lives of people such as Walker. Pasteur and Lister and germ theory, Marie Curie and X-rays, Virchow and his cells, Gregor Mendel's investigations of heredity, Darwin and evolution, Freud and the unconscious, even gene science, have all contributed to the lot and to the understanding of the intellectually disabled, as have popular education and recent legal reinforcements of the right of the disabled to live their own lives. But we still think "results" are the only reassuring measure of human success, and we still perpetrate injustices to maintain the illusion that we're producing results. As recently as 1964 Jean Vanier bought his small house for two intellectually disabled men because the conditions he found in institutions (in France, no less) alarmed him. It was only a year ago that I met Linda Pruessen over lunch one day in Toronto and she explained how her sister, Caroline, who is globally delayed and in her thirties, still lives at home with her parents, who are now both sixty-four years old and still trying to create a way for Caroline to live happily without them. For Pruessen's parents, arranging to see a movie on a Friday night is as complicated as planning a two-week vacation.

"The model we're given now is this idea of mainstreaming," Pruessen explained. "The idea is, get the disabled person into the community. But that breaks down at some point because my sister is never going to be able to be part of the community. It's noticeable, for instance, that she's physically different. If you take her into a hair salon, she's going to get looks. Is that fair to her? Is it not reasonable to expect her to be able to get a haircut without weird looks?" We spend eighteen years integrating people like Walker into public schools, and then at eighteen, when they come to the end of high school, we turn them back out into a society that is anything but integrated. Walker will be saved that fate because he has never been capable of being "integrated" in the first place.

These injustices abound. Specialized medical services for the disabled are still in such short supply in Saskatoon, Saskatchewan, that Julia Woodsworth, a twenty-year-old with CFC who lives with her mother, Pam, and her father, Eric, has had to wait as long as *three years* to get a dental appointment. "I feel like at every stage of Julia's life we've had to be trailblazers," Pam Woodsworth said. "But I haven't found there's been a real growth in some of the options where people with disabilities are concerned." Saskatoon is just a hundred miles east of Wilkie, Saskatchewan, where in 1993 Robert Latimer asphyxiated his quadriplegic twelve-year-old daughter, Tracy, because he couldn't stand to see her suffer any longer. He was sentenced to life for second-degree murder. "I think, as a family, I have a lot of empathy for the Latimers," Pam Woodsworth said to me the same day Latimer was denied parole. (The decision was reversed and parole granted months later.) "The big remaining question for me is, why isn't our province on trial? What he did was an act of despair. That family wasn't getting the support they needed. I'm really interested in how, as members of a civil society, we're all complicit in Tracy's death."

Now that the government in Ontario, which runs the provincial health care system where I live, is keen to be seen to be eliminating waiting times for surgery, if I want a new knee so I can ski better, I can have one in six months. If I know the right doctor, I can probably have the procedure in two weeks. Why, then, did it take seven years of looking and asking and begging to find a decent place where my son would be adequately cared for, where he could actually be the person he is?

These days, I have a fantasy of my own. In my fantasy, Walker and people like him live in a L'Arche-like community, with the help of assistants. It's a beautiful place, in a beautiful spot, with a view of the sea or the mountains, because for once, in this place, it isn't just those who can afford them who have access to the best views, but people who might need beauty even more, because they live with so much less. In my fantasy, this village is owned and inhabited by the disabled, on their schedule, at their pace, according to their standards of what is successful—not money or results, but friendship, and fellow feeling, and companionship. In my fantasy, it is the rest of us, the normals, who have to be "integrated" into their society, who have to adapt to *their* pace and their place. I can leave, I can go back to my more pressing and ambitious and even more interesting life, but I can also return to live with Walker, as Walker lives—slowly, and without much of an agenda beyond merely being himself.

Because in my fantasy lots of people *want* to visit and live in Walker's society for extended stretches at a time. Composers, writers, artists, students, MBA types doing their doctorates in business administration, researchers, executives on sabbatical—we too can enjoy the privilege of living in Walker's village for a few weeks or months at a time, in pleasant rooms of our own where we're encouraged to pursue our work, our art and our studies. Our only obligation is to integrate ourselves into the disabled world by eating lunch and dinner with them, and, once a week, by giving one of the residents a bath. The rest of the time we are free to think and write and paint and compose and analyze and calculate. But by then the disabled will have done their work, accomplished their goals, and changed the way we see the world. We will have benefited far more than we have benefited them, but they won't mind. Walker will have made his contribution, by simply being there. As I say, a fantasy.

Months passed after Walker's genetic tests before I stopped resenting genetics. I didn't resent Kate Rauen—her isolation of genes associated with CFC makes the syndrome easier to diagnose, which means early intervention therapies can begin sooner. I didn't resent the fact that a genetic cure for the symptoms of CFC is generations away, or even that Dr. Rauen was the only doctor I met who believed that the CFC gene would play a role in curing cancer.

What I resented was the idea of my son's life reduced to a typing error in a three-billion-long chain of letters, to one dinky nucleotide. The absolutism of genetics offended me. Eventually I met prominent geneticists who felt the same way. Craig Venter, the entrepreneur who helped create the Human Genome Project, and one of the few human beings whose genome has been fully sequenced, says as much in his biography, *A Life Decoded*. "Genes," he writes, "did not make us, body and mind."

At the University of Oxford, a renowned gene man named Denis Noble—the author of *The Music of Life: Biology Beyond the Genome*—went even further. It was one experimental thing, Noble said, to find a gene associated with a mutation, as Rauen and her fellow researchers had. "Beyond that, though, if people infer from that work that people can identify the function of that gene, that's going a step too far." The structure of the human genome has turned out to be much simpler than anticipated. But genetic physiology in humans—the way genes actually work—is exquisitely more complicated than anyone imagined.

More to the point, Noble insisted, understanding human beings as the product of genes alone, from the nucleotides up, is degrading. "The social and ethical implications of

understanding a human being from mere genes up are profound," he told me over the telephone from Oxford one
morning. He had a fantastic accent, one of those cosmically
articulate English jobs. "It does seem to me that one of the
main effects to have emerged since the bottom-up appeal of
genetic science is that, to the extent it unravels the human
body, it dehumanizes it."

As for the mind—the strange wisp I've looked for in my
boy, to only sporadic avail—Dr. Noble maintained that it had
nothing to do with genes. It's a controversial view, but Noble
insisted on it. "At the level of nerve cells and associated
molecules," he said, "the mind isn't there. You can't even
understand the idea of intentionality without the social networks we exist in, without communication with each other.
I think we'll find that the mind lies outside the body, in the
neural networks of social and cultural life." He preferred
the vision of "the Buddhists and the Taoists, who had this
notion that the mind was not an object. It was a process."

"The human genome is an elegant but cryptic store of
information," Roderick McInnes told me one afternoon.
McInnes was the director of genetics at the Canadian
Institutes of Health Research. He was a tall, friendly man
with a full head of brown hair and an office packed to the
ceiling with research papers and books and photographs of
his family. Outside his office, on the top floor of a new
research facility in downtown Toronto, dozens of geneticists
were crowded over computers. As he spoke, McInnes hunted
through papers and journals as well as in *Genetics in Medicine*
(7th edition), one of the main texts of the discipline, of which
he's a co-author. It struck me as unusual that a doctor would
need to consult his own work, but McInnes openly admitted

that the speed at which information about the genome is developing, and the complexity of what that information is revealing, makes the field almost impossible to grasp in its entirety and makes therapeutic progress rare. Sickle-cell anemia, he pointed out, was the first molecular (or "genetic") disease ever identified, way, way back in 1949. Sixty years later, there's still no cure. Geneticists are in general agreement about the number of protein-coding genes in the human genome—roughly 25,000—but there are at least another 32,000 non-coding genes that tell others what to do. There are feedback systems within feedback systems, and every day brings new discoveries and data. Even the genome itself is not fully sequenced. "There're still areas we can't sequence," he said, "because it's in a knot."

My problem, McInnes gradually persuaded me, wasn't with genetics, but with the nature of genetic disease. "There's something about genetic disease and kids," he said. "It's the permanent nature of it, the emotions associated with a mutation. Once you've got it, you've got it. Other diseases, you don't have them for life. I guess it's the inexorable nature of genetic disease that makes it striking. The blueprint's been changed." He paused. "And it has been changed in the way other people with the disease have been changed." Genetic disease felt like a particularly fierce form of fate. Most of Walker's doctors said, "See you in a week or two." His geneticist said, "See you in two years."

And Walker's mind? That was truly unfixable, from a genetic point of view. "The brain has 20 billion neurons," McInnes said. "Each neuron makes 1,000 contacts, and is touched by another 10,000. We're probably never going to understand the brain at the level of individual neurons. We'll probably have to look at it the way astrophysicists approach understanding a billion stars."

That, I find strangely comforting. Lying on my back, gazing up at the random sparkles of Walker's mind and speculating.

I keep speaking into that dotted black space, keep talking to him. Of course it's not Walker alone who needs to keep hearing me talk; it's me who needs to keep talking to Walker. I'm afraid of what will happen if I stop.

———

As it turned out, I tried one last time to find his mind. I applied for an MRI, a magnetic resonance image, a deep picture of his brain. Six months later, we were told to arrive at eight in the morning at the MRI department of the Toronto Hospital for Sick Children, my usual hangout. The MRI department was in the vast basement of the hospital, at the end of a long, long hall. The walls were beige or yellow or pastel blue, like all the walls in every hospital.

Walker and I were the first people to arrive. By eleven-thirty, three and a half hours later, we had still to see a doctor. It's one irritating thing to wait three and a half hours to see a doctor you were told to come and see at a particular time if you have even a well-behaved normal child. Three and a half hours with a severely screaming, hitting, disabled child is the sort of experience that makes grown men shout at receptionists. But this insight had yet to penetrate the minds of those at even the best children's hospital in the country.

Eventually a young female anaesthesiologist in royal blue scrubs appeared. She informed me she needed a recent report from Walker's cardiologist before she would administer the general anaesthetic he needed to have the MRI.

"No one told me," I said, as nonjudgmentally as I could. "Anyway, his murmur has been disappearing for years. It's practically non-existent."

"I still need a recent report."

"But he was here a month ago, having his teeth cleaned," I said. "They knocked him out then—you can look it up on his chart."

"That's not enough."

"You could call the dentist, he's a doctor here at the hospital, I'm sure he'd corroborate."

"I can't call the dentist."

So we went home. We waited another five, six, seven weeks for another MRI appointment, during which time I obtained a copy of a form that already existed in his file, a form in which the cardiologist repeated everything I already knew, and that every other doctor knew too, that Walker's heart murmur was insignificant. By then I had come to the conclusion that the young anaesthesiologist had simply been spooked by the look of my little freak boy; he scared her, she didn't know how far from normal he was.

We waited three hours again. The waiting room was more crowded this time, and more interesting: a five-year-old blind girl was reading aloud from a Braille version of the Bible, from Proverbs. Eventually, a nurse invited Walker and me into an anteroom, and into another anteroom, and into a third anteroom, and eventually they put him under and did the MRI.

Three weeks later I managed to persuade a radio-neurologist to tell me what he'd found. His name was Raybaud; he was French, from France, tanned, trim, precise. He had a habit of generalizing a lot of information into half a dozen words, a habit so overwhelming to a non-neurologist like me that I gradually began to think I needed an MRI as well.

Walker did not have neurofibromatosis. He did not have insufficient myelin sheathing his neurons. "His problems are at the functional level, not the physiological," the doctor said—the problem being that while neurologists understand more and more about brain physiology (thanks in large part to MRIs), they still understand very little about how the brain functions neurochemically.

"Are there any abnormalities in his brain?" I asked.

"Yes, lots."

"Do you know what they mean?"

"No. You either have a normal brain or an abnormal brain. Abnormal can mean overgifted or undergifted."

"Is Walker overgifted?" I said. I admit I said it with a touch of irony.

"No," Dr. Raybaud said, unironically.

The conversation went on like that. Raybaud was a pleasant man, and even helpful, but there were times when I wanted to open his own ultra-literal skull, possibly with a hatchet. It wasn't his fault, of course. He just wanted to stick to what he knew, and didn't want to speculate. But without speculating, Walker's brain was especially hard to fathom.

Then he showed me an image from my son's MRI.

It was a black-and-white image of the corpus callosum, the network of white matter that connects the left and right brain. Neurologists understand—this is a phrase one hears a lot from neurologists, brave scientists that they are—relatively little about the corpus callosum. Marsupials can do without it, and human beings have been known to function quite well with heavy damage to its structure, but in general mammals need it. "It's made of axons," Raybaud said— bundles of axons make up the nerve fibres that conduct electrical impulses away from a neuron's cell body—"hundred of billions of axons, and it connects to every part of the brain, except for vision and the fingertips." First the doctor showed me a side view cross-section of a normal corpus callosum: the part I could see looked like an oxbow lake, or a long balloon animal on a white plain.

Then he showed me Walker's. It didn't look like a lake or a balloon dachshund. It looked like a thin trickle of a stream with a tiny pool at its end, like a tendril, a single shoot off a sweet-pea plant, a fraction of the width of a normal corpus callosum.

It's hard to describe how quickly it crushed me. I realized I was panting slightly. "So that means there's a lack of connectivity in your son's brain. And specifically it affects coordination of functions between the hemispheres." The corpus callosum is the information highway of the brain; Walker's brain subscribed to a crappy Internet service that constantly broke down and misdelivered messages. His mind was hopelessly disorganized.

I could see everything in the MRI—his tongue, tonsils, throat, vertebrae, his little skull, the shadows of his frail and incomplete brain. He was like that: he revealed the state of his mind, such as it was, only indirectly, by inference and deduction, showing me what was not there, the shadows left by what blocked out the light. A boy I could see mostly in repose, only in what was left behind. Like love, sometimes. Like everything that turns out to one's surprise to be important. Like looking at a map, a strange ancient map from another epoch, or even further back—from another phase of time. No treasure, sadly. Only questions, on a magnetic image of a brain.

I must have been lost in the images; gradually I became aware Raybaud was speaking, the medieval-sounding labels of brain parts rolling off his tongue as he toured more pictures of Walker's head. Walker had large cerebrospinal cavities, but within the range of normal. "Fifty percent of the brain is white matter, and he doesn't have much. I would say the forebrain is a bit small." His hippocampus, particularly his medial temporal lobe, had too few sulci, or furrows. That grey matter of the brain, the crenellated surface, is where the content of our thoughts and associations originates (my memory of the smell of dried formula, my mental picture of Walker's crying face); the white matter delivers the content here and there (the smell of dried formula makes me see Walker in my mind's eye). Walker also had less grey matter than most people, Raybaud explained, so that even if his information delivery system had been sound, his content was very likely rudimentary to start with. "The brain"—Raybaud admitted he called it "the brain" to give him distance from the child he was describing—"is too small." Beyond that, it was hard to say what was wrong. For all the physiological flaws the MRI revealed, the functional problem in Walker's brain, its misdirected electrical activity, was invisible.

I had saved my investigation of Walker's brain for last, hoping it might reveal him. But his brain had even less to tell me about who Walker was and how the world appeared to him than I knew myself. The fancy pictures told me less than I could figure out from ten minutes in his company, and there was no fine grade to these pictures, no subtlety. It was a technical report on the hardware, not that it wasn't grave enough. "Just from one bug, you can make the whole Internet stop," Raybaud said, by way of analogy. He compared the pictures on the computer screen—I'm not making this up—to the brain of a dog.

"The dog has the same memory as you have. The dog has the same affective intelligence as you. But he cannot operate a computer. He cannot do math or context very well. Dogs don't have these anterior frontal lobes."

"But Walker has them," I pointed out.

"But they may not be properly connected." It was possibly the work of the RAS pathway, transposing small parts of the brain to places they weren't supposed to be, over-building where it ought not to have built, under-building where it ought to have built. There was no health in that. Walker had all the parts: the primitive brain, the somatosensory stuff; he had the secondary meat, the processing and anticipating bits; he even had the parts, if somewhat diminished, that did the brain's cross-associating, the radar dishes normally associated with intelligence. "But to know what to do with all of it—to place shapes in time and space—you need tertiary functions. He has it all, but it doesn't work properly."

Walker's intellectual shortcomings, I learned several weeks later from Dr. Robert Munn, his neurologist, occurred most likely in his neurons, at a neurochemical level—the level science cannot yet see, much less understand. There was some new evidence, Munn said, that some children whose faces develop abnormally have abnormal brain stems as well, with the result that their serotonin uptake mechanism is flawed—making it harder for them to feel pleasure, and possibly harder for them to learn. "But we don't know much about the brain," Munn said. (There was that phrase again.) "The neuropathways we can't see very easily. There are all sorts of changes in Walker's brain that are neurochemical. And that's the next path we have to take." The very nature of the brain has stymied research into the brain. Brain matter, Munn explained, was too jelly-like even to be dissected in its natural state, and the chemicals that made it cuttable altered the crucial neurochemicals within. Because of the body's brain-blood barrier these neurochemicals aren't present in blood samples, either. Even spinal fluid, another potential way to study the neurochemical brain, is altered by the sedation necessary to draw the fluid in the first place. It was as if Walker's brain didn't want to be studied.

Munn was a youthful-looking man in his forties, casually dressed, with an office out on the edge of the city, not too far from where Walker lived. He often made house calls to the home: several of the residents suffered seizures. Walker didn't, usually, but his self-mutilation was a mystery. "I think it's a compulsive need to create a sensation," Munn said, "whether it's pleasant or unpleasant. And I think there are elements of frustration." But that was speculation.

"Seems hopeless," I said.

"Nobody's hopeless to me," Munn said. "If you pick up a kid in a wheelchair and make him or her smile, you've done something. You don't have to be a hero."

His wife had died of cancer early in their marriage, and now he devoted himself to the brains of disabled children. From one unanswerable question to another.

———

Without a knowable brain, was Walker a knowable boy? If he wasn't knowable, what was his value? I talked about it endlessly at home, but Johanna didn't see the point. He was the boy he was, she was his mother. Without Walker in the house all the time, soaking up her every minute, she had begun writing more again, concentrating on Hayley, exercising. I wondered what shape the missing boy took in her head, in her body. She took compulsively to crosswords, sudoku, Brain Age, a massive two-thousand-piece jigsaw of Munch's *The Scream*, any pastime that required close obsessive attention. I tried to read Foucault's *History of Madness* and watched her secretly from across the room, wondering if she was bored.

Had there ever been a point in Walker's infancy when the doctors realized how hard his life would be? If so, they never mentioned it. Quite the opposite, in fact: in the early days of Walker's life, when he struggled to put on weight and survive, the only urging I ever received from his doctors was to greater and more assiduous effort. The words of his pediatrician, Norman Saunders, still rang in my ears: *We do want this boy to survive, don't we?* It turns out we did, though I wasn't always sure at the time.

Dr. Bruce Blumberg, a member of the team of geneticists that first identified CFC syndrome, has counselled parents on similar genetic dilemmas for thirty years, most of them at Kaiser Permanente Hospital in Oakland, California. He admits optimism is the default position of his profession. Imagine the scene, after all: the distraught parent of a seriously compromised child, exhausted from riding the Internet all night and full of fear; the life of a baby is hanging in balance. "More often than not," Blumberg told me, "to achieve a balance point, I need to emphasize the positive. At the same time, the parents are keen to hope. And it's easier to be positive. It's easier to smile. I've been through stuff with patients. It's hard. So I think for doctors it's avoidance at times." If he couldn't solve the problem, at least the parents could be reassured. If Blumberg urged parents to have such a child, he risked sentencing them to a life of hell.

But that dilemma is also artificial. The real problem, Dr. Blumberg said to me that morning in his office in Oakland, lies in our unwillingness to accept that a handicapped life has real value as is—especially if the value requires that you get down on your hands and knees and look for it. "Families often do find raising a handicapped child a gift, despite the hardship," he said. "It creates new relationships, reveals new capabilities. The trick is to give up the idea of the potential child and accept the actual child."

Blumberg is familiar with medical catastrophe. He was blinded in one eye as a boy while helping his father spread fertilizer. He went on to become a doctor via some of the best universities in the world. "It's arrogant of us to assume that these states are inferior to the normal state," he said. "If you have an IQ of 60, that's a serious handicap in our society. But if you're a migrant farm worker, it might be fine, plenty. So who is to say that the state of non-verbal rapture you describe in your son—who is to say that that is inferior? Who is to say that? We're arrogant enough to believe that sentience is all that counts. It's not all that counts. A sequoia is not a sentient being. But they count. There is nothing more magnificent. It doesn't require me to think about it to be in awe of it. I don't want to minimize the difficulty of raising a handicapped child. It says something about the place we have reached as a society that doing so creates a serious handicap in these contexts. But it's just a mistake to think of them as *lesser than*. There's no lesser than. There's just different from. It isn't just great minds that matter. It's great spirits too."

———

Every time we meet someone who is severely handicapped, Jean Vanier believes, they ask two questions: Do you consider me human? Do you love me? The more we meet the handicapped on their own ground, Vanier believes, the more our answers evolve. We begin in fear of their appearance and behaviour; move on through pity; pass through the stage where we help them and respect them, but still see them as lesser beings; until finally we experience "wonderment and thanksgiving," and "discover that, by becoming close to disabled people and entering an authentic relationship with them, they transform us."

In Vanier's last and highest stage of consciousness, "we see the face of God within the disabled. Their presence is a sign of God, who has chosen 'the foolish in order to confound the strong, the proud and the so-called wise of our world.' And so those we see as weak or marginalized are, in fact, the most worthy and powerful among us: they bring us closer to God."

I wish I could believe in Vanier's God. But the truth is, I do not see the face of the Almighty in Walker. Instead, I see the face of my boy; I see what is human, and lovely and flawed at once. Walker is no saint and neither am I. I can't bear to watch him bash himself every day, but I can try to understand why he does it. The more I struggle to face my limitations as a father, the less I want to trade him. Not just because we have a physical bond, a big simple thing; not just because he's taught me the difference between a real problem and a mere complaint; not just because he makes me more serious, makes me appreciate time and Hayley and my wife and friends, and all the sweetness that one day ebbs away. I have begun simply to love him as he is, because I've discovered I can; because we can be who we are, weary dad and broken boy, without alteration or apology, in the here and now. The relief that comes with such a relationship still surprises me. There is no planning with this boy. I go where he goes. He may be a deleterious effect of evolution as far as a geneticist is concerned, but he has few peers as a route to developing what Darwin himself in *The Descent of Man* called the evolutionary advantages of "the social instincts . . . love, and the distinct emotion of sympathy." Darwin's opponents pointed out that man was weaker than the apes, and so there was no logical way he, man, could be the result of the survival of the fittest. But evolution is smarter than that, Darwin replied. "We should . . . bear in mind that an animal possessing great size, strength, and ferocity, and which, like the gorilla, could defend itself from all enemies, would not perhaps have become social: and this would most effectually have checked the acquirement of the higher mental facilities, such as sympathy and the love of his fellows. Hence it might have been an immense advantage to man to have sprung from some comparatively weak creature."

My own goals are modest: to step from time to time into Walker's world; to come to know a few intellectually disabled people (rather than simply permitting them to live in my milieu); to face my fear of the broken people who are

The Other—not to fix them or even save them, but merely to be with them until I stop wanting to run away. At my most optimistic and confident I hope those might qualify as a few steps toward what the evolutionary biologist Julian Huxley imagined when he wrote his famous essay "Evolutionary Ethics" in 1943. A clearer ethical vision as human beings, Huxley writes, will never "prevent us from suffering what we feel as injustice at the hands of the cosmos—congenital deformity, unmerited suffering, physical disaster, the early death of loved ones. Such cosmic injustice represents the persistence of chance and its amorality in human life: we may gradually reduce its amount but we assuredly shall never abolish it. Man is the heir of evolution: but he is also its martyr.

"But man is not only the heir of the past and the victim of the present: he is also the agent through whom evolution may unfold its further possibilities. . . . He can inject his ethics into the heart of evolution."

The face of God? Sorry, no. Walker is more like a mirror, reflecting much back, my choices included. For me—and this is the grandest and yet most consistent way I can think of him, amid all the others, head bonker and beagle and hyperkinetic maniac and gurgling drooler and intermittently curious boy and sad sweet son—Walker is like the vessel Wallace Stevens wrote about:

I placed a jar in Tennessee,
And round it was, upon a hill.
It made the slovenly wilderness
Surround that hill.
The wilderness rose up to it,

And sprawled around, no longer wild.
The jar was round upon the ground
And tall and of a port in air.
It took dominion every where.
The jar was gray and bare.
It did not give of bird or bush,
Like nothing else in Tennessee.

I realize it's not much to go on, not much of a light to see by. It easily wavers. But it's the best I can do.

We waited for hours again when we returned for that second try at an MRI of Walker's brain. Once again I wheeled him up and down the halls in his fancy red stroller, up and down and out the door into the longer hall and back, up to the coffee stand and back. Three hours ticked by.

I finally abandoned the stroller, and sat down with my back to the glazed brick wall in the hall next to the waiting room. Walker was standing two feet away, where the wall turned a corner. Olga was somewhere behind him.

Suddenly he swooned, and fell, like a slipping stack of plates, into my arms. I saw him look and aim himself. There was no mistaking what was happening: he was having a seizure. I had heard accounts of seizures in other CFC children, and the staff at his home had thought on two occasions he might have had a mild attack. But I had never seen anything like this, not in Walker. His eyes began to twitch back and forth like metronomes; his arms jerked faintly. His heart, I could feel it through my legs, was racing like a robin's. He was trying to look into my eyes. He looked scared.

"Do you need some help?" another parent asked from the vestibule, but I shook my head no. I knew what to do. I knew to cradle his wan body in my strong body, wait with him while the shuddering passed, be there when his twitchy eyes found me again. Two minutes went by. It was unlike any other thing. A random and uncontrolled firing of neurons: that is the medical explanation of a seizure.

But it wasn't that which filled my mind. I held him in my arms as quietly as I could, and I thought: this is what it will be like if he dies. It will be like this. There was nothing much to do. I didn't fear it. I was already as close as I could be to him; there was no space between my son and me, no gap or air, no expectation or disappointment, no failure or success: only what he was, a swooned boy, my silent sometimes laughing companion, and my son. I knew I loved him, and I knew he knew it. I held that sweetness in my arms, and waited for whatever was going to happen next. We did that together.

acknowledgements

I wrote this book with the help of deep ranks of people too numerous to mention here. In addition to the people who spoke to me for this book, to explain the complications and implications of Walker's condition, I am especially grateful for the specific help of the late Dr. Norman Saunders, Walker's pediatrician, and Sally Chalmers, his head nurse; Dr. Saunders' successors, Dr. Nessa Bayer and Dr. Joseph Telch; Diane Doucette and Tyna Kasapakis and the legion of children and grown-ups who have befriended and helped Walker at Stewart Homes in Toronto; Minda Latowsky, Lisa Benrubi, Paul McCormack and DeLisle Youth Services; Alana Grossman and her teachers at Beverley Junior Public School in Toronto; Dr. Giovanni Neri, director of the Institute of Genetic Medicine at the Università Cattolica del Sacro Cuore in Rome; Dr. Edmund Kelly at Mount Sinai Hospital, and Judith John at the Hospital for Sick Children in Toronto. I have been continuously grateful, as well, for the unerring counsel and steady encouragement of Dr. Bruce Barnes. I owe Jean-Louis Munn, of L'Arche Canada, a good French meal, as well.

It took a long time to write this book because it has taken a long time to live it. The generosity of my colleagues at the *Globe and Mail* has been bracing, to say nothing of a godsend. Editor-in-chief Edward Greenspon and deputy editor Sylvia Stead granted me time away from my regular responsibilities at the newspaper. Carl Wilson edited an early version of some sections of this book, which became a series in the newspaper. Cathrin Bradbury, my longtime editor and friend, was the person who convinced me to write about Walker in the first place, and who later steered that writing into a book; her keen eye and alert editorial judgment have been Walker's best advocate ever since. What Cathrin started, Anne Collins, my editor at Random House Canada, finished, with the able assistance of Allyson Latta, peerless copy-editor. Anne's skill in helping me find this book's through-line was surpassed only by her patience, which is so immense it warrants genetic analysis on its own.

At the very edge of my composure, I must thank some dear friends, who not only kept us company through the darker moments of Walker's struggles, but more importantly became his friends and made him part of their lives. Their kindness has become my definition of grace. Before Olga de Vera, Hayley's and then Walker's nanny, I am, quite frankly, speechless. My pal and colleague Colin MacKenzie and his wife Lorrie Huggins were the reason we finally found lasting care for Walker. My brother, Timothy Brown, and his partner, Frank Rioux, befriended Walker literally from the moment he was born, without a blink of hesitation or qualm; took us on holidays, cooked us meals, gave me a place to write, loved the boy. Two couples—Allan Kling and Tecca Crosby, and John Barber and Cathrin Bradbury—have been the best friends Walker could have: they shared summer cottages, took him on weekends, became his and our favourite refuge, and never accepted a word of thanks. Their children—Daisy Kling, and Kelly and Mary Barber—were equally decent, and treated Walker like their (always) little brother. Don't think I didn't notice.

Finally, I must do the impossible and describe my gratitude to my daughter, Hayley, and my wife, Johanna, Walker's sister and mother—my steadies, my best advisers, my sweetest solace in those darkest nights, and Walker's favourite companions. For good reason: their love knew no hesitation, no start and no finish.

Toronto, Canada
April 23, 2009

1. In *The Boy in the Moon*, Ian Brown describes the many effects the birth of his disabled son, Walker, had on the life of their family. In what ways did Walker change the lives of Brown, his wife, Johanna, and their daughter, Hayley?

2. One of Brown's main emotions throughout the book is guilt. Why does he feel so guilty, especially if Walker's problems are caused by a random genetic mutation? Does the fact that Walker was kept alive by new medical technologies change Brown's responsibilities as a father? He admits that he sometimes thought of committing suicide, and of taking Walker with him. Can you understand his reasoning? What stopped him, in your opinion?

3. Brown claims that while he has no concrete proof, he suspects Walker has an inner life, complete with aspirations, desires, urges, and even a point of view, albeit an unconventional one. What does he present as evidence for this inner life? Did you find it convincing?

4. What, if anything, is the value of Walker's "broken life"? What is the value of believing that Walker has an inner, personal life?

5. Thanks to prenatal testing and a simple blood test, Brown points out, a woman can now know early in her pregnancy whether her fetus will be born with any number of serious and debilitating genetic afflictions. Some experts believe Down syndrome will be a thing of the past by 2030. Would that be a good development? Would it be a good development for people with Down syndrome? After reading *The Boy in the Moon*, what are the reasons for aborting a genetically afflicted child? What, according to the book, are the reasons against aborting a disabled fetus?

6. Would prenatal tests still be desirable if we took better care of the disabled? Brown claims that his wife, Johanna, is unlike most mothers of disabled children because she says she would have changed Walker if she could have, to the most average child. For whose sake would she have changed him? What would you have done in her circumstances?

St. Martin's
Griffin

7. In the course of the book, Walker's mother, Johanna, visits a native shaman to find out what the shaman can tell her about Walker's future and purpose. Describe the shaman's vision and how it relates to Walker's life. Why does Walker want to see his own reflection in the well? What does his reflection represent? Johanna believes that the native vision of Walker's life is the most humane one she has ever heard. Why? How would our view of the intellectually disabled be different if we saw them through the eyes of the shaman?

8. Charles Darwin believed that the human capacity for speech and empathy may have evolved from our comparative fragility, and not from our being fittest of all the animals. Has Walker's fragility bestowed any evolutionary benefit on us? Is fragility the same as weakness? Brown claims that Walker has helped him far more than Brown has been able to help Walker. What does he mean? What is the value, if any, of imperfection?

9. Jean Vanier, the founder of L'Arche, a system of communities for the disabled, was a successful professor when he gave up his job to start L'Arche. Why do you think he did it? What do you think he hoped to find? How do communities like L'Arche differ from group homes?

10. Throughout *The Boy in the Moon,* Brown values his physical togetherness with Walker at least as much as he values their emotional or intellectual togetherness. But are they really that different? Does Ian Brown "know" his disabled, non-talking fifteen-year-old son as well as another father can know his normal fifteen-year-old teenager? Is there anything you envy about Walker's life?

11. Brown claims at one point to be surprised when a geneticist refers to Walker's future wife. Why? Were you surprised? Do you automatically think, as Brown admits he sometimes does, that marriage is out of the question for Walker? Why do we resist the idea that the disabled have normal desires?

12. Brown says we tend to ignore the disabled, or sweep them out of sight, because we are afraid of them. Why? What do the disabled represent? He also says they expect much less from us than we think we owe them. Why is that?

13. Brown claims that Walker's care, which requires twenty-four-hour supervision, costs $200,000 a year. In Canada, most of that is paid for by the government and therefore through taxes revenue. Do you think that's fair to people who don't have disabled children? Walker would have died if nature had taken its course, but was instead kept alive by sophisticated new medical technologies. Does this change your opinion of how much responsibility a society has to look after its disabled?

14. At one point in *The Boy in the Moon*, Brown says that disability is always against the status quo, always radical, always antiestablishment. How so? Do you agree?

15. Walker Brown is seriously disabled, intellectually and physically; his father, the writer, is not. Neither are most of the people who buy *The Boy in the Moon*. How do you think you would react to the book if you were disabled? Do you have to be disabled, or the relative of a disabled person, to appreciate the book? In what ways is it a universal story?

*A
Reading
Group
Guide*

*For more reading group suggestions,
visit www.readinggroupgold.com*

St. Martin's
Griffin